DEDICATION

Thank you for taking a time-out to explore the wonder of PEJETALES©. I am confident you will find it informative, entertaining and educational.

This book is dedicated to my precious little wonders. My children are my pride and joy. I look forward to the day when they each realize what an inspiration they have been in my life.

This version of PEJETALES© will help parents and faculty assist children, of all ages, become familiar with state flags, names, abbreviations, capitals, nicknames and more. I hope you will find this book so fun and informative, you will be encouraged to share it with everyone you know.

Sincerely,

Patrick Malcolm
Author/Motivational Speaker

Alabama

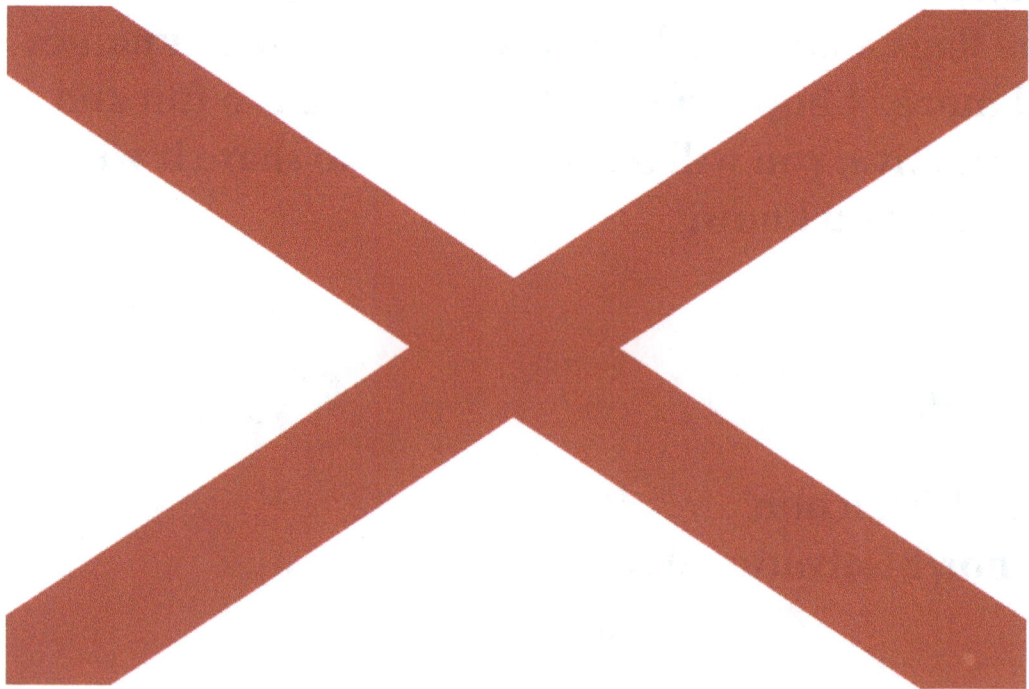

Printed in the United States of America
Copyright© 2016 by Peje-Patrick Malcolm Publishing
ISBN No.: 978-0-9890237-3-3

Interior and Exterior Graphic Design
provided by Irene Michel
illestr8tor@gmail.com

Answer each multiple choice question and write the state capital.

DID YOU KNOW?

The state flower is a:
Camellia

The state bird is a:
Yellowhammer

Alabama
Abbreviation:
a. (AM)
b. (AL)
c. (AA)
Capital:
a. Montgomery
b. Mobile
c. Birmingham
Nickname:
a. The Mobile State
b. The Civil Right State
c. Yellowhammer State

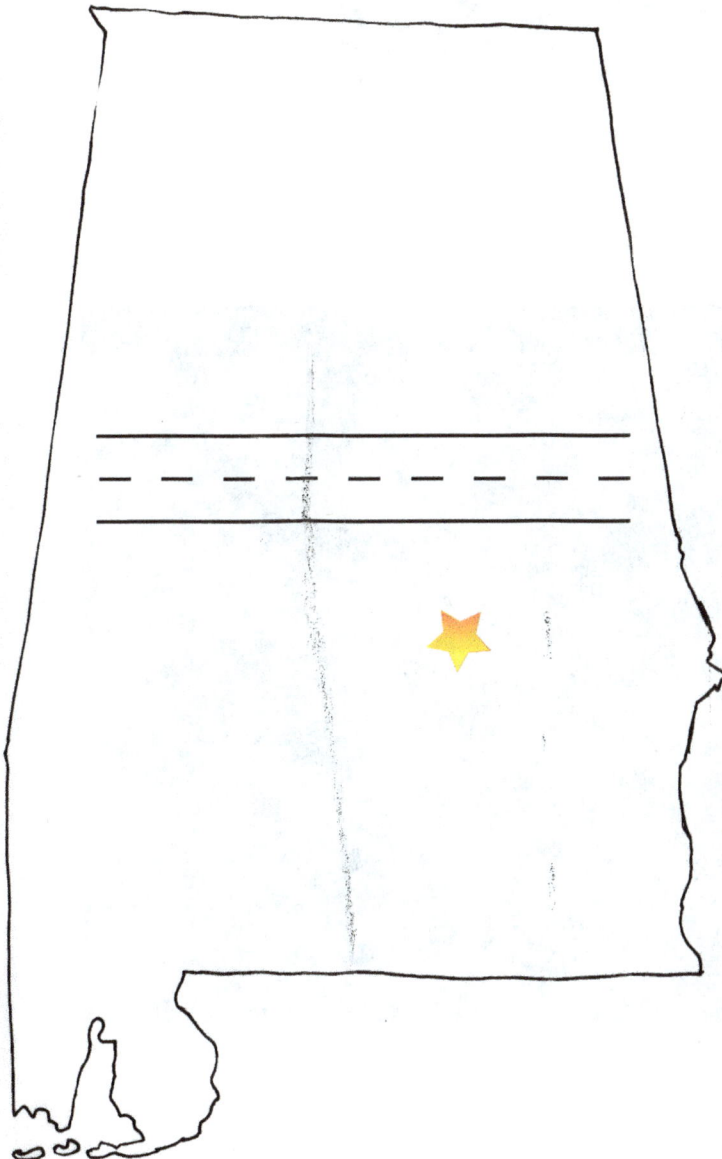

Alaska

Answer each multiple choice question and write the state capital.

DID YOU KNOW?

The state flower is a:
Forget-Me-Not

The state bird is a:
Willow Ptarmigan

Alaska

Abbreviation:
a. (AS)
b. (AL)
c. (AK)

Capital:
a. Anchorage
b. Juneau
c. Fairbanks

Nickname:
a. The Last Frontier
b. The Ice State
c. The Salmon Run

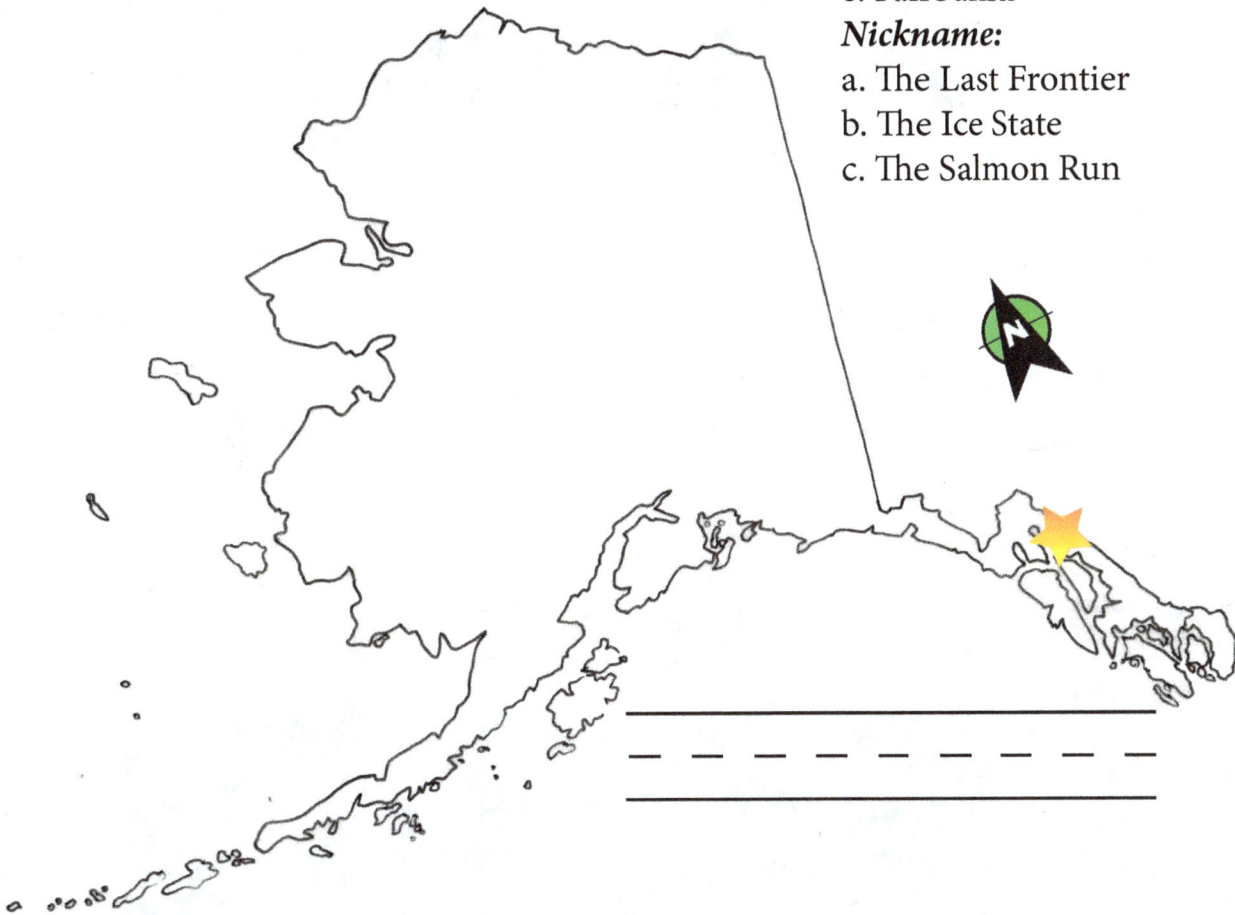

Arizona

Answer each multiple choice question and write the state capital.

DID YOU KNOW?

The state flower is a:
Saguaro Cactus Flower

The state bird is a:
Cactus Wren

Arizona
Abbreviation:
a. (AZ)
b. (AR)
c. (AA)
Capital:
a. Tucson
b. Phoenix
c. Tombstone
Nickname:
a. The Diamond Back State
b. Death Valley
c. The Grand Canyon State

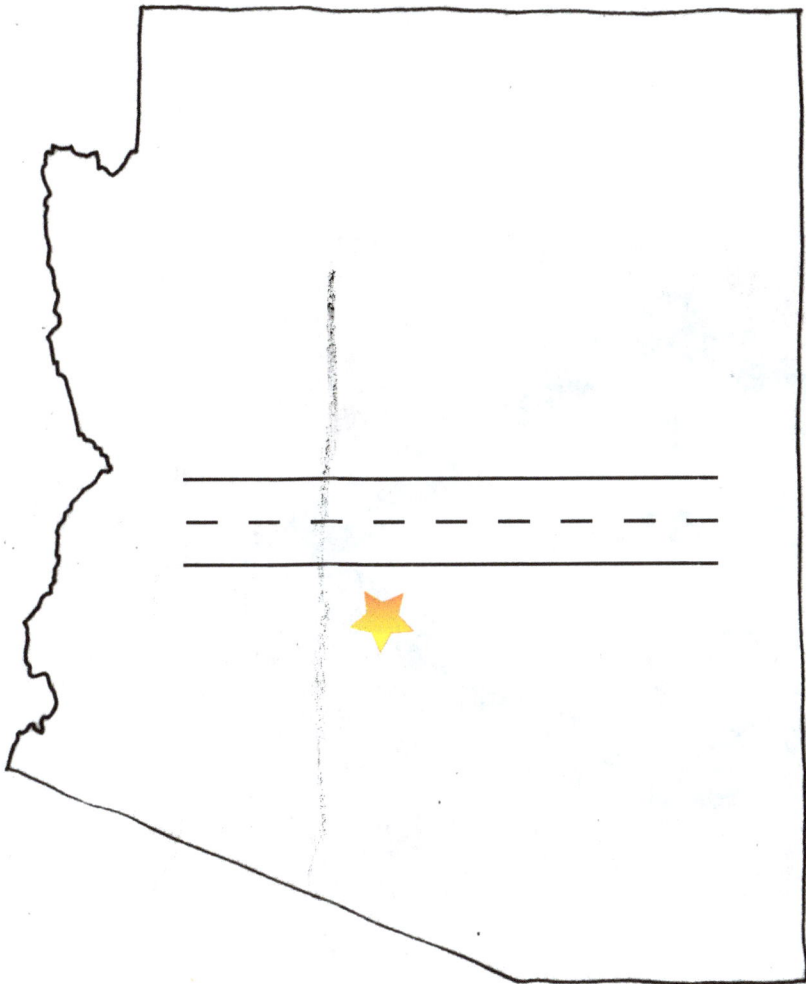

Arkansas

Answer each multiple choice question and write the state capital.

DID YOU KNOW?

The state flower is an:
Apple Blossom

The state bird is a:
Mockingbird

Arkansas
Abbreviation:
a. (AK)
b. (AS)
c. (AR)
Capital:
a. Hot Springs
b. Little Rock
c. Hope
Nickname:
a. The Plantation State
b. The Mineral State
c. The Natural State

California

CALIFORNIA REPUBLIC

Answer each multiple choice question and write the state capital.

DID YOU KNOW?

The state flower is a:
Golden Poppy

The state bird is a:
California Valley Quail

California
Abbreviation:
a. (CF)
b. (CL)
c. (CA)
Capital:
a. Sacramento
b. Hollywood
c. Los Angeles
Nickname:
a. The Gold Rush State
b. The Golden State
c. Golden Poppy State

Colorado

Answer each multiple choice question and write the state capital.

DID YOU KNOW?

The state flower is a:
Rocky Mountain Columbine

The state bird is a:
Lark Bunting

Colorado

Abbreviation:
a. (CD)
b. (CO)
c. (CL)

Capital:
a. Colorado Springs
b. Rocky Mountain
c. Denver

Nickname:
a. Centennial State
b. Black Canyon State
c. The Columbine State

Connecticut

QUI TRANSTULIT SUSTINET

Answer each multiple choice question and write the state capital.

DID YOU KNOW?

The state flower is a:
Mountain Laurel

The state bird is an:
American Robin

Connecticut

Abbreviation:
a. (CT)
b. (CO)
c. (CN)

Capital:
a. New Haven
b. Massachusetts
c. Hartford

Nickname:
a. The Connection State
b. Constitution State
c. Legislative State

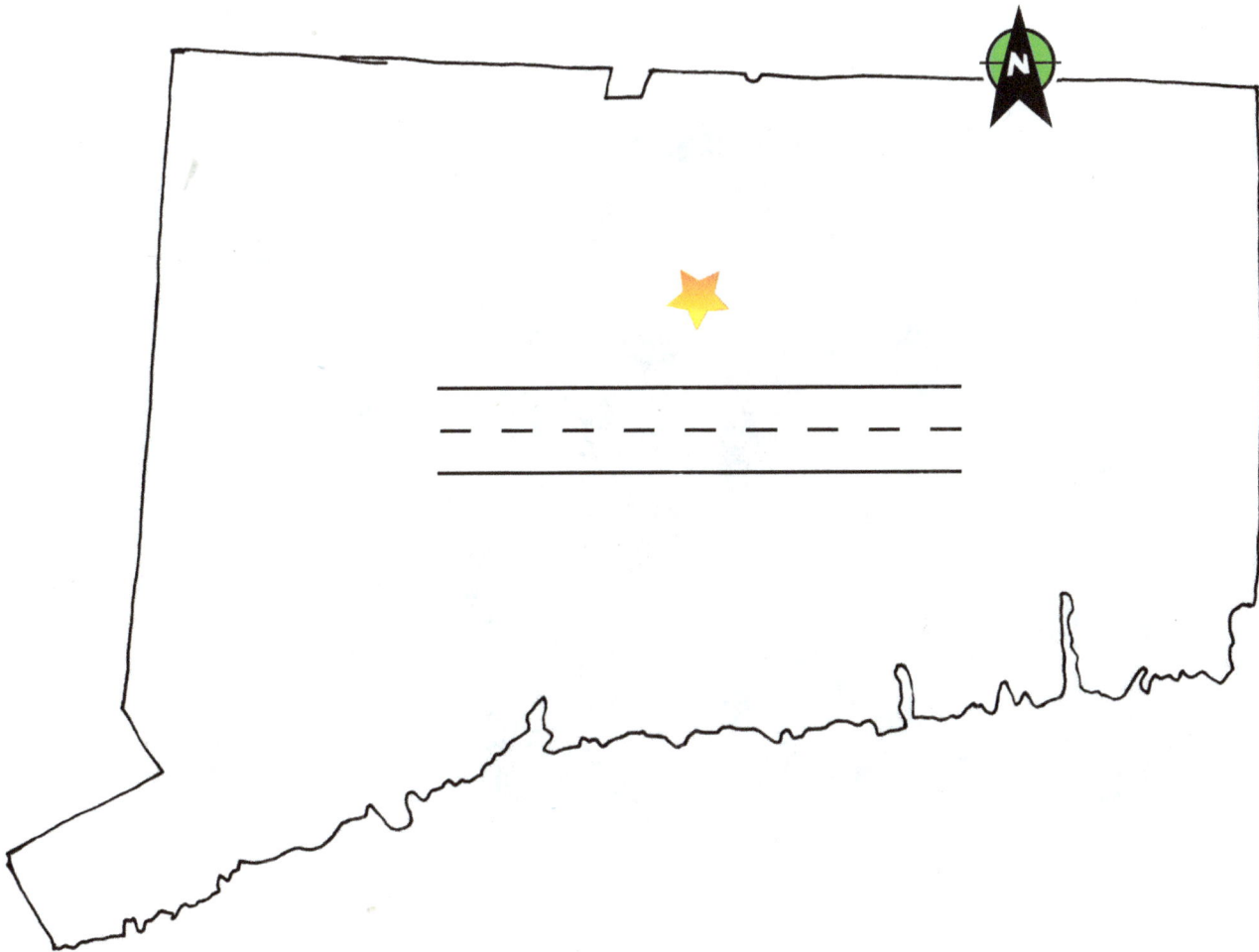

Delaware

DECEMBER 7, 1787

Answer each multiple choice question and write the state capital.

DID YOU KNOW?

The state flower is a:
Peach Blossom

The state bird is a:
Blue Hen Chicken

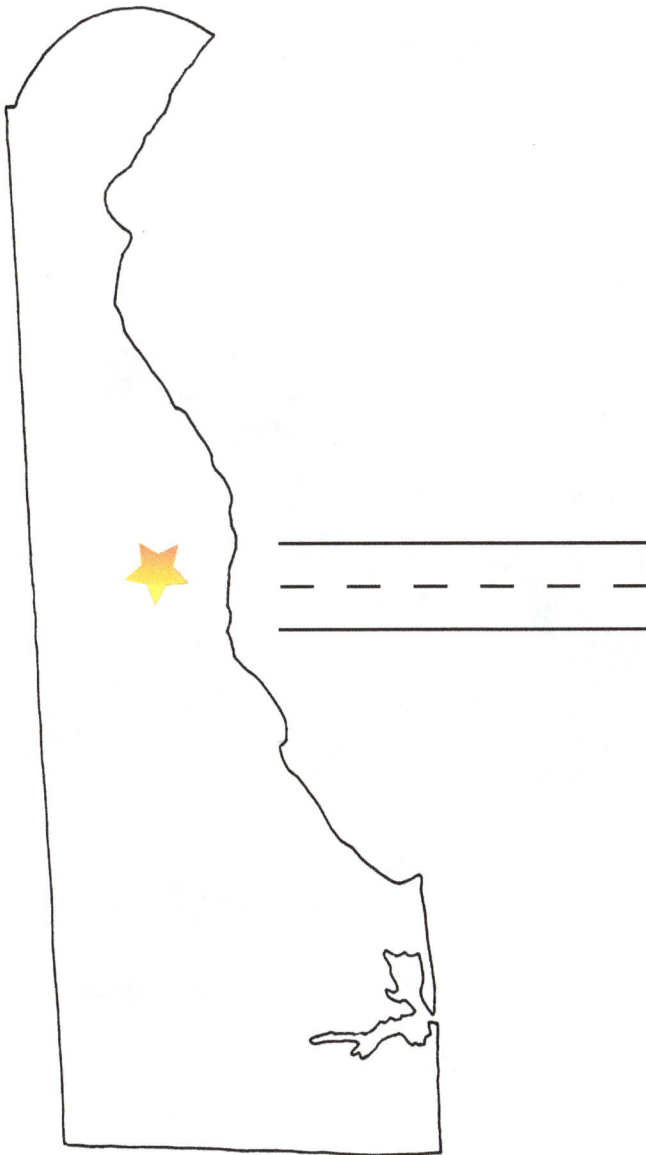

Delaware
Abbreviation:
a. (DE)
b. (DL)
c. (DW)
Capital:
a. Wilmington
b. Dover
c. New Castle
Nickname:
a. Diamond; First State
b. Free Tax State
c. The Finance State

Florida

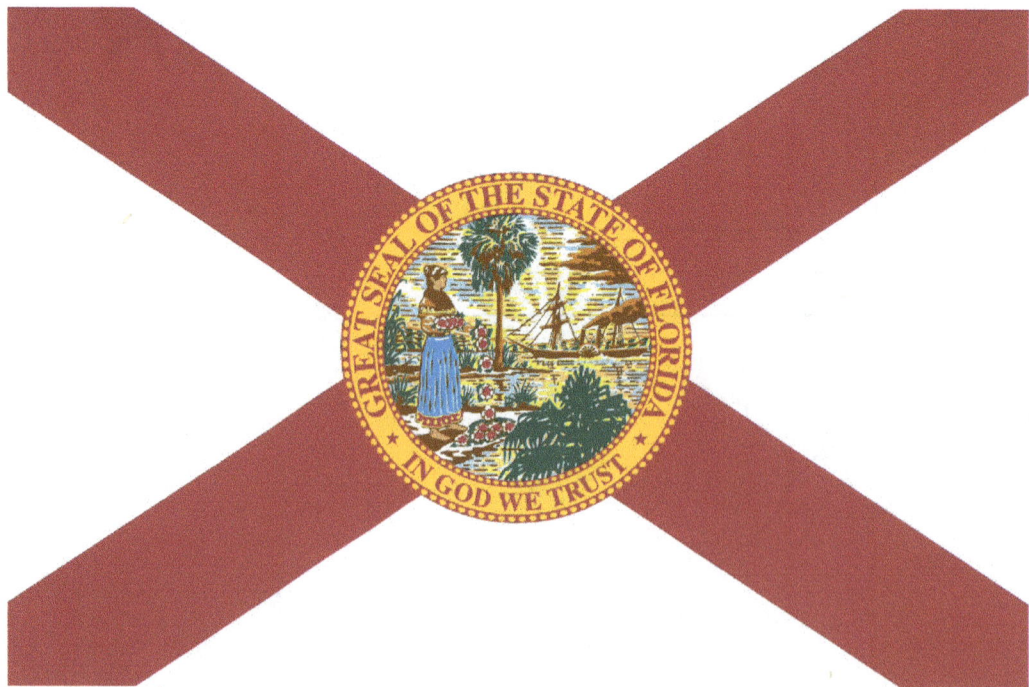

Answer each multiple choice question and write the state capital.

DID YOU KNOW?

The state flower is an:
Orange Blossom

The state bird is a:
Mockingbird

Florida

Abbreviation:
a. (FA)
b. (FD)
c. (FL)

Capital:
a. Orlando
b. Miami
c. Tallahassee

Nickname:
a. The Gator Glades
b. Sunshine State
c. Citrus State

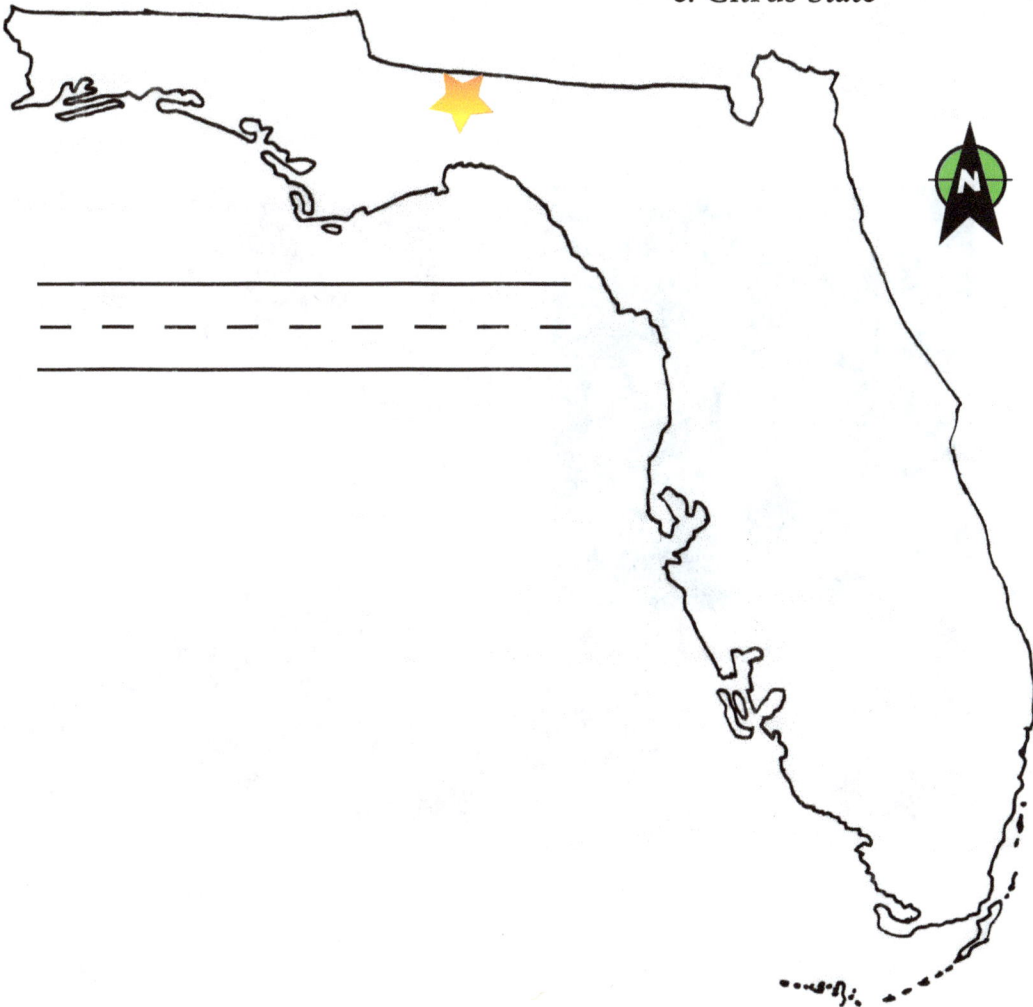

Georgia

Answer each multiple choice question and write the state capital.

DID YOU KNOW?

The state flower is a:
Cherokee Rose

The state bird is a:
Brown Thrasher

Georgia
Abbreviation:
a. (GE)
b. (GA)
c. (GR)
Capital:
a. Savannah
b. Atlanta
c. Augusta
Nickname:
a. The Civil State
b. The Rosewood State
c. Peach State

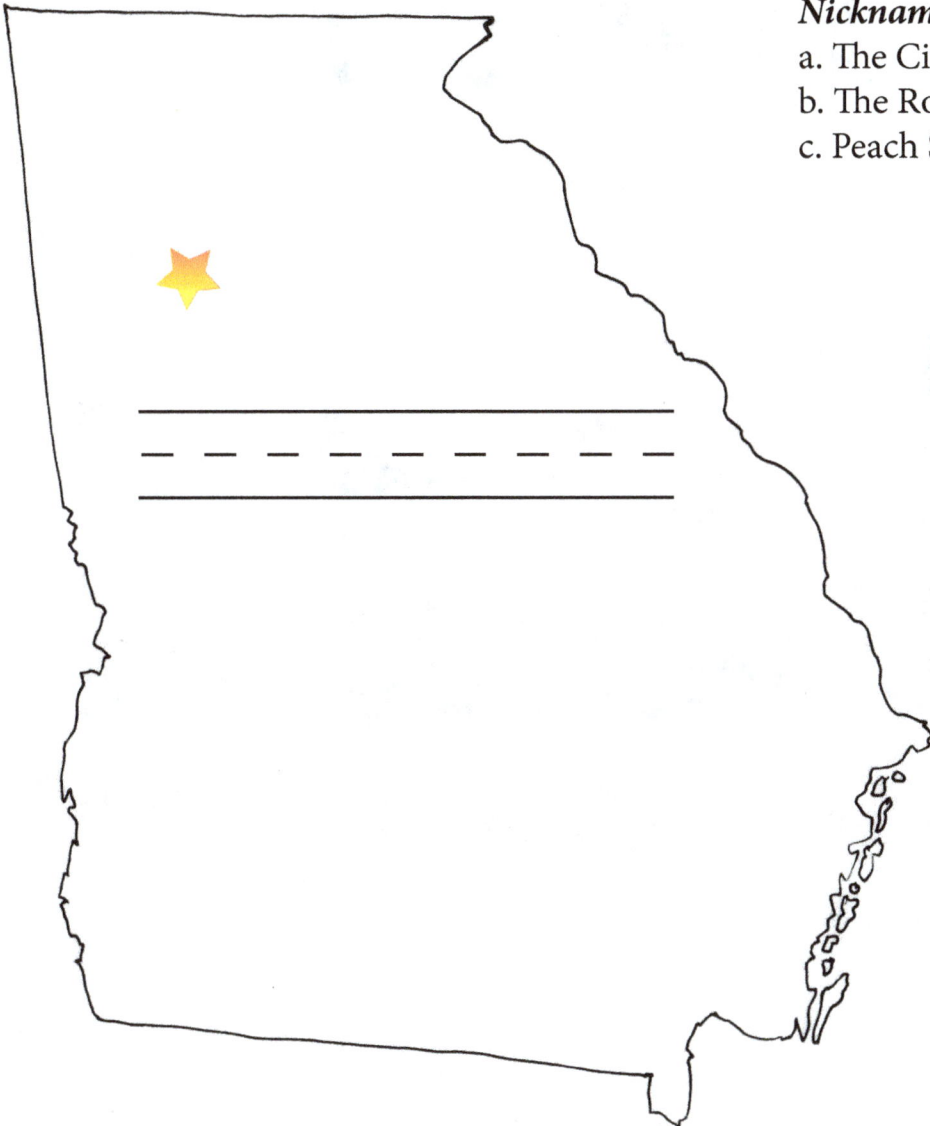

Hawaii

Answer each multiple choice question and write the state capital.

DID YOU KNOW?

The state flower is a:
Hibiscus

The state bird is a:
Nene (Hawaiian Goose)

Hawaii

Abbreviation:
a. (HI)
b. (HW)
c. (HA)
Capital:
a. Honolulu
b. Pearl Harbor
c. Maui
Nickname:
a. Aloha State
b. The Tahitian State
c. Kahoolawe State

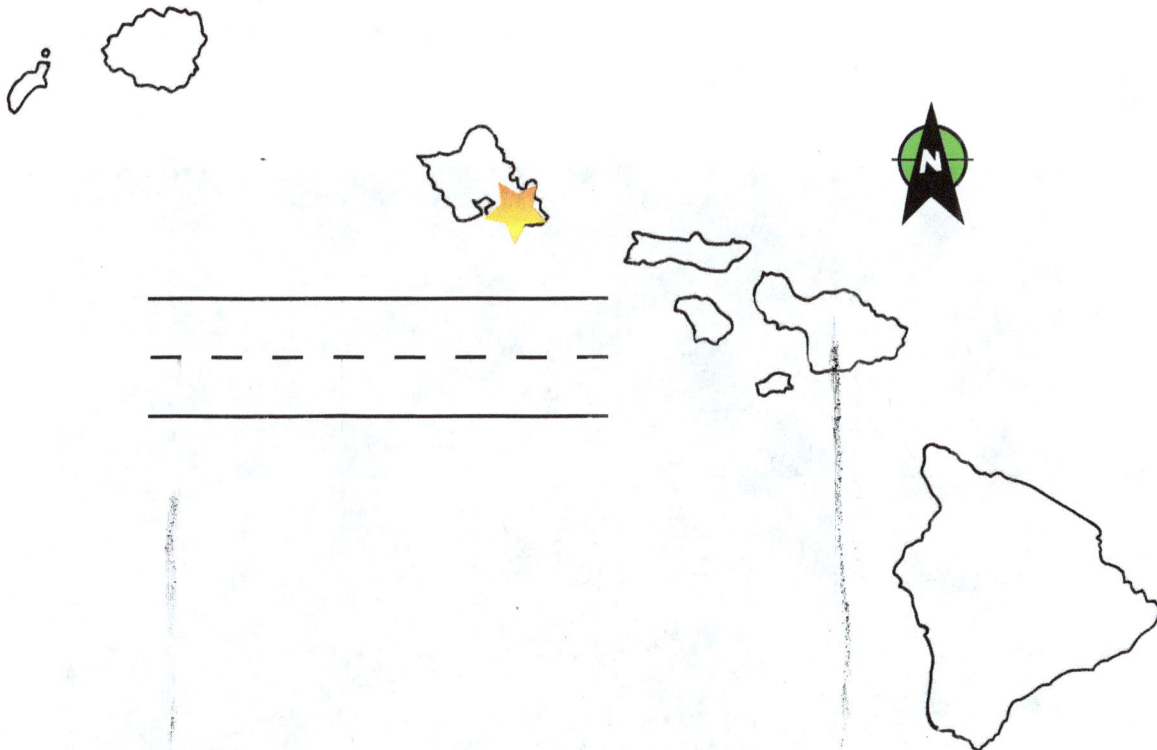

Idaho

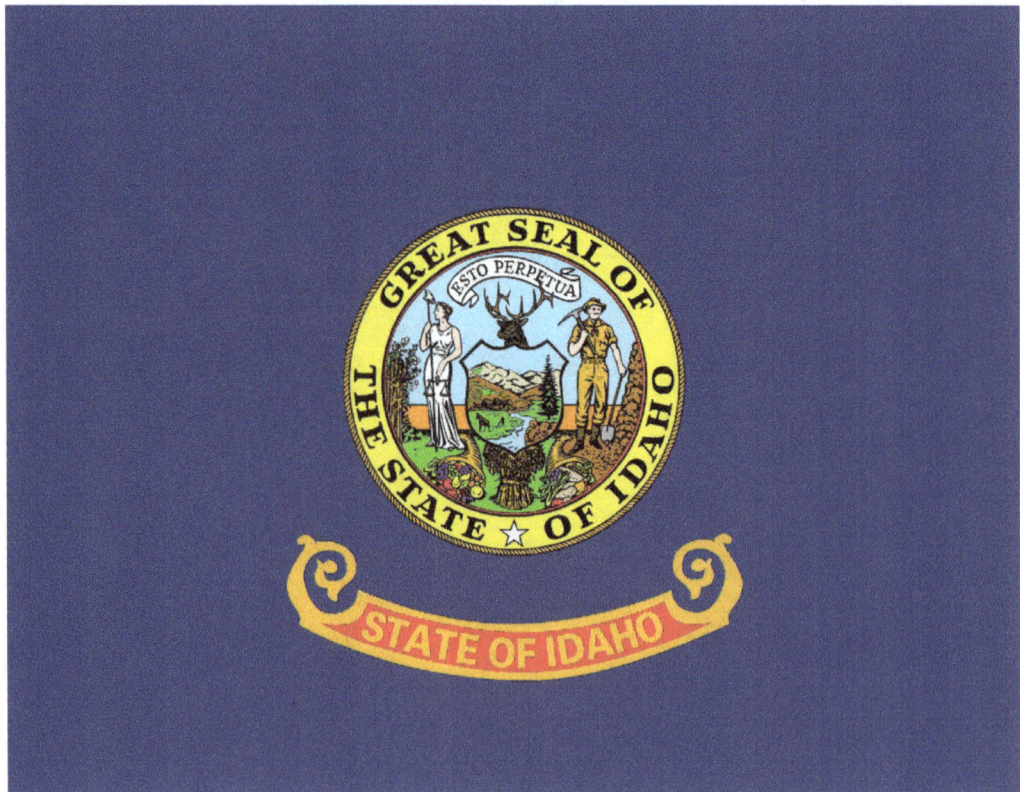

Answer each multiple choice question and write the state capital.

DID YOU KNOW?

The state flower is a:
Syringa

The state bird is a:
Mountain Bluebird

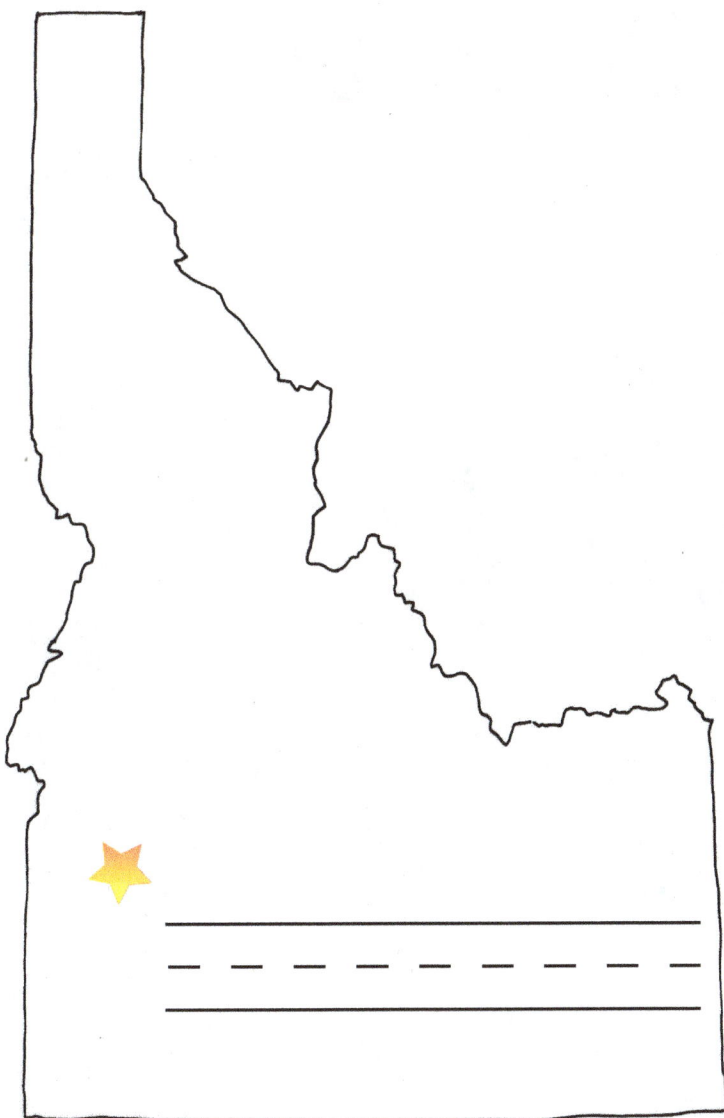

Idaho
Abbreviation:
a. (IO)
b. (ID)
c. (IH)
Capital:
a. Kellogg
b. Twin Falls
c. Boise
Nickname:
a. Gem State
b. The Produce State
c. Potatoe State

Illinois

ILLINOIS

Answer each multiple choice question and write the state capital.

DID YOU KNOW?

The state flower is a:
Violet

The state bird is a:
Cardinal

Illinois

Abbreviation:
a. (IS)
b. (IN)
c. (IL)
Capital:
a. Indiana
b. Springfield
c. Chicago
Nickname:
a. Prairie State
b. Hog State
c. The Shrine State

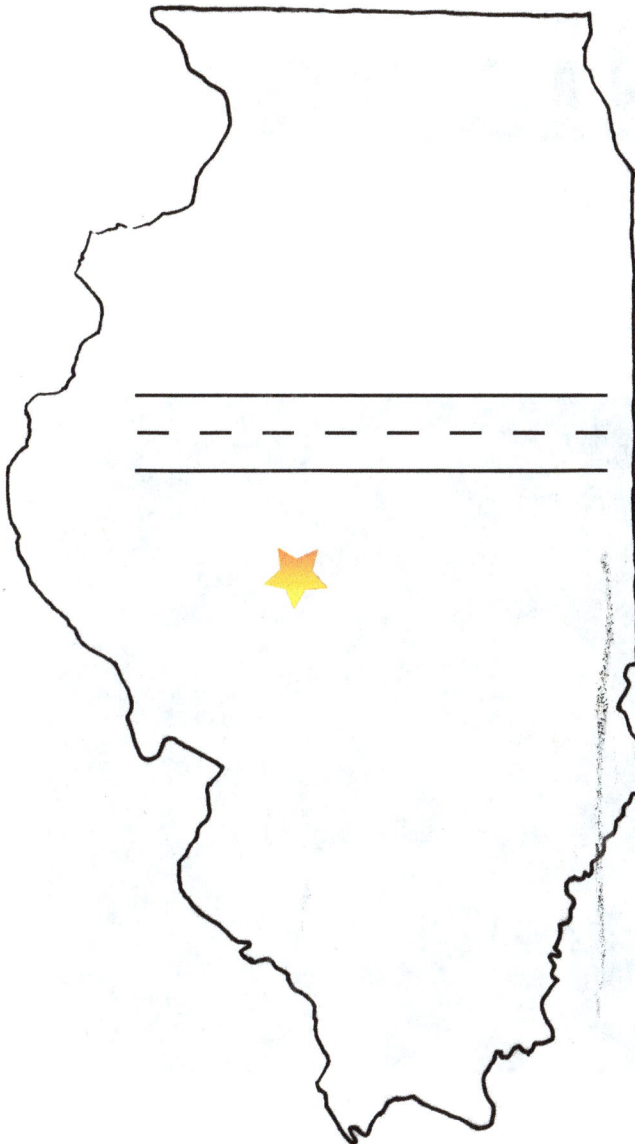

Indiana

Answer each multiple choice question and write the state capital.

DID YOU KNOW?

The state flower is a:
Peony

The state bird is a:
Cardinal

Indiana

Abbreviation:
a. (IA)
b. (IN)
c. (ID)

Capital:
a. Anapolis
b. New Albany
c. Indianapolis

Nickname:
a. Timber State
b. Hoosier State
c. The Waterfront State

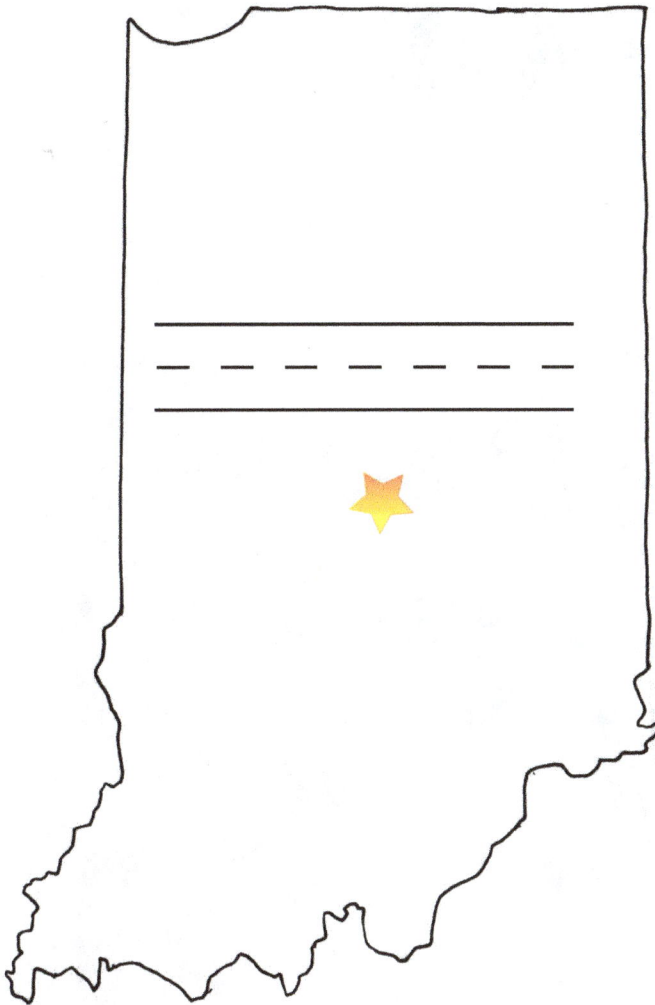

Iowa

Answer each multiple choice question and write the state capital.

DID YOU KNOW?

The state flower is a:
Wild Rose

The state bird is an:
Eastern Goldfinch

Iowa

Abbreviation:
a. (IA)
b. (IO)
c. (IW)

Capital:
a. Iowa City
b. Waterloo
c. Des Moines

Nickname:
a. Black Hawk State
b. Hawkeye State
c. The Agricultural State

Kansas

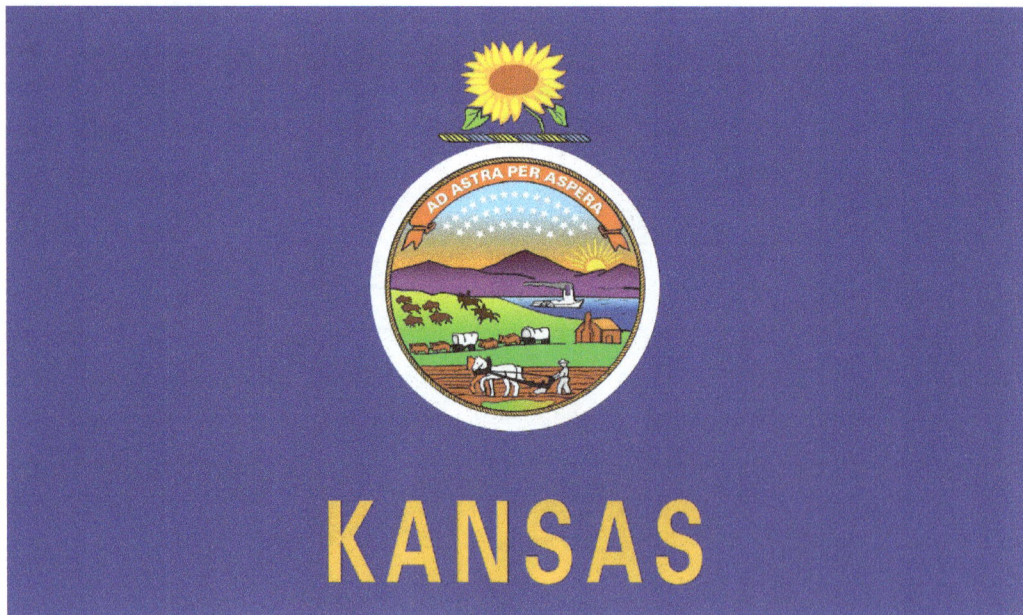

Answer each multiple choice question and write the state capital.

DID YOU KNOW?

The state flower is a:
Sunflower

The state bird is a:
Western Meadowlark

Kansas

Abbreviation:
a. (KN)
b. (KA)
c. (KS)

Capital:
a. Kansas City
b. Wichita
c. Topeka

Nickname:
a. Sunflower State
b. Helium State
c. The Oats & Barley State

Kentucky

Answer each multiple choice question and write the state capital.

DID YOU KNOW?

The state flower is a:
Goldenrod

The state bird is a:
Kentucky Cardinal

Kentucky

Abbreviation:
a. (KY)
b. (KE)
c. (KT)

Capital:
a. Lexington-Fayette
b. Frankfort
c. Richmond

Nickname:
a. Fried Chicken State
b. Bluegrass State
c. The Tobacco State

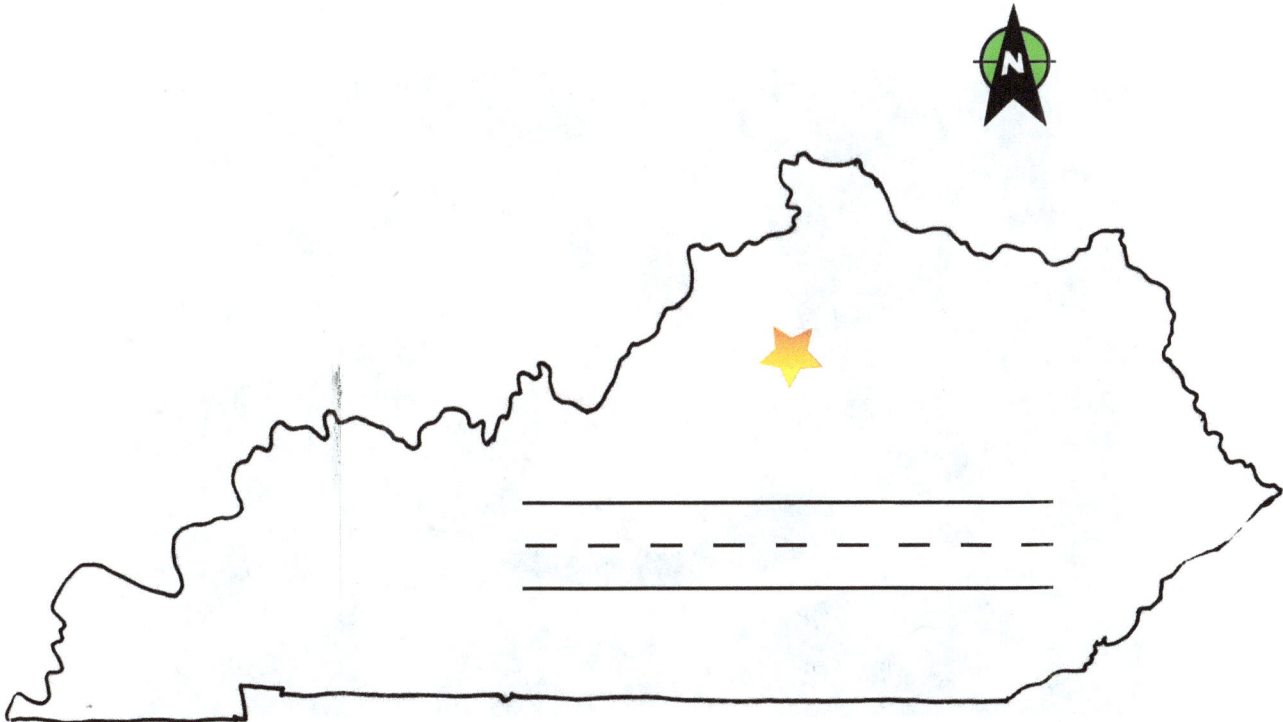

Louisiana

35

Answer each multiple choice question and write the state capital.

DID YOU KNOW?

The state flower is a:
Magnolia

The state bird is an:
Eastern Brown Pelican

Louisiana

Abbreviation:
a. (LO)
b. (LA)
c. (LI)

Capital:
a. Baton Rouge
b. New Orleans
c. Lafayette

Nickname:
a. The Cajun State
b. Pelican State
c. The Bourbon Magic State

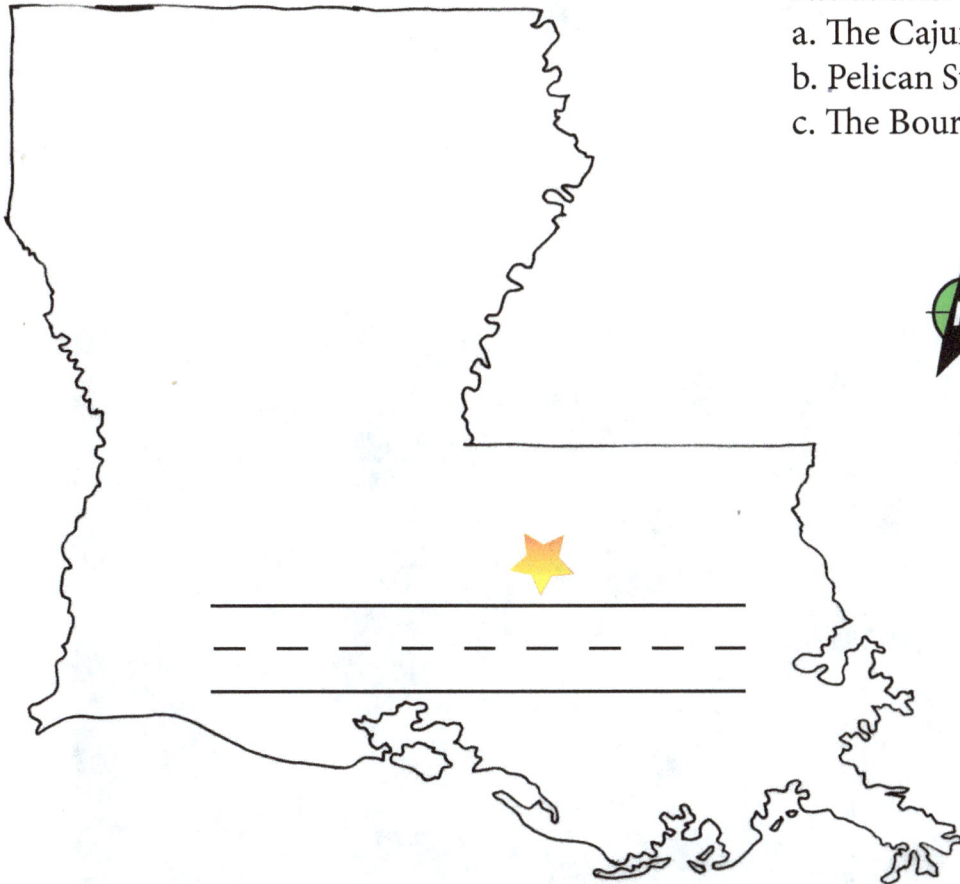

Maine

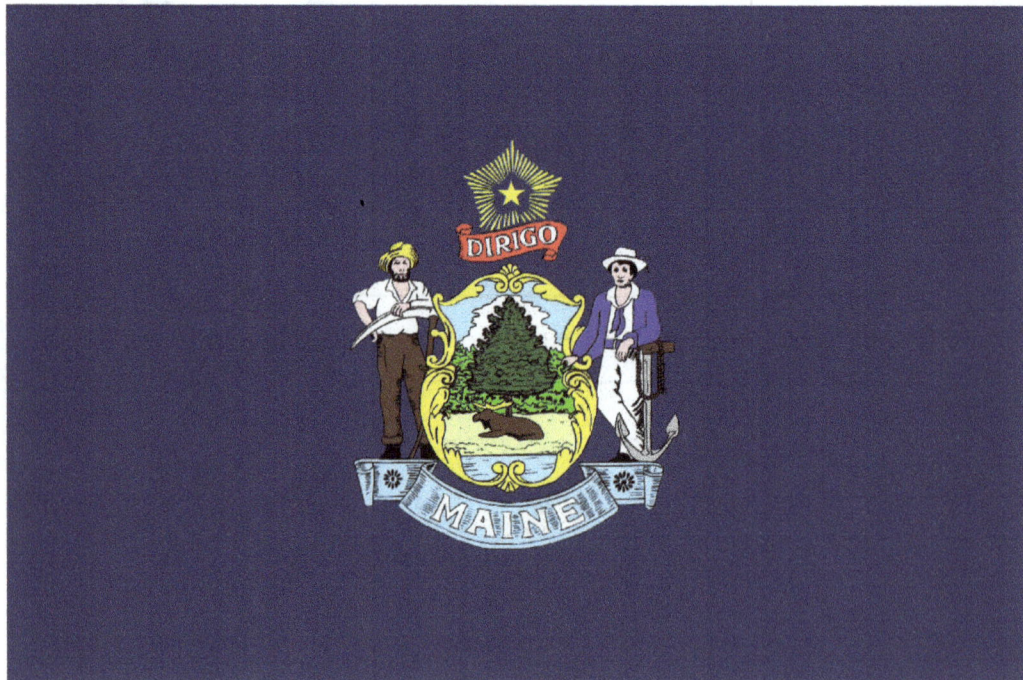

Answer each multiple choice question and write the state capital.

DID YOU KNOW?

The state flower is a:
White Pine Cone & Tassel

The state bird is a:
Chickadee

Maine

Abbreviation:
a. (MA)
b. (ME)
c. (MN)

Capital:
a. Auburn
b. Augusta
c. Portland

Nickname:
a. Pine Tree State
b. The Wilderness State
c. Lobster Tail State

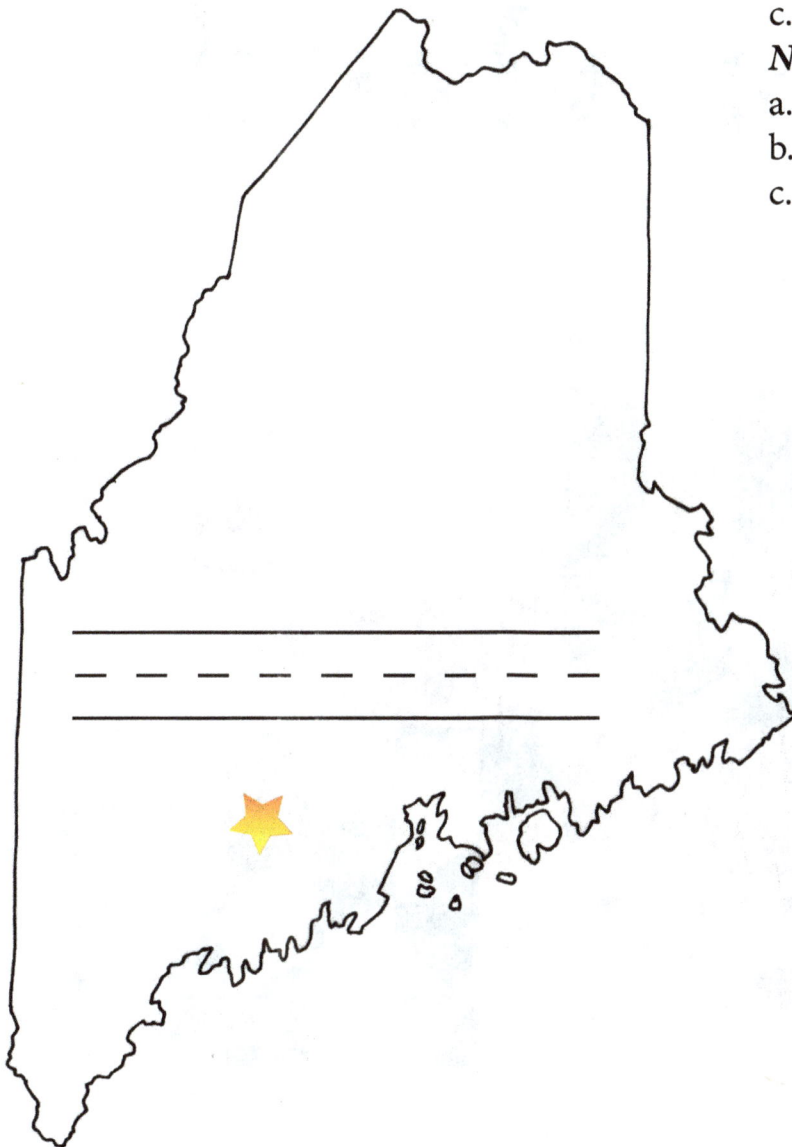

Maryland

Answer each multiple choice question and write the state capital.

DID YOU KNOW?

The state flower is a:
Black-Eyed Susan

The state bird is a:
Baltimore Oriole

Maryland

Abbreviation:
a. (MD)
b. (MA)
c. (MY)
Capital:
a. Annapolis
b. Baltimore
c. Frederick
Nickname:
a. Star-Spangled Banner State
b. Free State; Old Line State
c. The Nursery State

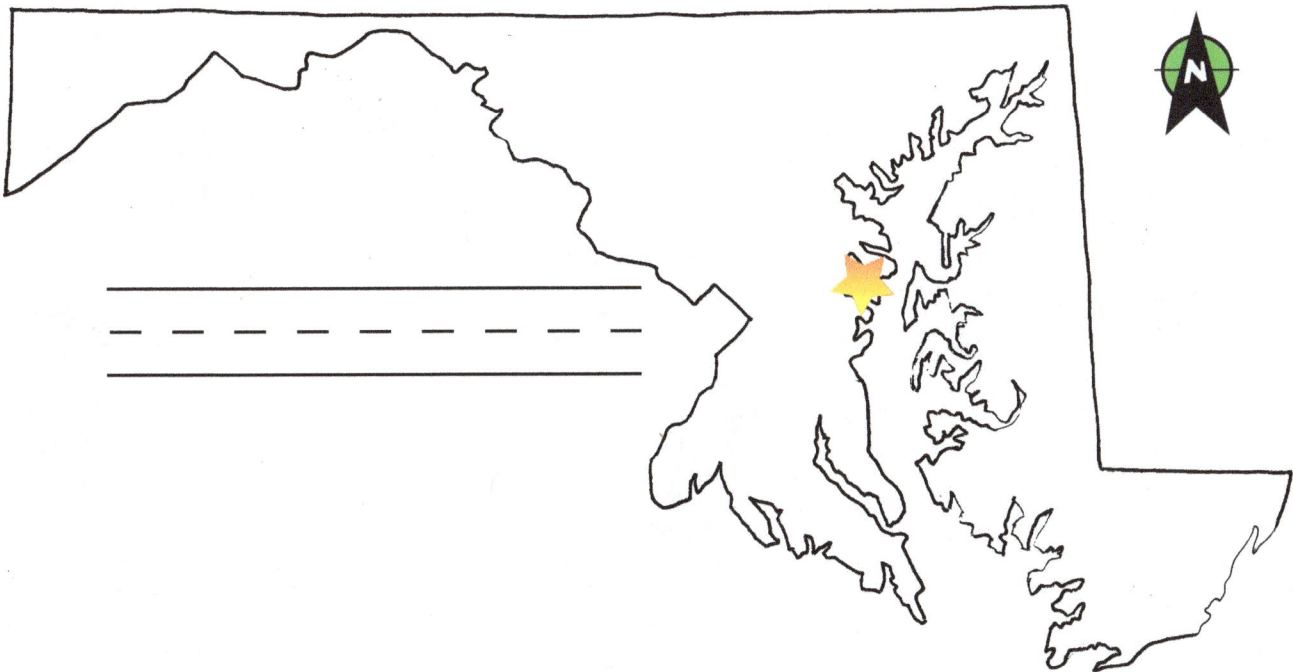

Massachusetts

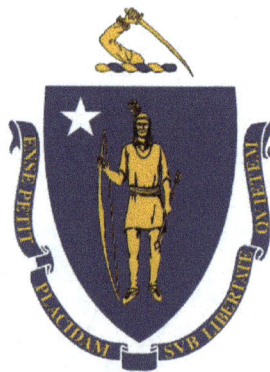

Answer each multiple choice question and write the state capital.

DID YOU KNOW?

The state flower is a:
Mayflower

The state bird is a:
Chickadee

Massachusetts

Abbreviation:
a. (MA)
b. (MS)
c. (MC)
Capital:
a. Cape Cod
b. Boston
c. Springfield
Nickname:
a. Bay State
b. Pilgrim State
c. Minute Men State

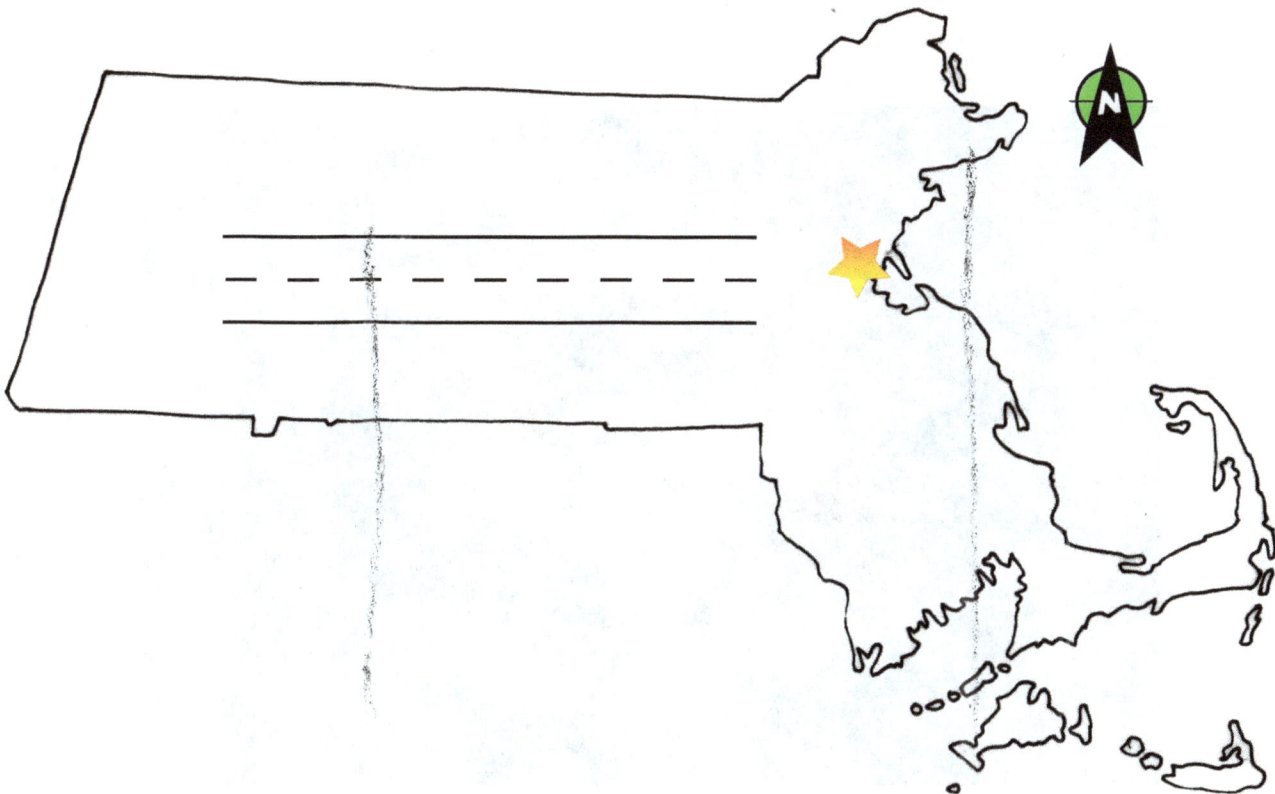

Michigan

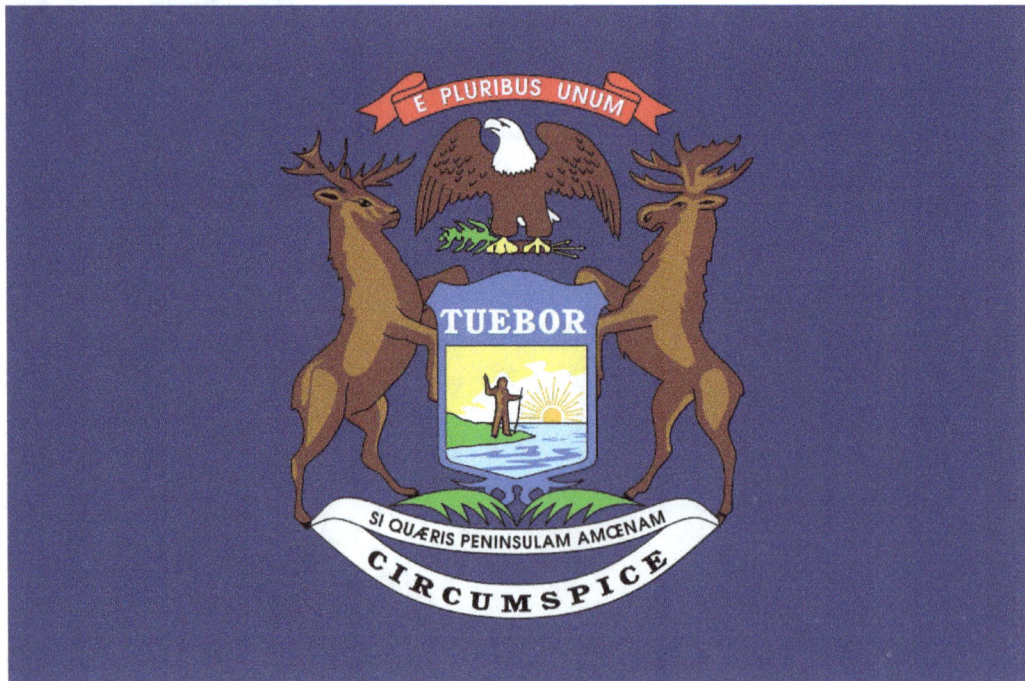

Answer each multiple choice question and write the state capital.

DID YOU KNOW?

The state flower is a:
Apple Blossom

The state bird is a:
Robin

Michigan
Abbreviation:
a. (MC)
b. (MN)
c. (MI)
Capital:
a. Detroit
b. Lansing
c. Grand Rapids
Nickname:
a. Motor City
b. The Great Lakes State
c. Wolverine State

Minnesota

Answer each multiple choice question and write the state capital.

DID YOU KNOW?

The state flower is a:
Lady Slipper

The state bird is a:
Common Loon ("Great Northern Diver")

Minnesota

Abbreviation:
a. (MI)
b. (MN)
c. (MA)

Capital:
a. Minneapolis
b. St. Paul
c. Rochester

Nickname:
a. The Wolves State
b. North Star State;
   Gopher State;
   Land of 10,000 Lakes State
c. 10,000 Lakes State

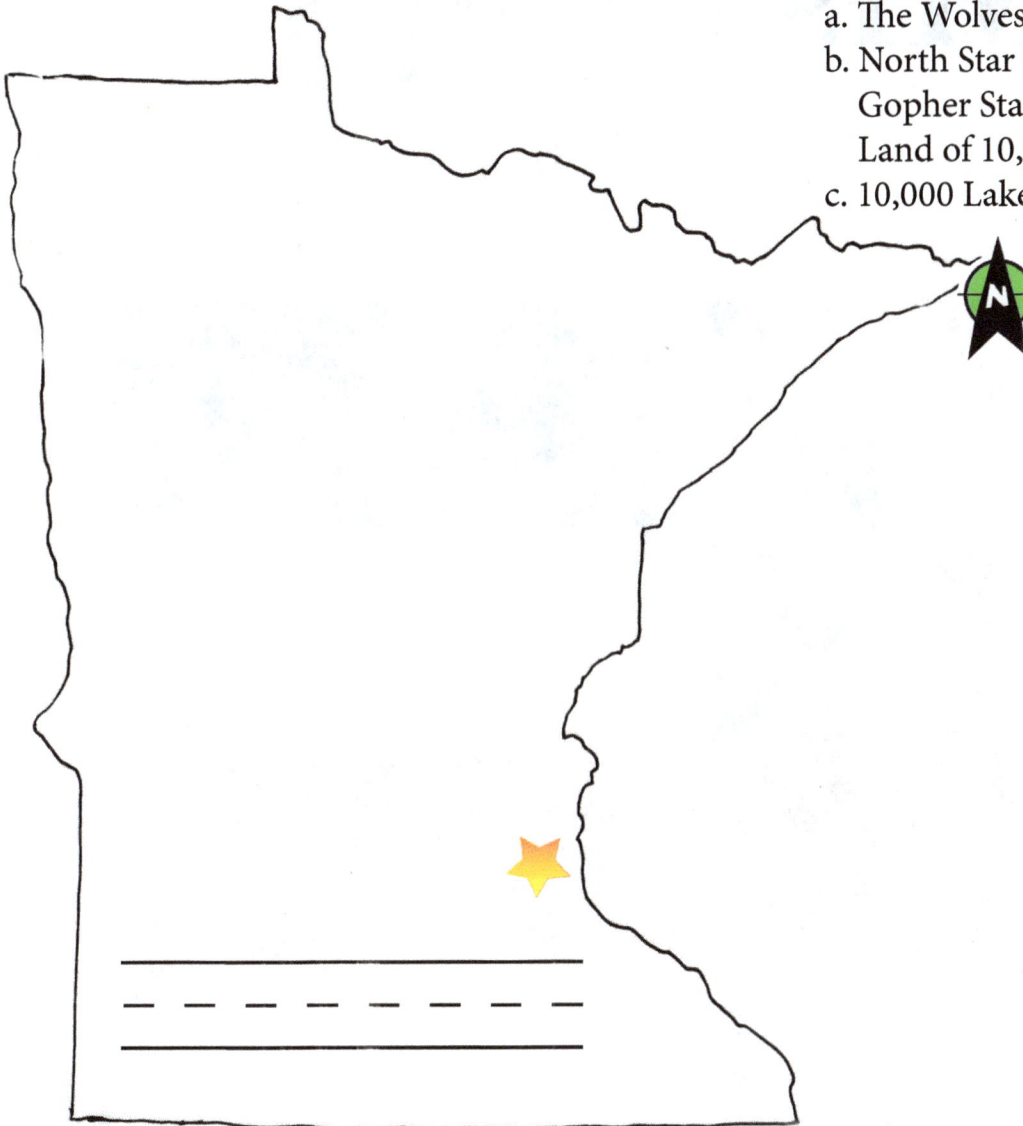

Mississippi

Answer each multiple choice question and write the state capital.

DID YOU KNOW?

The state flower is a:
Bloom of the Magnolia

The state bird is a:
Mockingbird

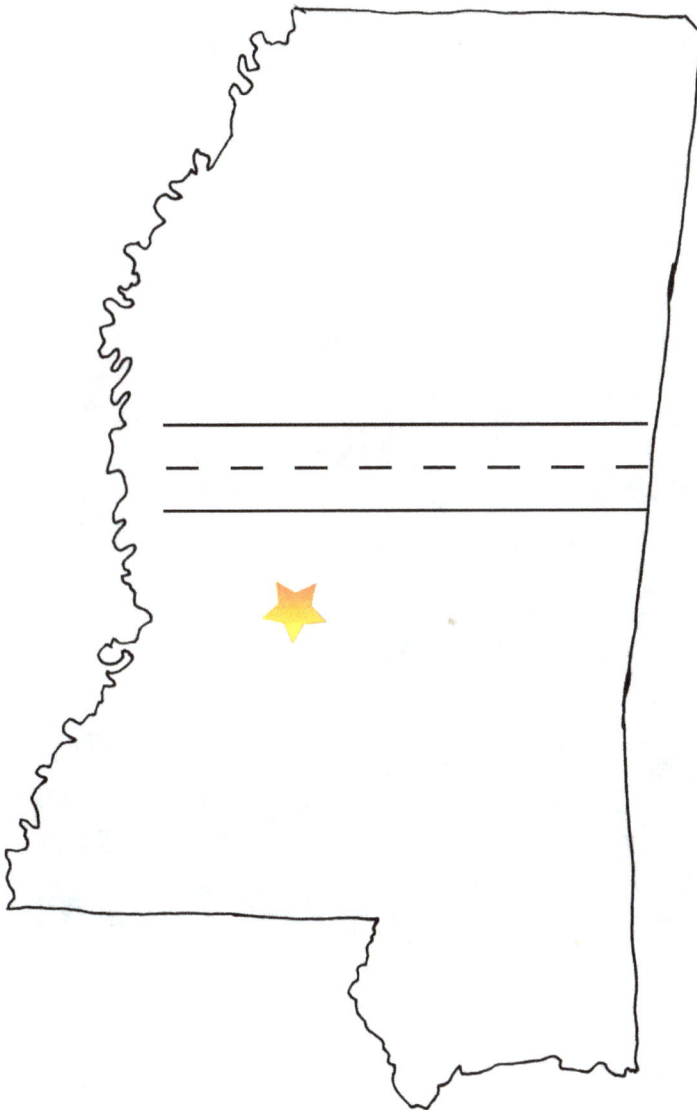

Mississippi
Abbreviation:
a. (MI)
b. (MP)
c. (MS)
Capital:
a. Jackson
b. Greenville
c. Hattiesburg
Nickname:
a. The Confederate State
b. Magnolia State
c. The Cotton State

Missouri

Answer each multiple choice question and write the state capital.

DID YOU KNOW?

The state flower is a:
Hawthorn

The state bird is a:
Bluebird

Missouri
Abbreviation:
a. (MS)
b. (MI)
c. (MO)
Capital:
a. St. Louis
b. Jefferson City
c. Kansas City
Nickname:
a. Show-Me-State
b. Pony Express State
c. Cattle State

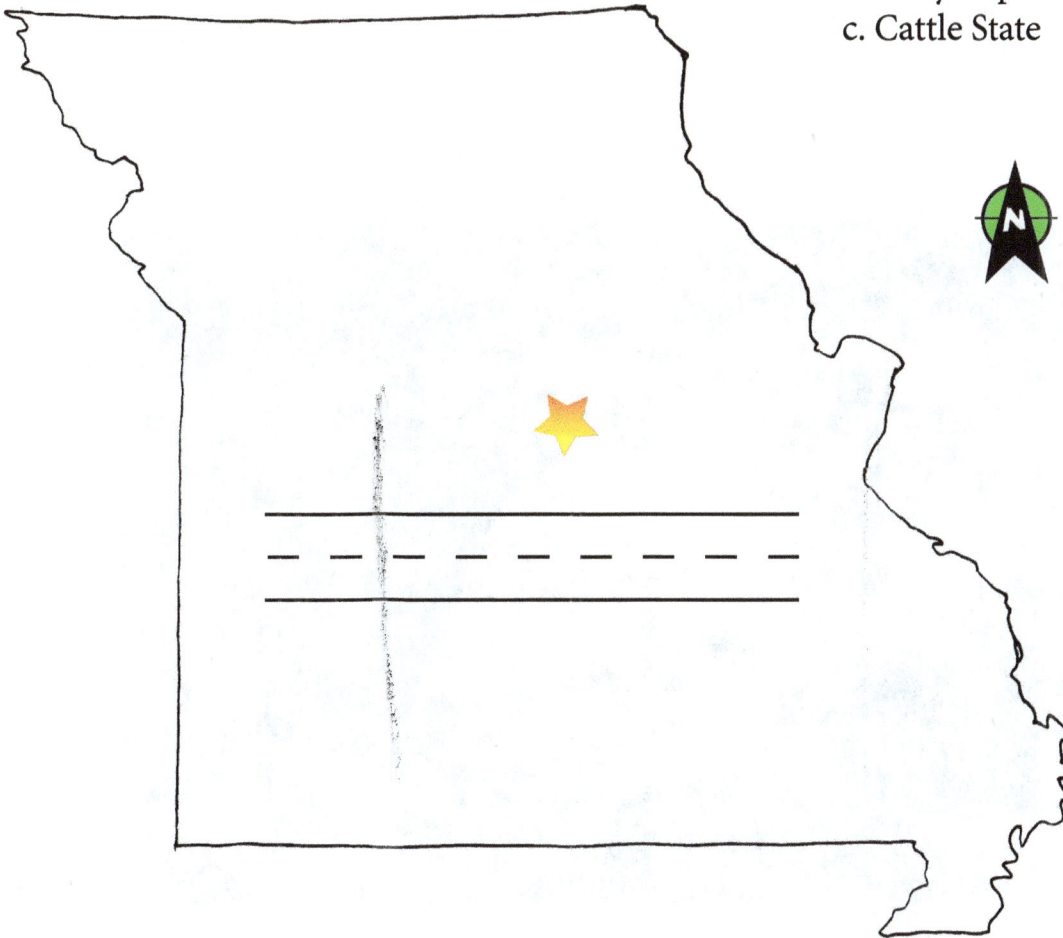

Montana

Answer each multiple choice question and write the state capital.

DID YOU KNOW?

The state flower is a:
Bitterroot

The state bird is a:
Western Meadowlark

Montana
Abbreviation:
a. (MA)
b. (MT)
c. (MO)
Capital:
a. Helena
b. Great Falls
c. Billings
Nickname:
a. Little Big Horn State
b. Yellowstone Valley State
c. Treasure State

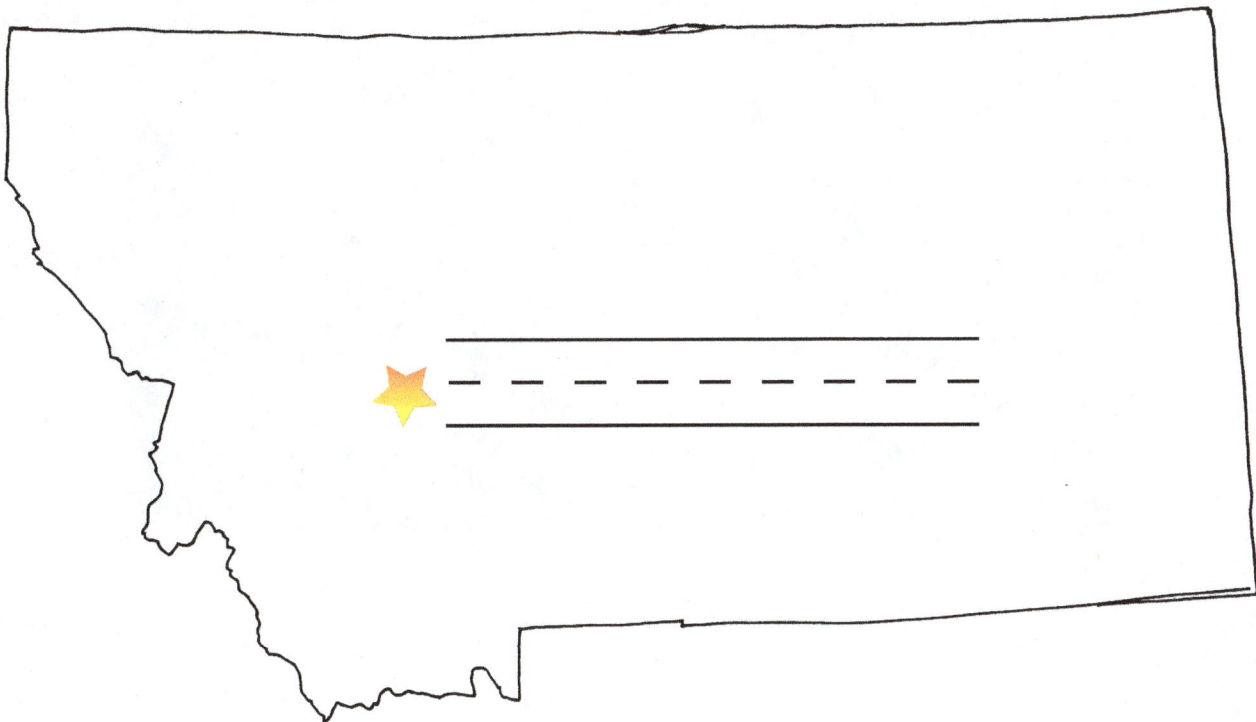

Nebraska

Answer each multiple choice question and write the state capital.

DID YOU KNOW?

The state flower is a:
Goldenrod

The state bird is a:
Western Meadowlark

Nebraska

Abbreviation:
a. (NE)
b. (NB)
c. (NA)

Capital:
a. Kearney
b. Omaha
c. Lincoln

Nickname:
a. Whitetail State
b. Cornhusker State
c. Fossil Bed State

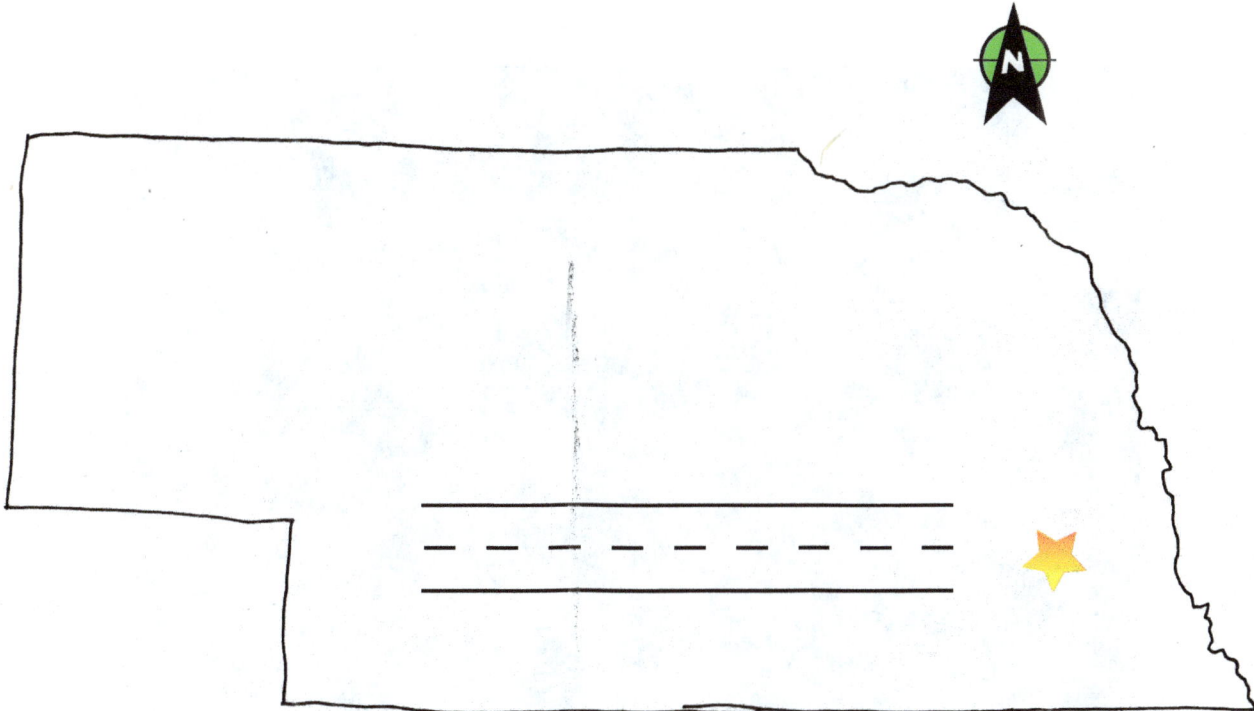

Nevada

Answer each multiple choice question and write the state capital.

DID YOU KNOW?

The state flower is a:
Sagebrush

The state bird is a:
Mountain Bluebird

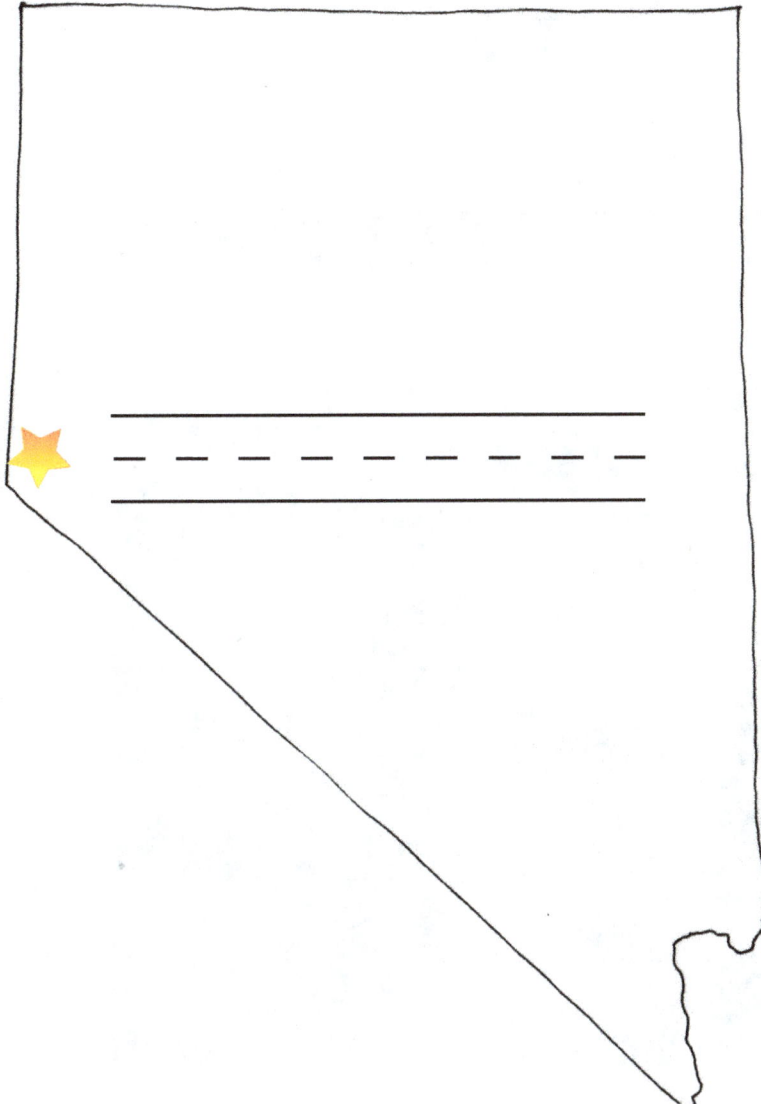

Nevada
Abbreviation:
a. (NV)
b. (NA)
c. (ND)
Capital:
a. Las Vegas
b. Carson City
c. Reno
Nickname:
a. Hoover Dam State
b. Comstock Lode State
c. Silver State; Sagebrush State
   Battle Born State

New Hampshire

Answer each multiple choice question and write the state capital.

DID YOU KNOW?

The state flower is a:
Purple Lilac

The state bird is a:
Purple Finch

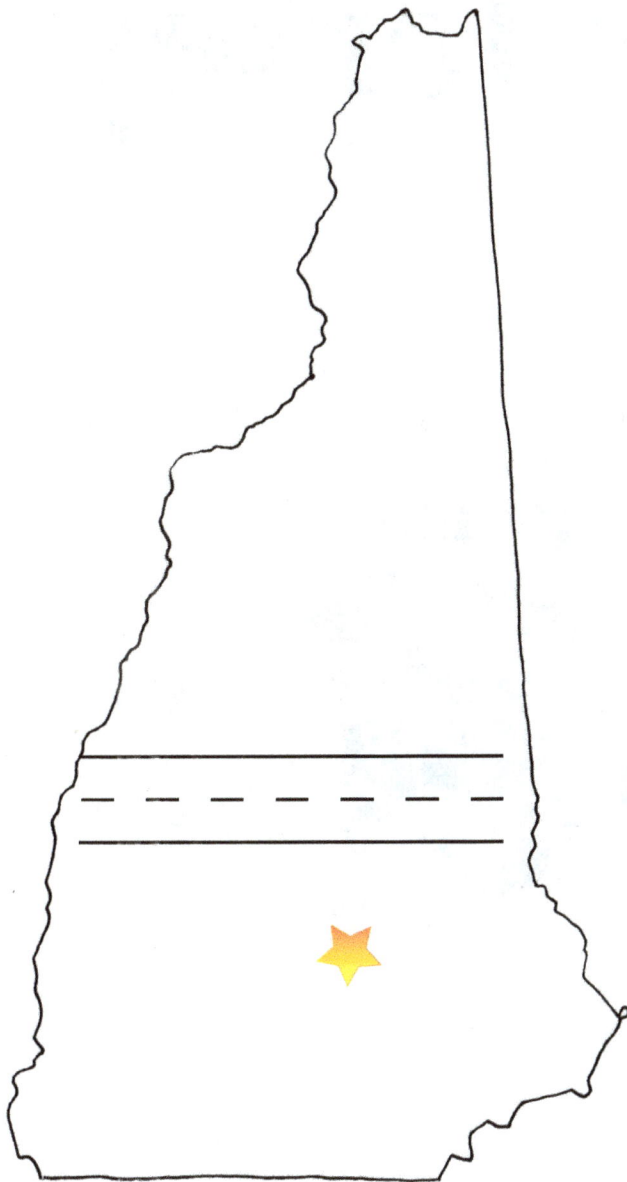

New Hampshire

Abbreviation:

a. (NP)

b. (NH)

c. (NE)

Capital:

a. Salem

b. Concord

c. Manchester

Nickname:

a. Old Man of the
   Mountain State

b. The Industrial State

c. Granite State

New Jersey

Answer each multiple choice question and write the state capital.

DID YOU KNOW?

The state flower is a:
Purple Violet

The state bird is an:
Eastern Goldfinch

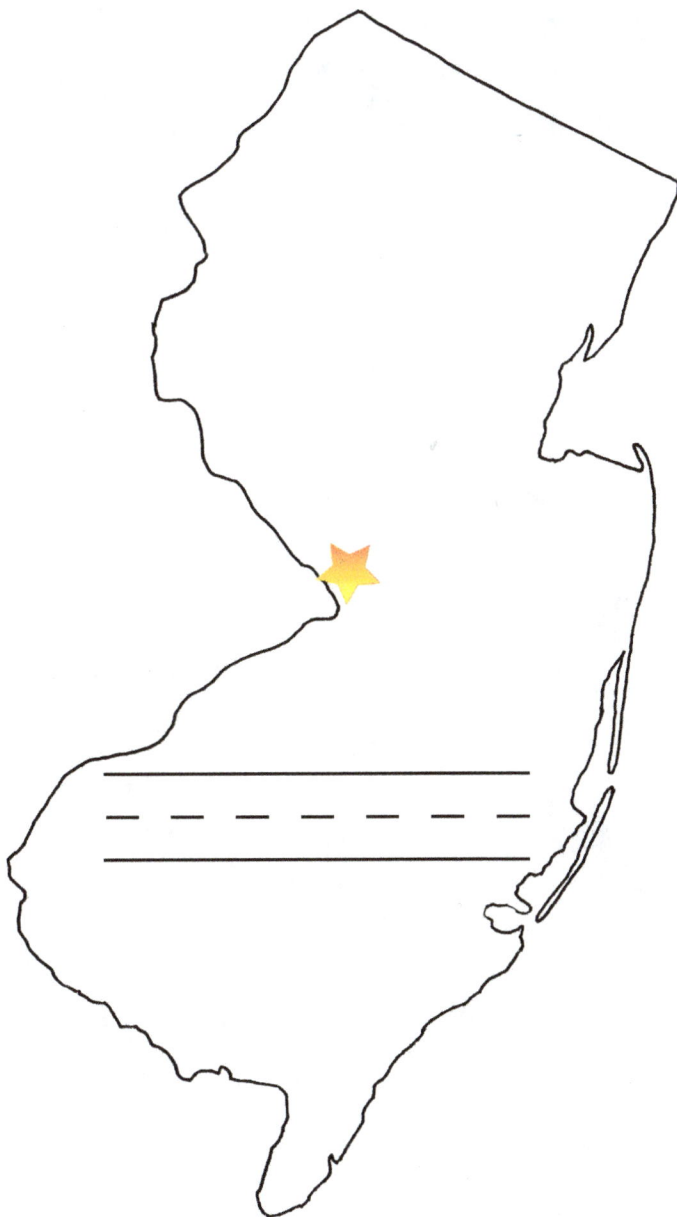

New Jersey

Abbreviation:
a. (NS)
b. (NR)
c. (NJ)

Capital:
a. Jersey City
b. Trenton
c. Newark

Nickname:
a. Boardwalk State
b. The Produce State
c. Garden State

New Mexico

Answer each multiple choice question and write the state capital.

DID YOU KNOW?

The state flower is a:
Yucca

The state bird is a:
Roadrunner

New Mexico

Abbreviation:
a. (NX)
b. (NM)
c. (NO)

Capital:
a. Albuquerque
b. Las Cruces
c. Santa Fe

Nickname:
a. The Apache State
b. Land of Enchantment
c. Rio Grande State

New York

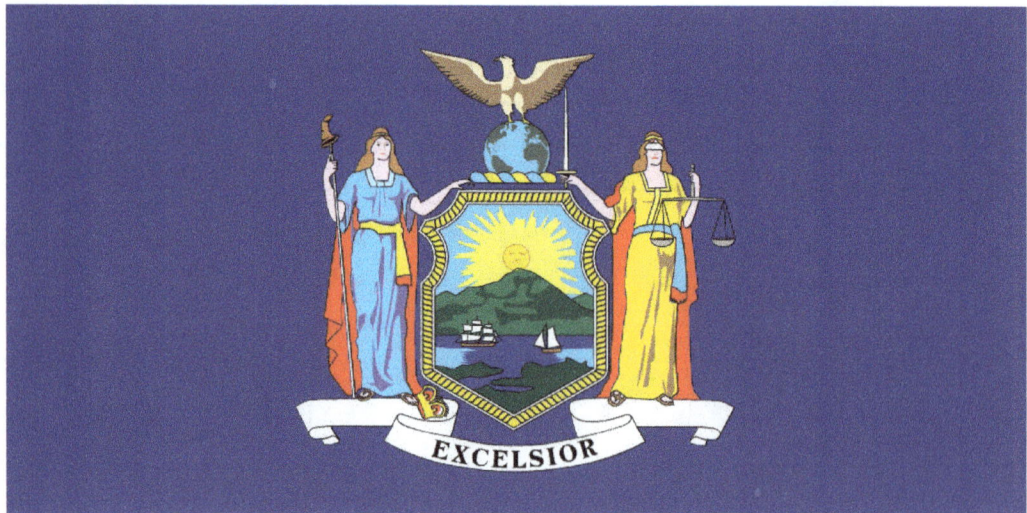

Answer each multiple choice question and write the state capital.

DID YOU KNOW?

The state flower is a:
Rose

The state bird is a:
Bluebird

New York

Abbreviation:
a. (NY)
b. (NO)
c. (NK)

Capital:
a. New York City
b. Albany
c. Manhattan

Nickname:
a. The Big Apple
b. Empire State
c. Concrete Jungle

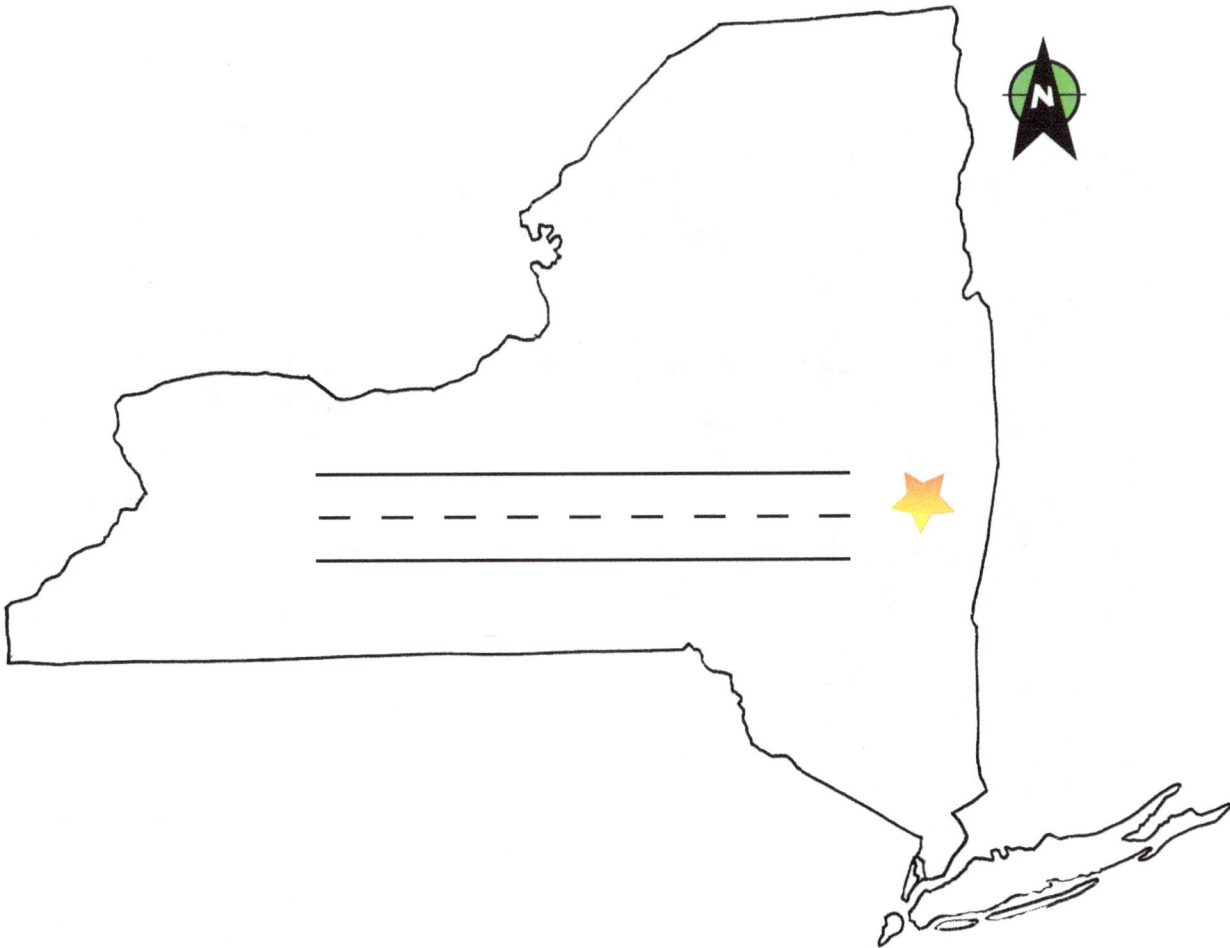

North Carolina

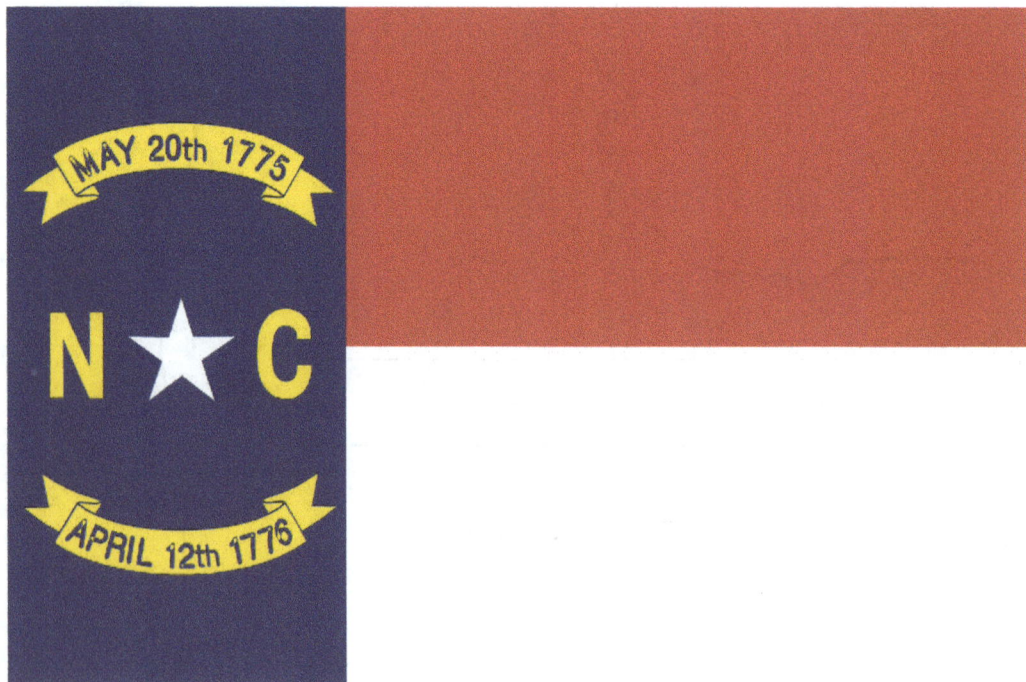

Answer each multiple choice question and write the state capital.

DID YOU KNOW?

The state flower is a:
Dogwood

The state bird is a:
Cardinal

North Carolina

Abbreviation:
a. (NC)
b. (NA)
c. (NO)

Capital:
a. Raleigh
b. Greensboro
c. Charlotte

Nickname:
a. Tar Heel State
b. Blue Ridge Mountain State
c. Life Science State

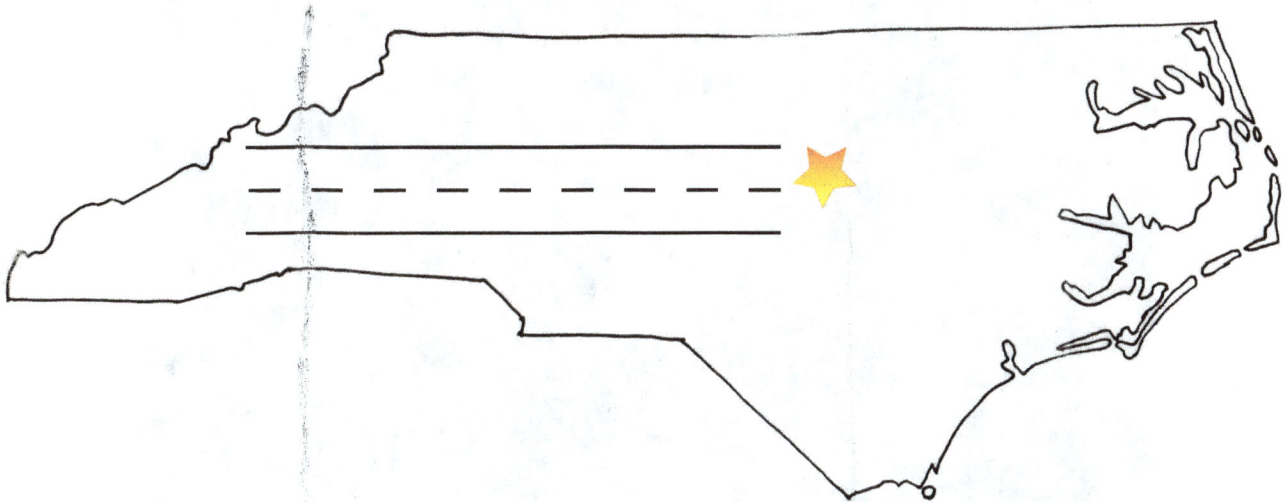

North Dakota

Answer each multiple choice question and write the state capital.

DID YOU KNOW?

The state flower is a:
Wild Prairie Rose

The state bird is a:
Western Meadowlark

North Dakota

Abbreviation:
a. (NK)
b. (ND)
c. (NA)

Capital:
a. Williston
b. Fargo
c. Bismarck

Nickname:
a. Peace Garden State; Sioux State; Flickertail State; Rough Rider State
b. The Crude State
c. The Prairie State

Ohio

Answer each multiple choice question and write the state capital.

DID YOU KNOW?

The state flower is a:
Scarlet Carnation

The state bird is a:
Cardinal

Ohio
Abbreviation:
a. (OH)
b. (OO)
c. (OI)
Capital:
a. Cleveland
b. Cincinnati
c. Columbus
Nickname:
a. The Fertile State
b. Buckeye State
c. The Carnation State

Oklahoma

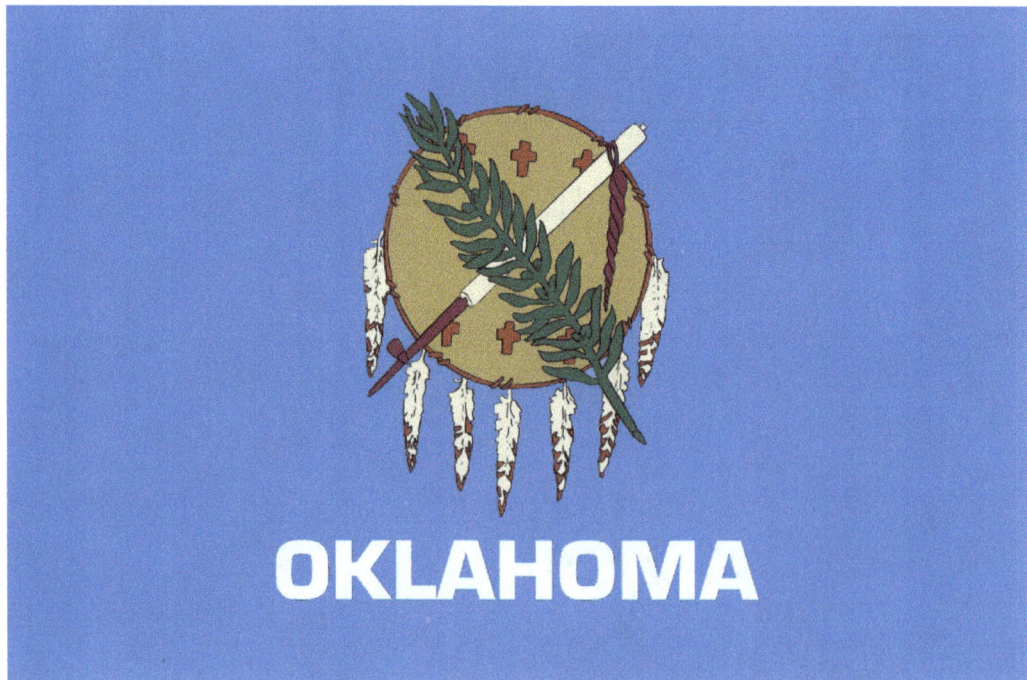

Answer each multiple choice question and write the state capital.

DID YOU KNOW?

The state flower is a:
Mistletoe

The state bird is a:
Scissor-Tailed Flycatcher

Oklahoma

Abbreviation:
a. (OA)
b. (OL)
c. (OK)

Capital:
a. Norman
b. Tulsa
c. Oklahoma City

Nickname:
a. Tornado Alley
b. Broken Arrow State
c. Sooner State

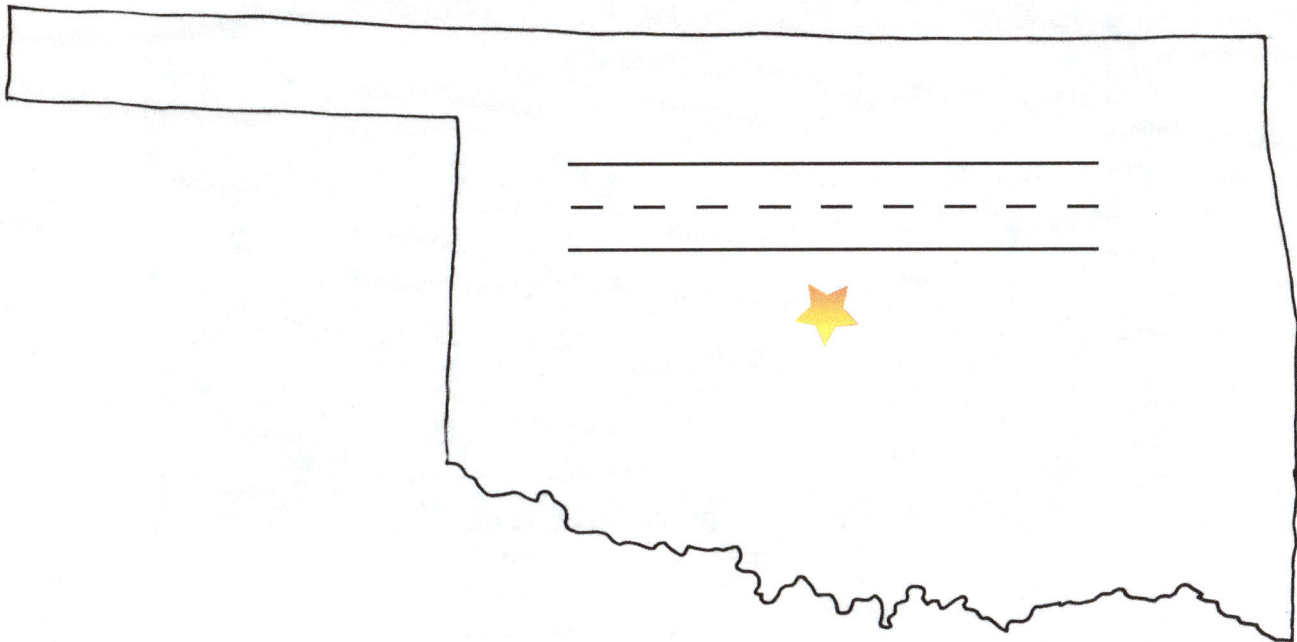

Oregon

Answer each multiple choice question and write the state capital.

DID YOU KNOW?

The state flower is a:
Oregon Grape

The state bird is a:
Western Meadowlark

Oregon

Abbreviation:
a. (ON)
b. (OR)
c. (OG)

Capital:
a. Salem
b. Beaverton
c. Portland

Nickname:
a. Elk State
b. Beaver State
c. Coyote State

Pennsylvania

Answer each multiple choice question and write the state capital.

DID YOU KNOW?

The state flower is a:
Mountain Laurel

The state bird is a:
Ruffed Grouse

Pennsylvania

Abbreviation:
a. (PE)
b. (PA)
c. (PN)

Capital:
a. Harrisburg
b. Philadelphia
c. Pittsburgh

Nickname:
a. Mountain Laurel State
b. The Quaker State
c. Keystone State

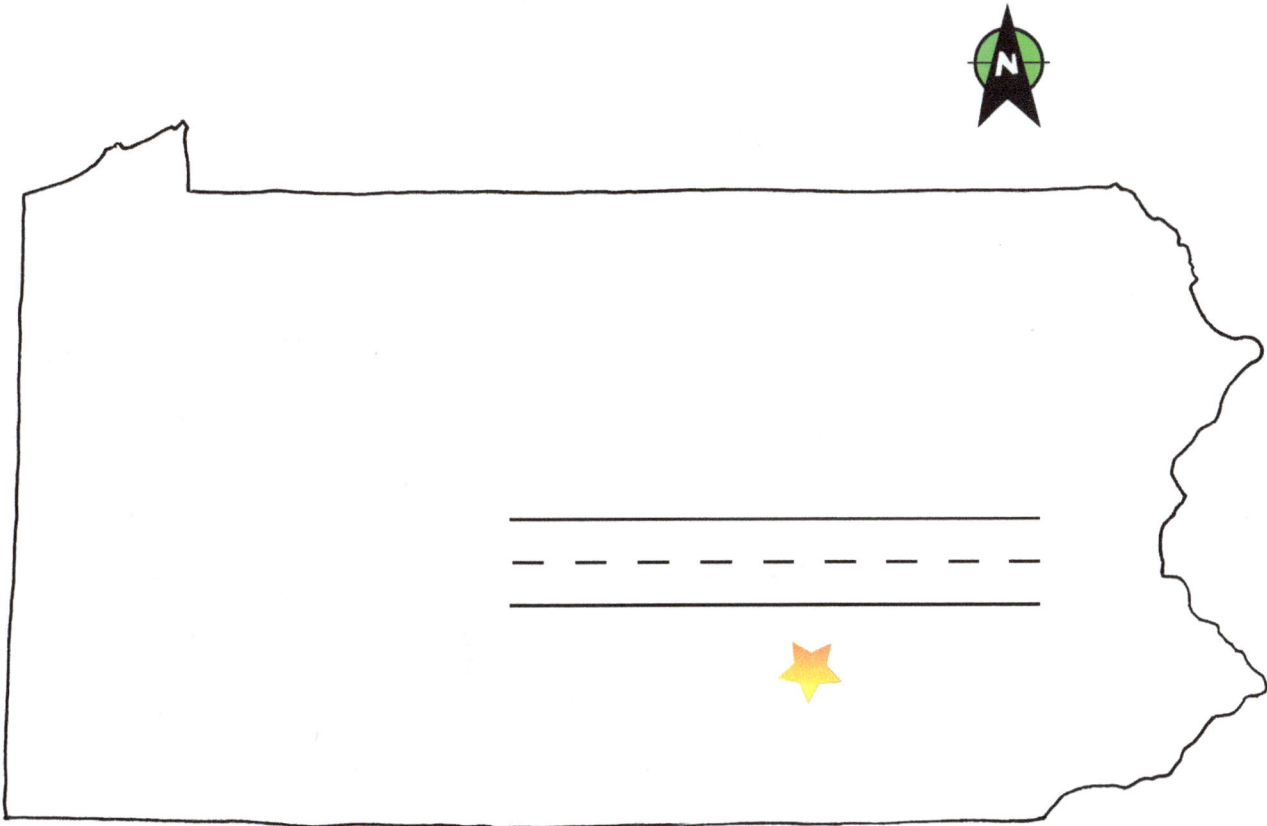

Rhode Island

Answer each multiple choice question and write the state capital.

DID YOU KNOW?

The state flower is a:
Violet

The state bird is a:
Rhode Island Red Hen

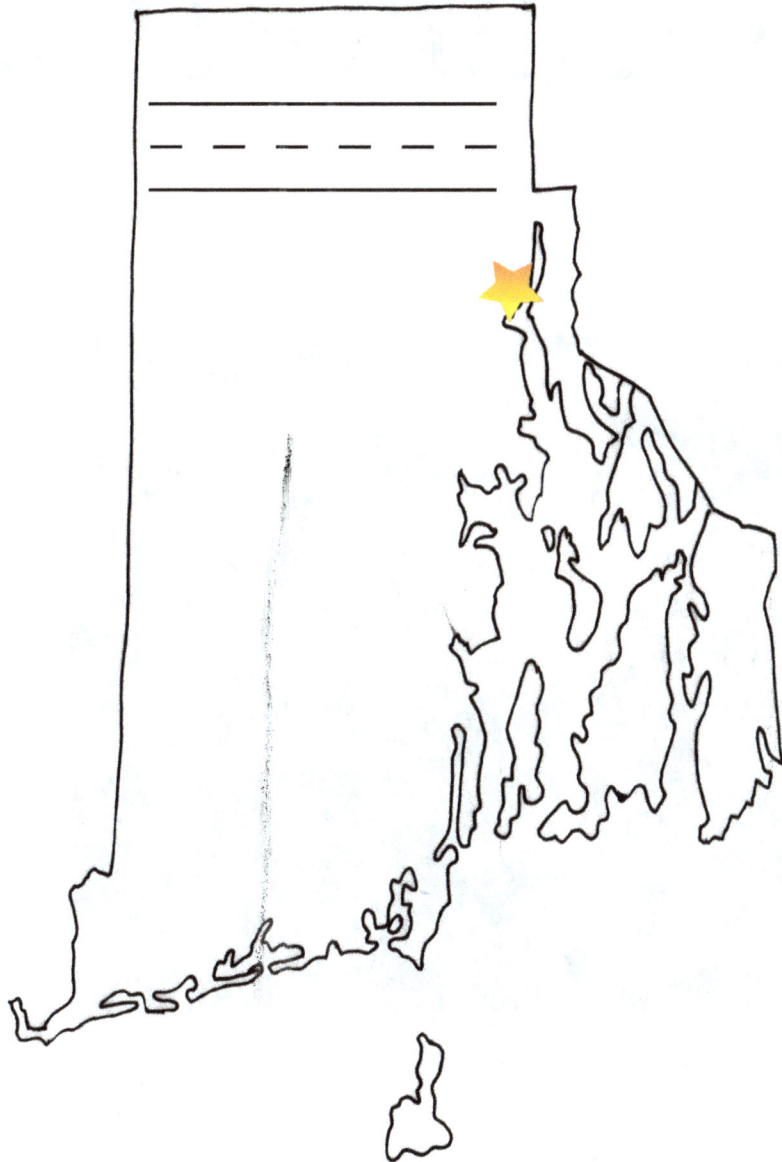

Rhode Island
Abbreviation:
a. (RI)
b. (RD)
c. (RH)
Capital:
a. Providence
b. Warwick
c. East Providence
Nickname:
a. The Block Island
b. The Ocean State
c. Greek Island of Rhodes

South Carolina

Answer each multiple choice question and write the state capital.

DID YOU KNOW?

The state flower is a:
Carolina Yellow Jessamine

The state bird is a:
Carolina Wren

South Carolina
Abbreviation:
a. (SA)
b. (SO)
c. (SC)
Capital:
a. Columbia
b. Charleston
c. Greenville
Nickname:
a. Production State
b. Plantation State
c. Palmetto State

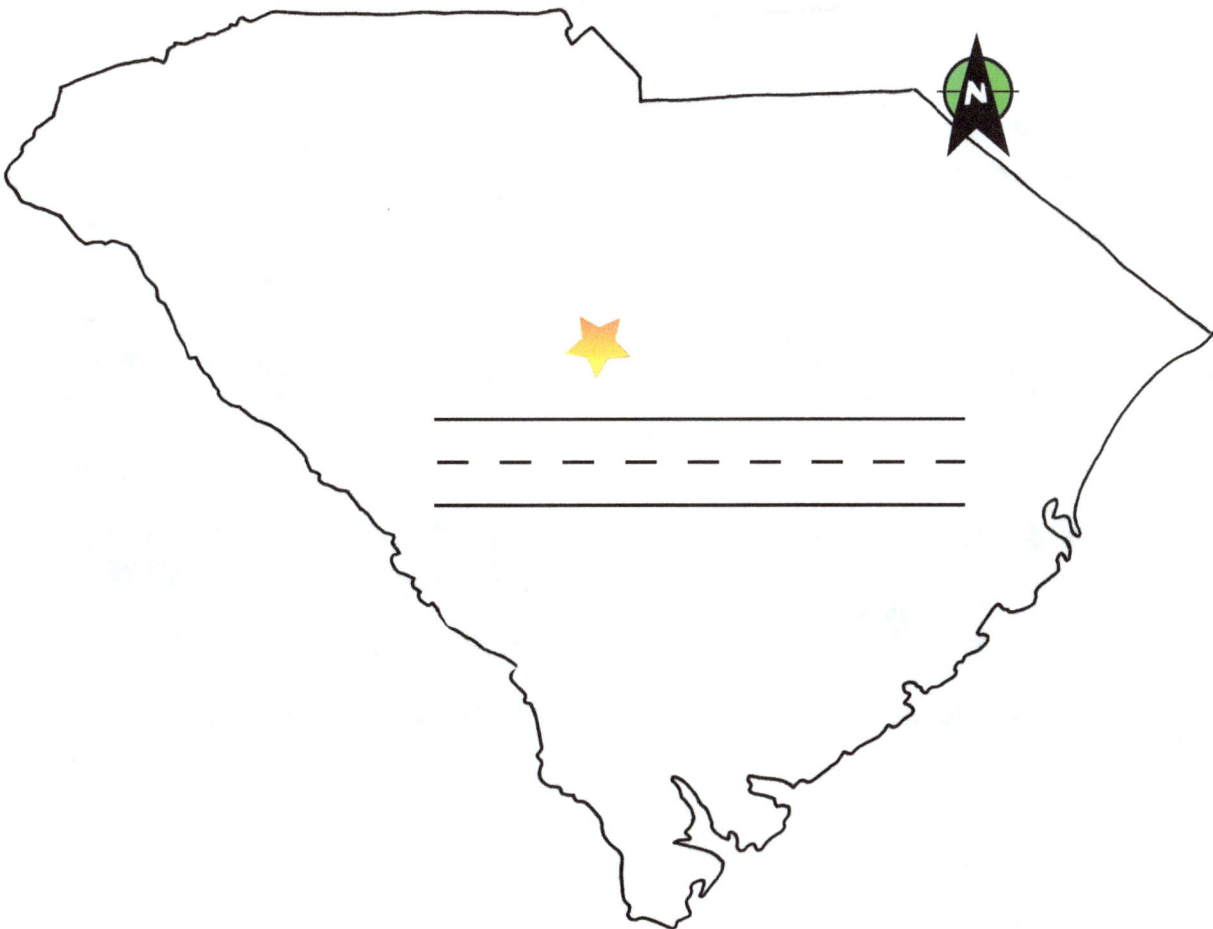

South Dakota

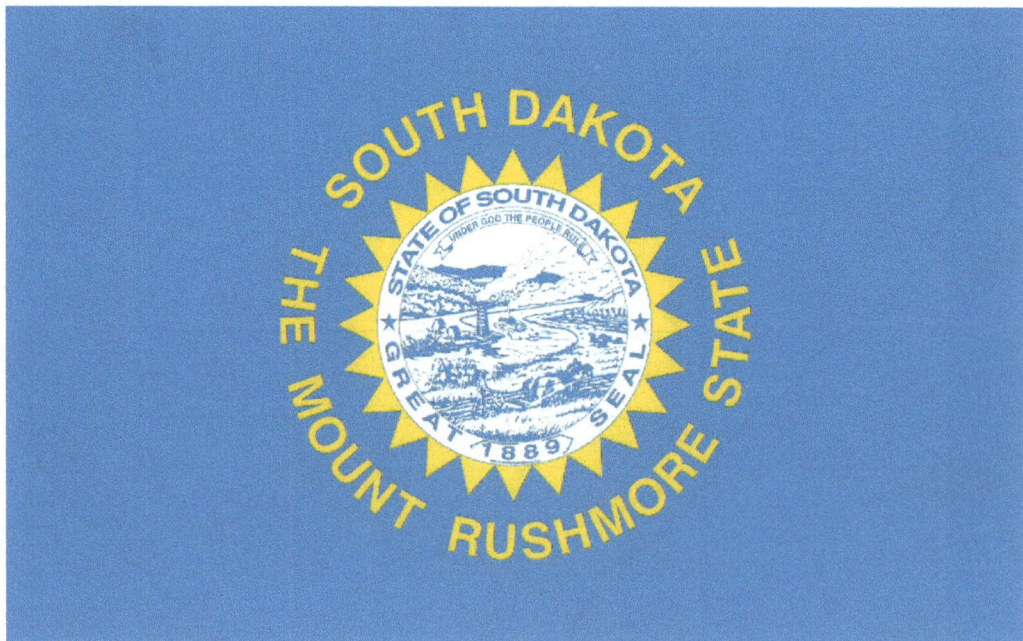

Answer each multiple choice question and write the state capital.

DID YOU KNOW?

The state flower is an:
American Pasqueflower

The state bird is a:
Ring-Necked Pheasant

South Dakota

Abbreviation:
a. (SD)
b. (SK)
c. (SA)

Capital:
a. Rapid City
b. Pierre
c. Sioux Falls

Nickname:
a. Mount Rushmore State;
   Coyote State
b. Black Hills State
c. Badlands State

Tennessee

Answer each multiple choice question and write the state capital.

DID YOU KNOW?

The state flower is an:
Iris

The state bird is a:
Mockingbird

Tennessee

Abbreviation:
a. (TS)
b. (TE)
c. (TN)

Capital:
a. Memphis
b. Nashville
c. Chattanooga

Nickname:
a. Smoky Mountain State
b. Commerce State
c. Volunteer State

Texas

Answer each multiple choice question and write the state capital.

DID YOU KNOW?

The state flower is a:
Bluebonnet

The state bird is a:
Mockingbird

Texas

Abbreviation:
a. (TE)
b. (TS)
c. (TX)

Capital:
a. Austin
b. Dallas
c. Houston

Nickname:
a. Lone Star State
b. Alamo State
c. Cowboy State

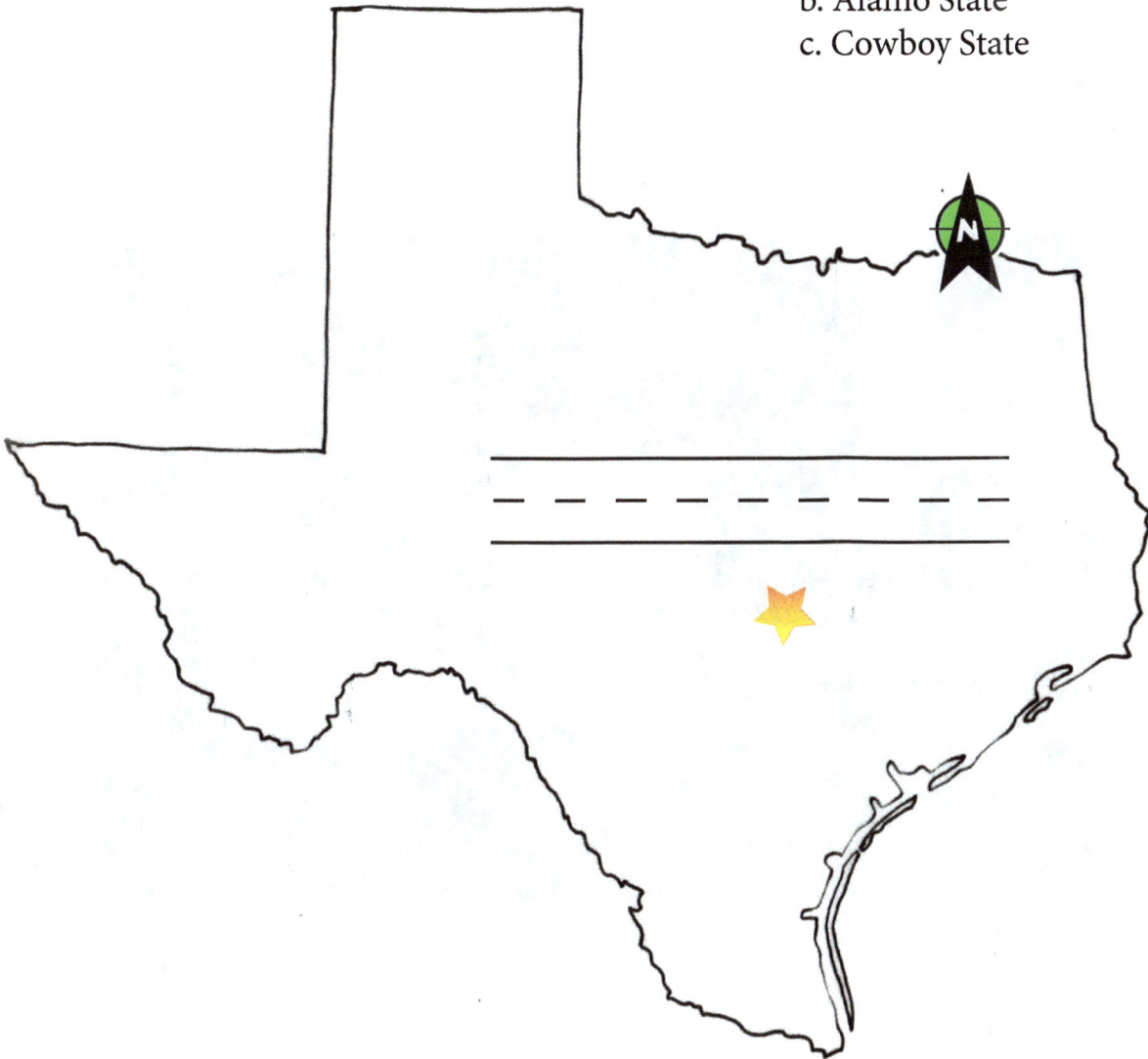

Utah

Answer each multiple choice question and write the state capital.

DID YOU KNOW?

The state flower is a:
Sego Lilly

The state bird is a:
California Gull

Utah
Abbreviation:
a. (UT)
b. (UH)
c. (UA)
Capital:
a. Salt Lake City
b. Park City
c. Provo
Nickname:
a. Mormon State
b. Beehive State
c. Salt Flat State

Vermont

Answer each multiple choice question and write the state capital.

DID YOU KNOW?

The state flower is a:
Red Clover

The state bird is a:
Hermit Thrush

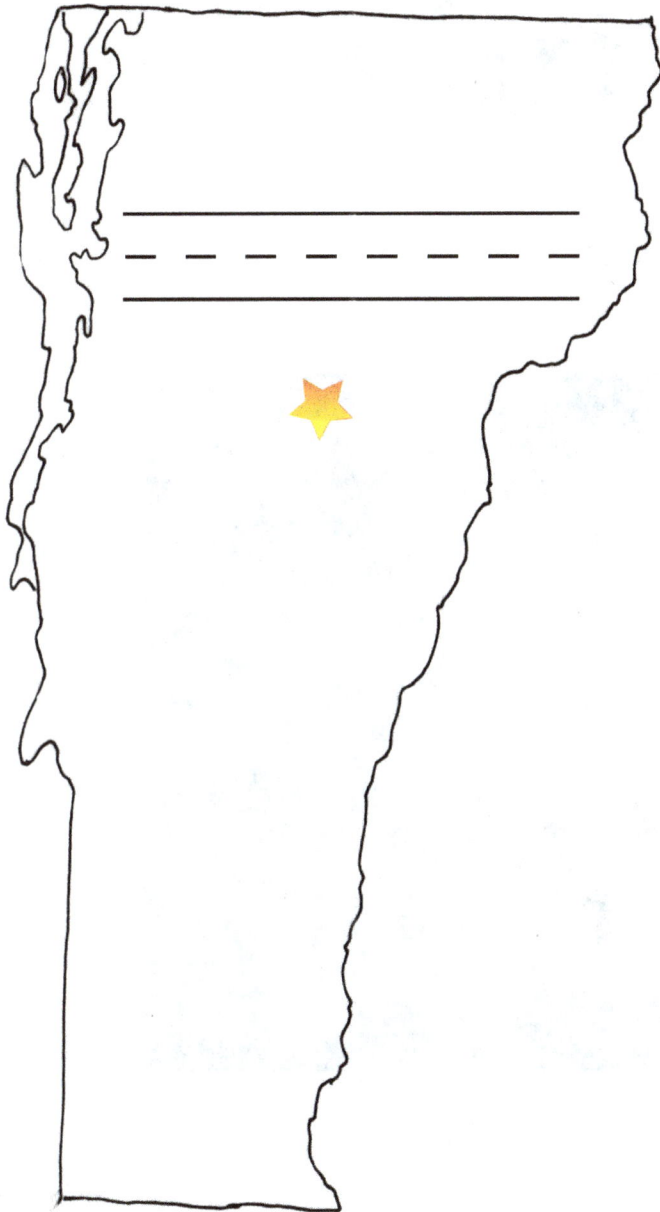

Vermont
Abbreviation:
a. (VM)
b. (VT)
c. (VE)
Capital:
a. Burlington
b. Montpelier
c. Rutland
Nickname:
a. Homestead State
b. Green Mountain State
c. Red Clover State

Virginia

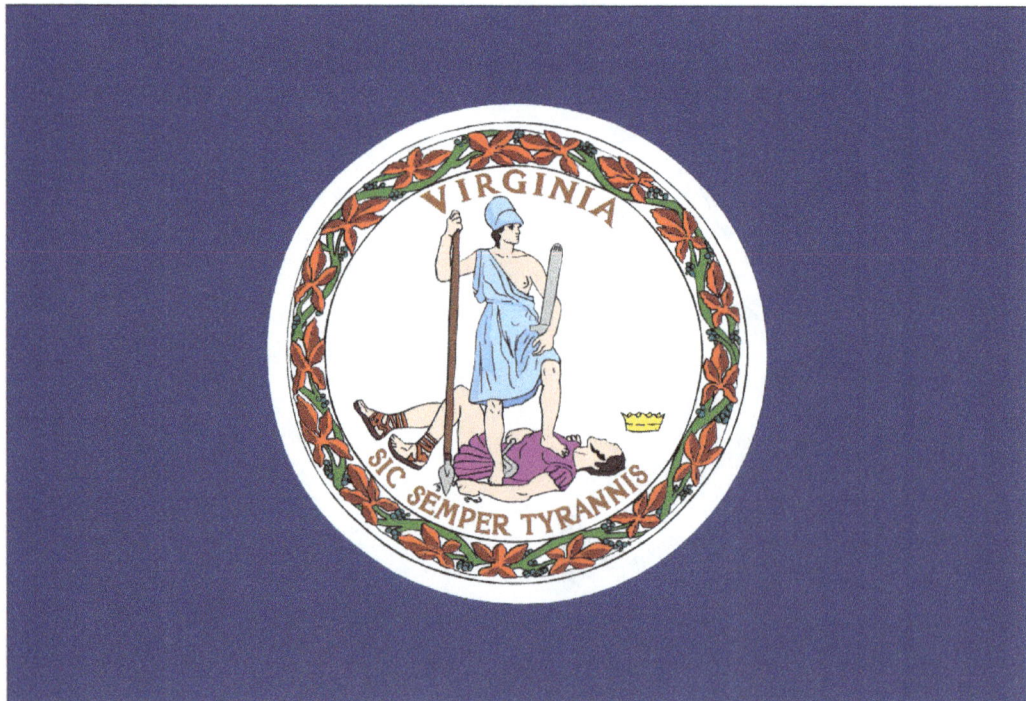

Answer each multiple choice question and write the state capital.

DID YOU KNOW?

The state flower is an:
American Dogwood

The state bird is a:
Cardinal

Virginia
Abbreviation:
a. (VA)
b. (VI)
c. (VG)
Capital:
a. Virginia Beach
b. Norfolk
c. Richmond
Nickname:
a. Tobacco State
b. The Old Dominion;
   Mother of Presidents
c. Revolution State

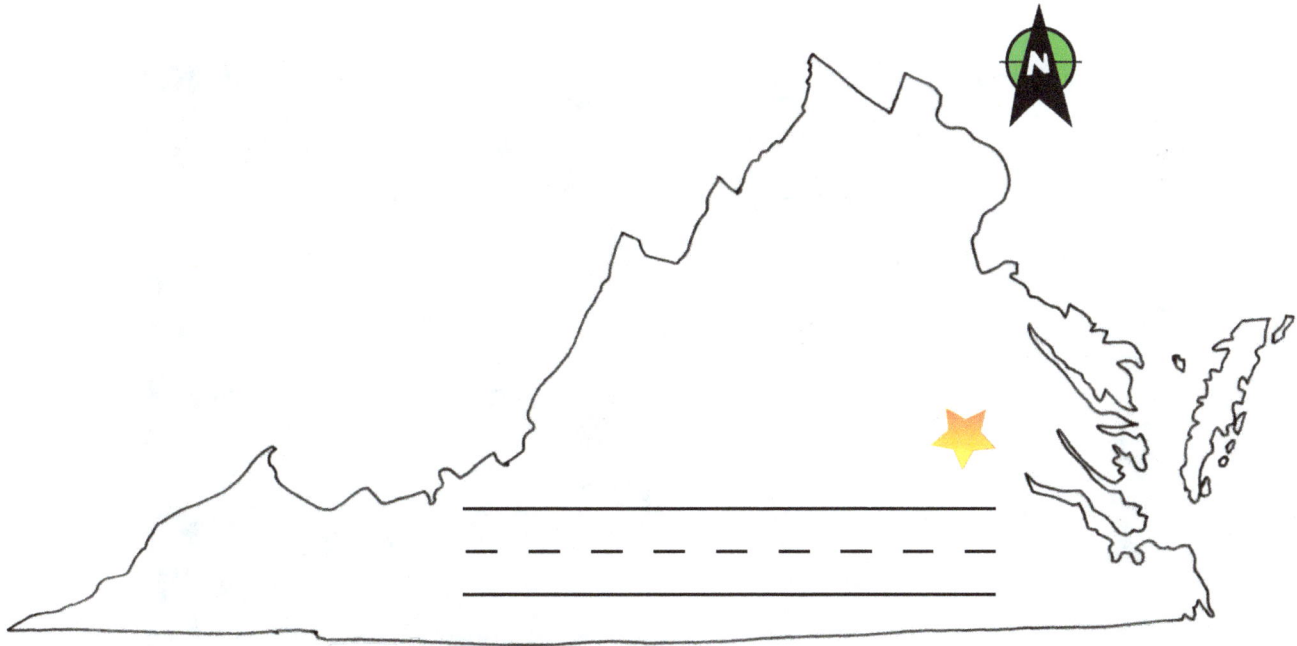

Washington

Answer each multiple choice question and write the state capital.

DID YOU KNOW?

The state flower is a:
Coast Rhododendron

The state bird is a:
Willow Goldfinch

Washington
Abbreviation:
a. (WN)
b. (WT)
c. (WA)
Capital:
a. Seattle
b. Tacoma
c. Olympia
Nickname:
a. Evergreen State
b. The Rain State
c. George Washington State

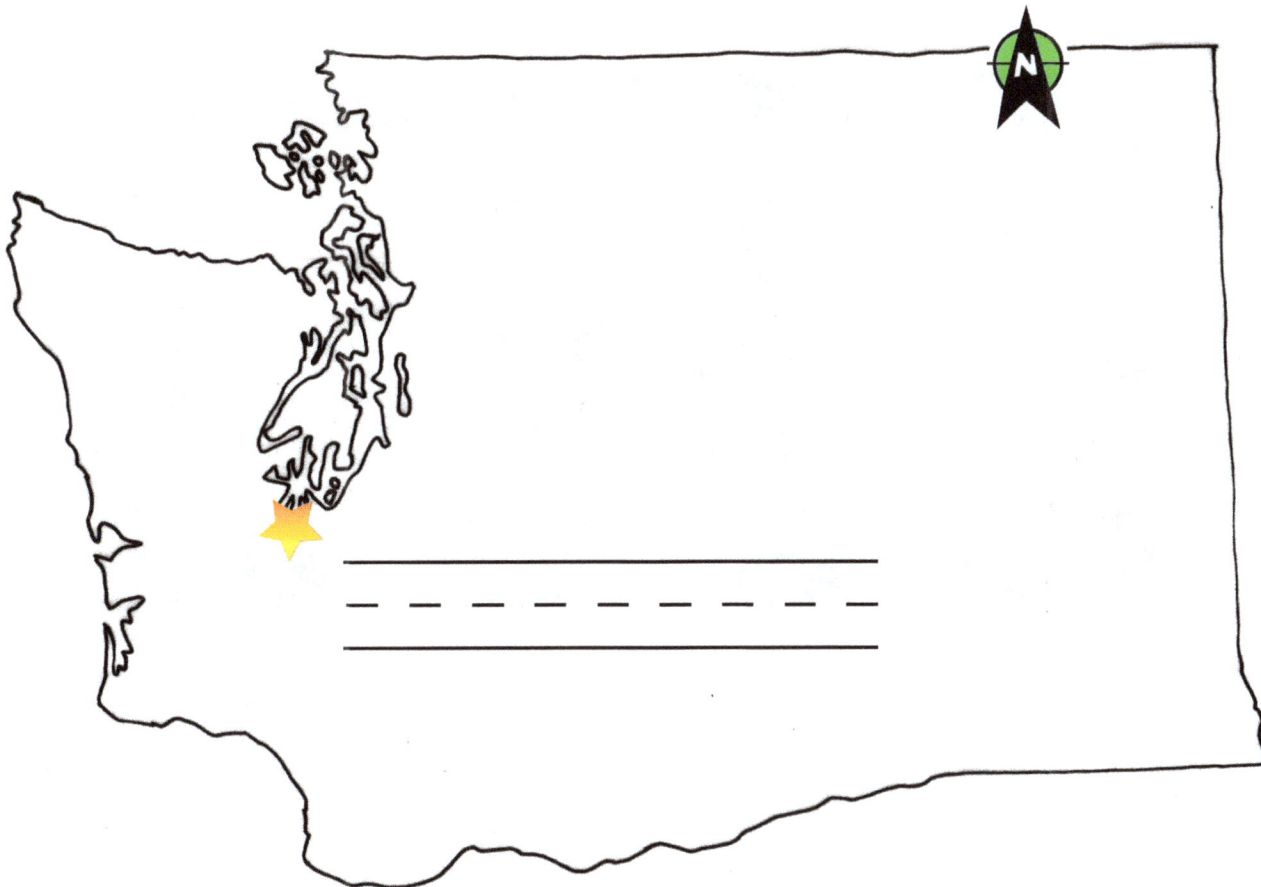

West Virginia

Answer each multiple choice question and write the state capital.

DID YOU KNOW?

The state flower is a:
Rhododendron

The state bird is a:
Cardinal

West Virginia

Abbreviation:
a. (WG)
b. (WV)
c. (WN)

Capital:
a. Charleston
b. Huntington
c. Clarksburg

Nickname:
a. Coal State
b. The Hardwood Forest State
c. Mountain State

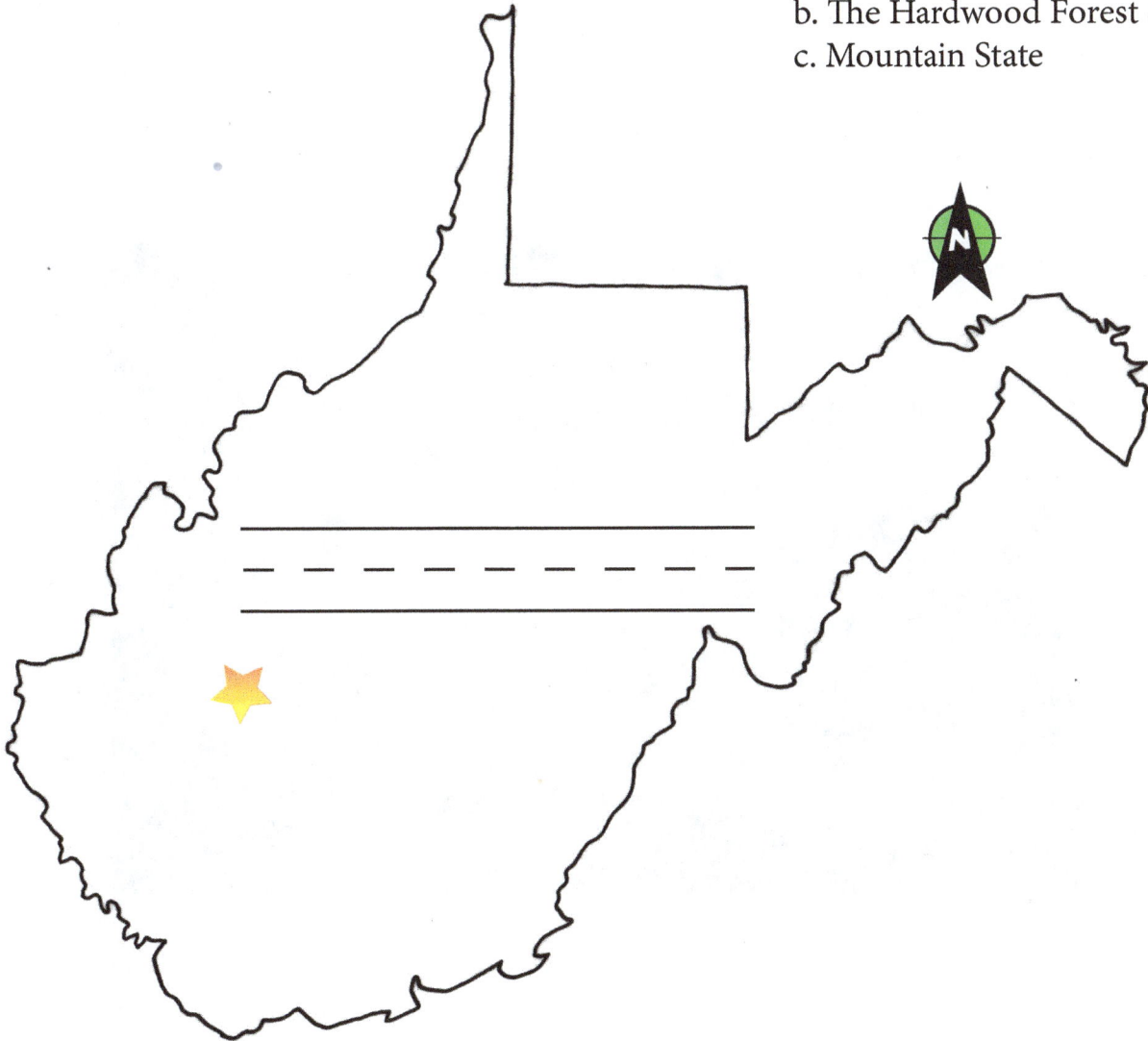

Wisconsin

Answer each multiple choice question and write the state capital.

DID YOU KNOW?

The state flower is a:
Wood Violet

The state bird is a:
Robin

Wisconsin

Abbreviation:
a. (WC)
b. (WI)
c. (WS)

Capital:
a. Madison
b. Appleton
c. Oshkosh

Nickname:
a. Badger State
b. 14,000 Lakes State
c. The Winnebago State

Wyoming

Answer each multiple choice question and write the state capital.

DID YOU KNOW?

The state flower is an:
Indian Paintbrush

The state bird is a:
Western Meadowlark

Wyoming
Abbreviation:
a. (WM)
b. (WY)
c. (WG)
Capital:
a. Casper
b. Cheyenne
c. Rocky Springs
Nickname:
a. Yellowstone State
b. Equality State
c. Valley State

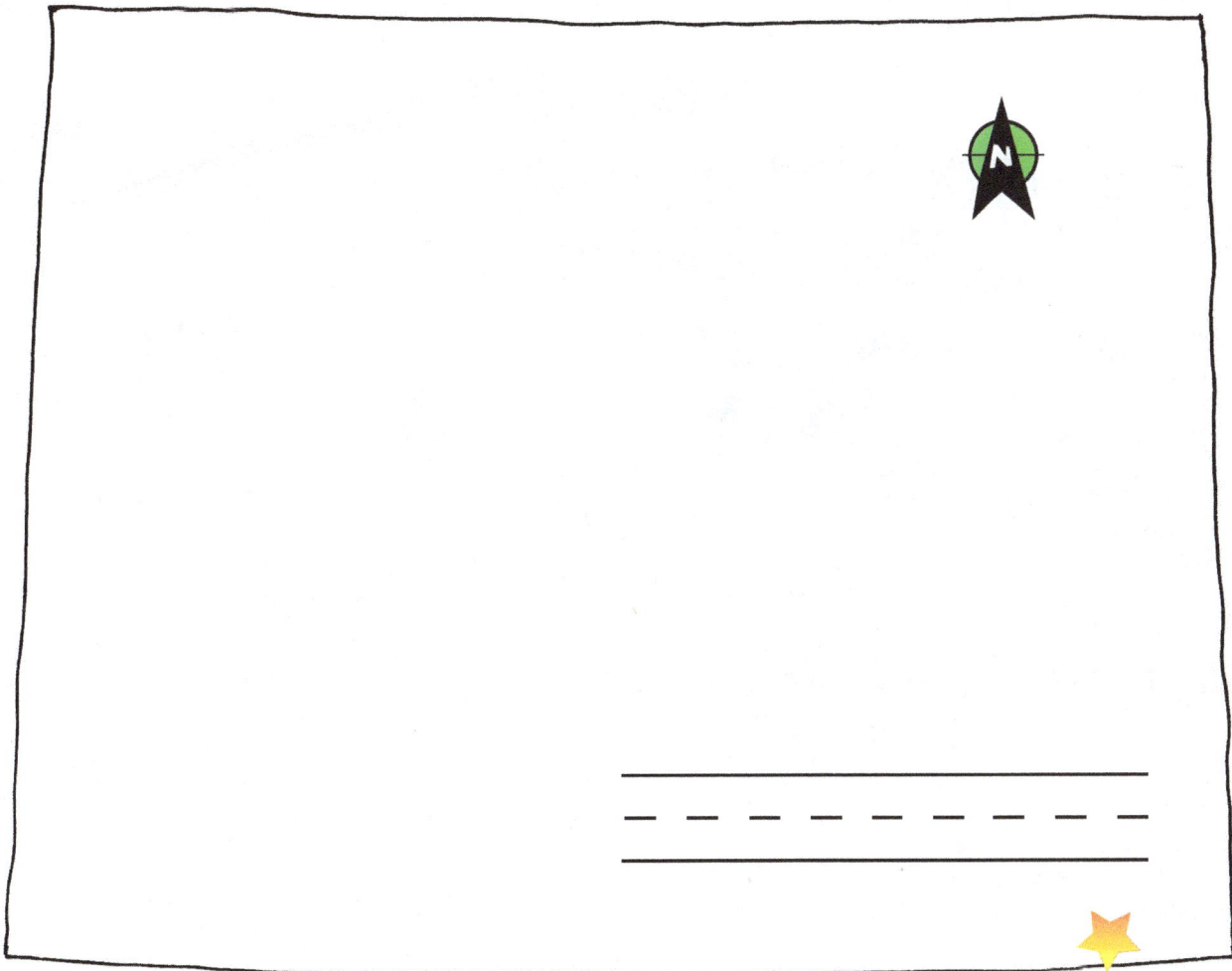

United States of America

DID YOU KNOW?

Washington, D.C.* is the capital of the United States of America which can be found within the state of Maryland along the border of Virginia. *D.C. stands for District of Columbia.

This city has many historic sites and landmarks such as: The White House, The National Mall, The United States Capital, The Lincoln Memorial, The Washington Monument, The Supreme Court Building, The Martin Luther King Jr. Memorial and many more.

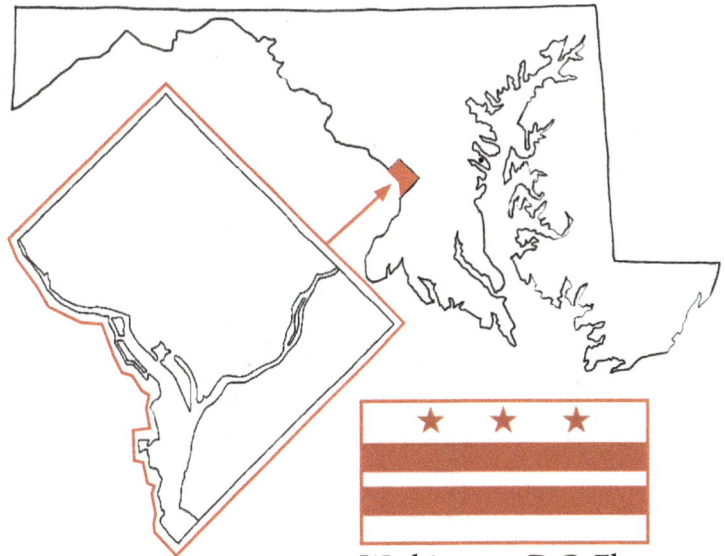

Washington, D.C. Flag

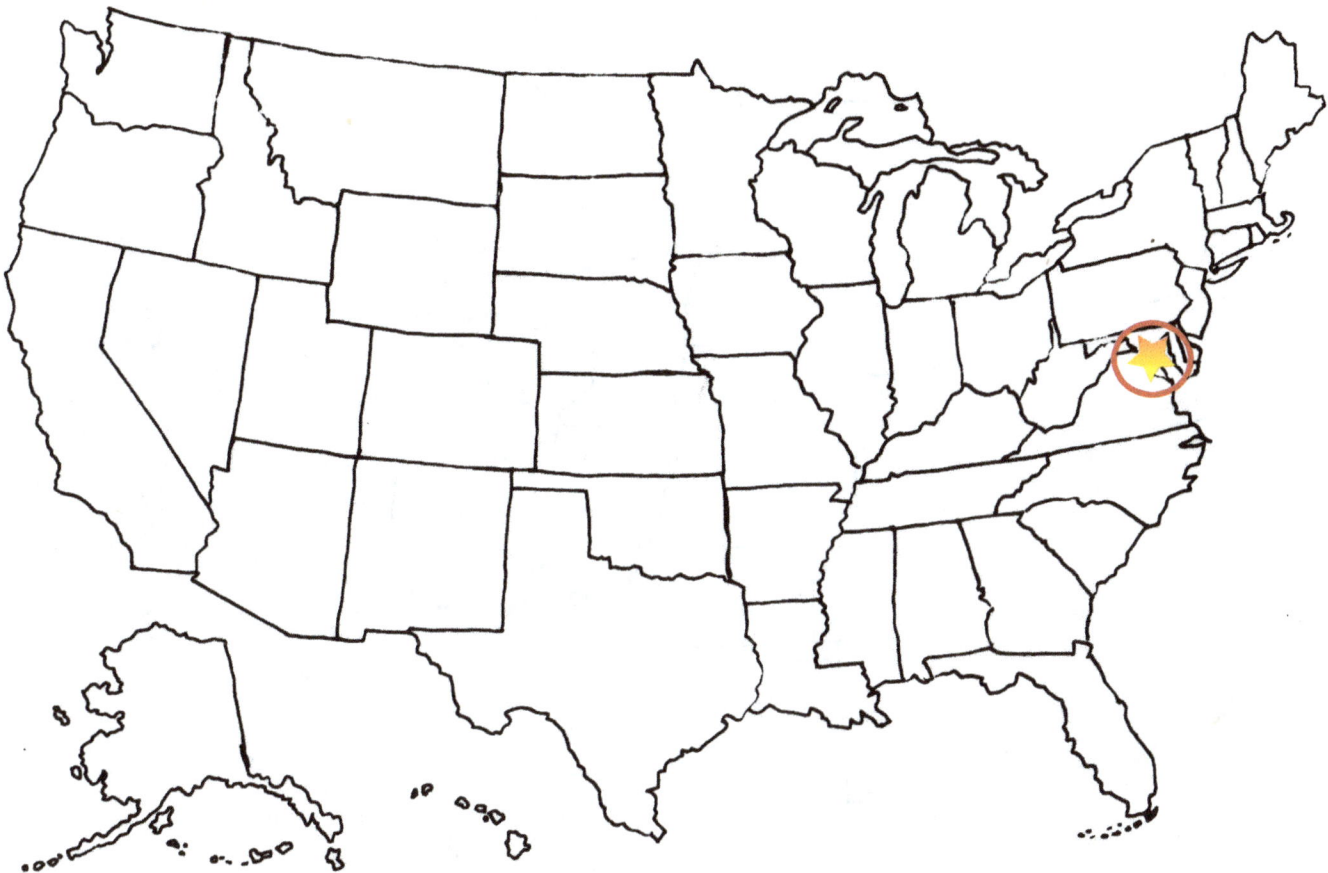

PEJETALES©

Each state has been numbered, identify and abbreviate each state.

1. (WA)
2. _____
3. _____
4. _____
5. _____
6. _____
7. _____
8. _____
9. _____
10. _____

11. _____
12. _____
13. _____
14. _____
15. _____
16. _____
17. _____
18. _____
19. _____
20. _____

21. _____
22. _____
23. _____
24. _____
25. _____
26. _____
27. _____
28. _____
29. _____
30. _____

31. _____
32. _____
33. _____
34. _____
35. _____
36. _____
37. _____
38. _____
39. _____
40. _____

41. _____
42. _____
43. _____
44. _____
45. _____
46. _____
47. _____
48. _____
49. _____
50. _____

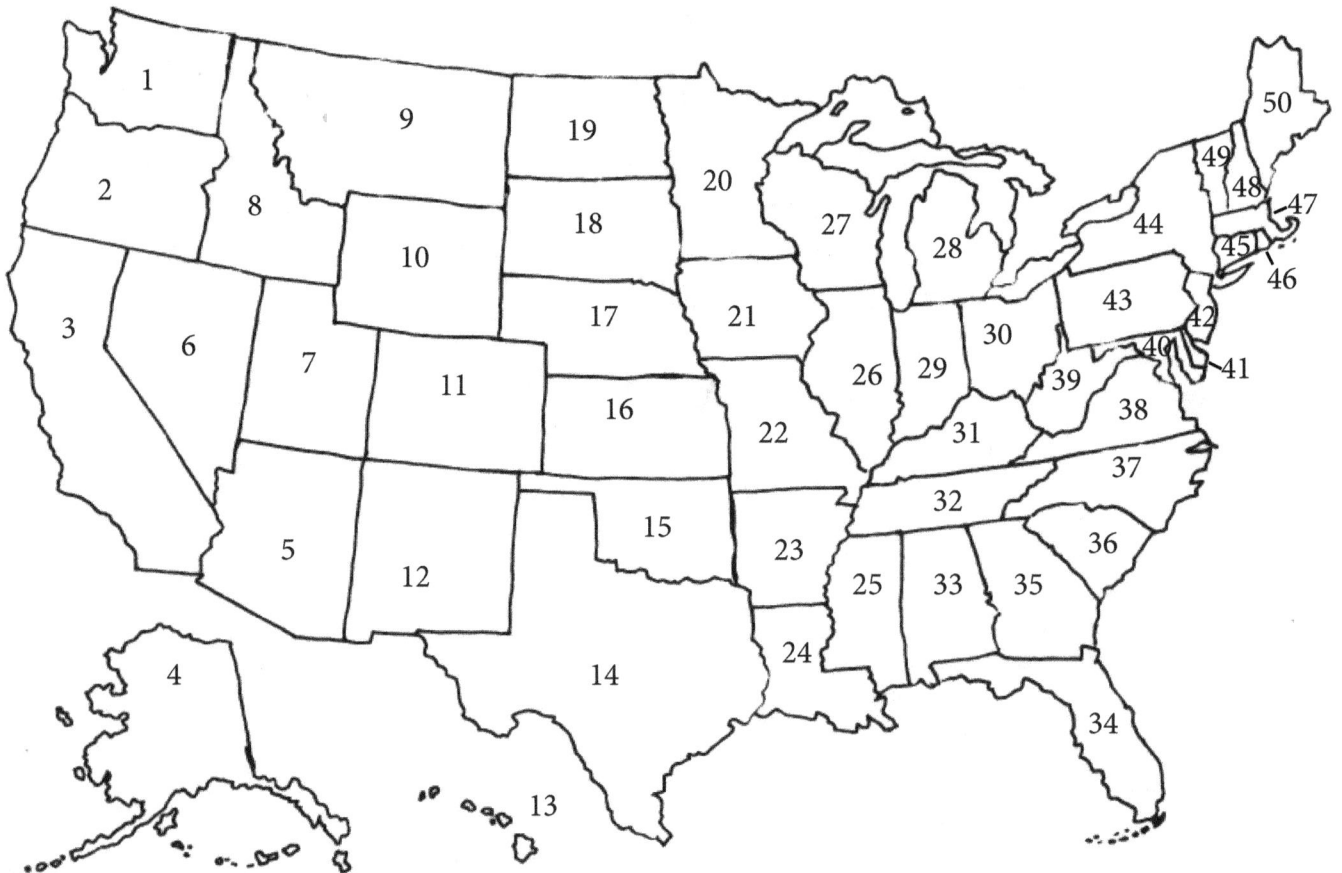

The West Region

PEJETALES©

Each state has been abbreviated, identify and name each state.

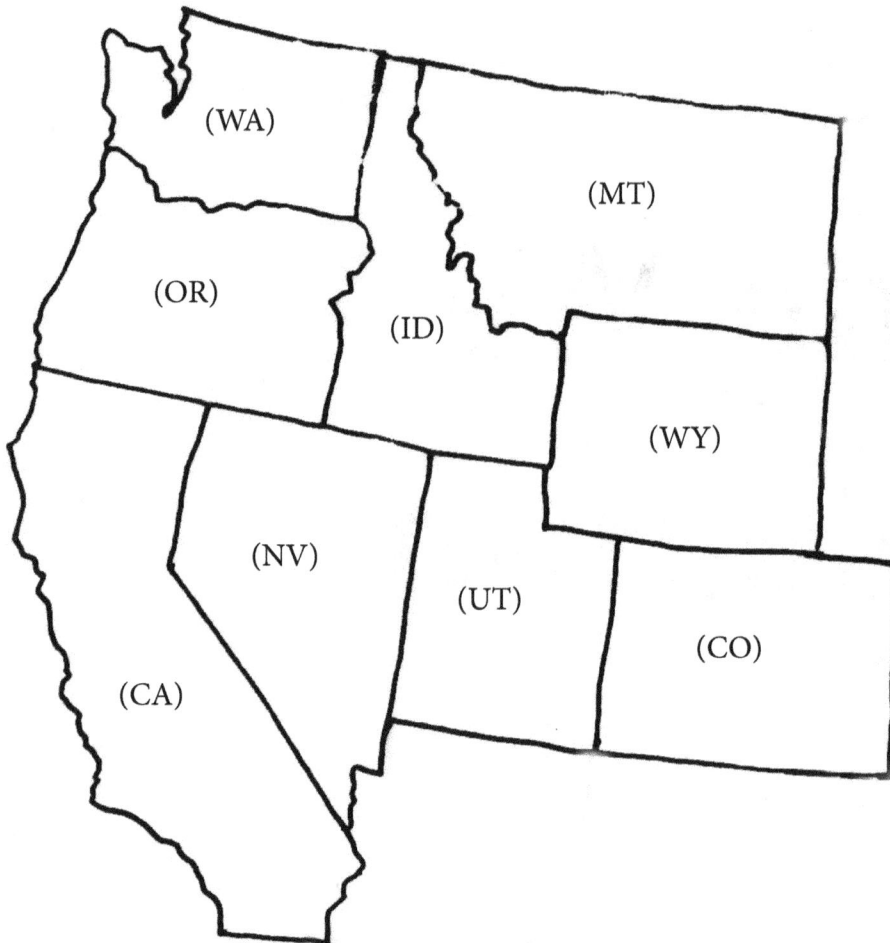

1. (AK) Alaska _____

2. (CA) _____

3. (CO) _____

4. (HI) _____

5. (ID) _____

6. (MT) _____

7. (NV) _____

8. (OR) _____

9. (UT) _____

10. (WA) _____

11. (WY) _____

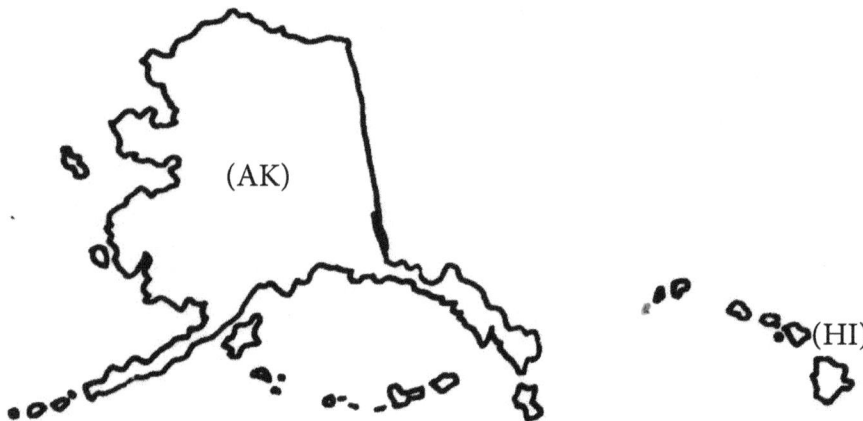

The Southwest Region

Each state has been abbreviated, identify and name each state.

1. (AZ) _____

2. (NM) _____

3. (OK) _____

4. (TX) _____

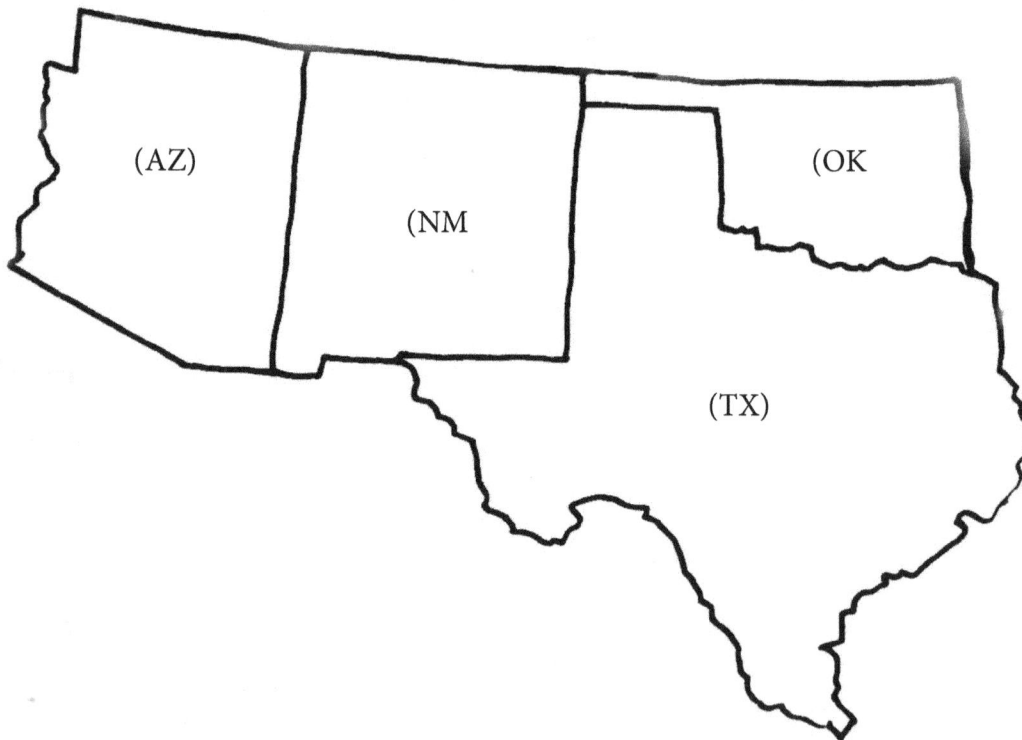

The Midwest Region

PEJETALES©

Each state has been abbreviated, identify and name each state.

1. (IL) _____

2. (IN) _____

3. (IA) _____

4. (KS) _____

5. (MI) _____

6. (MN) _____

7. (MO) _____

8. (NE) _____

9. (ND) _____

10. (OH) _____

11. (SD) _____

12. (WI) _____

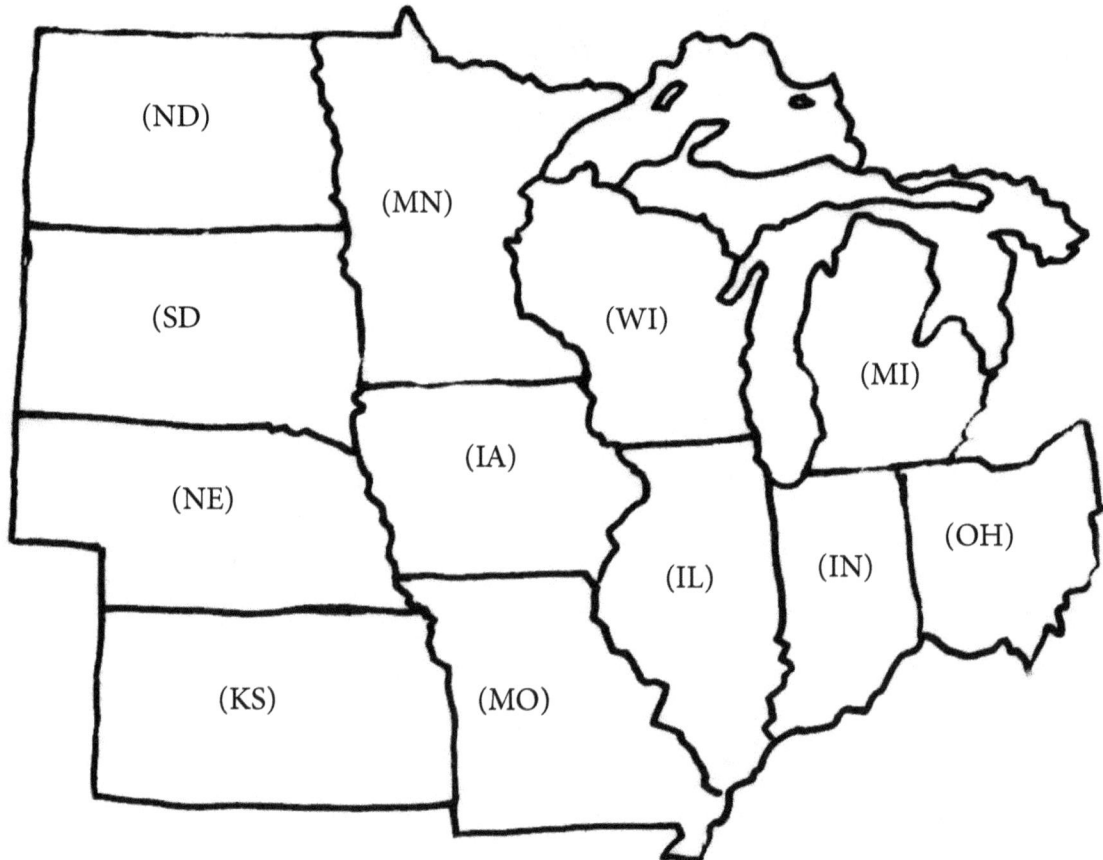

The Southeast Region

Each state has been abbreviated, identify and name each state.

1. (AL) _____

2. (AR) _____

3. (FL) _____

4. (GA) _____

5. (KY) _____

6. (LA) _____

7. (MS) _____

8. (NC) _____

9. (SC) _____

10. (TN) _____

11. (VA) _____

12. (WV) _____

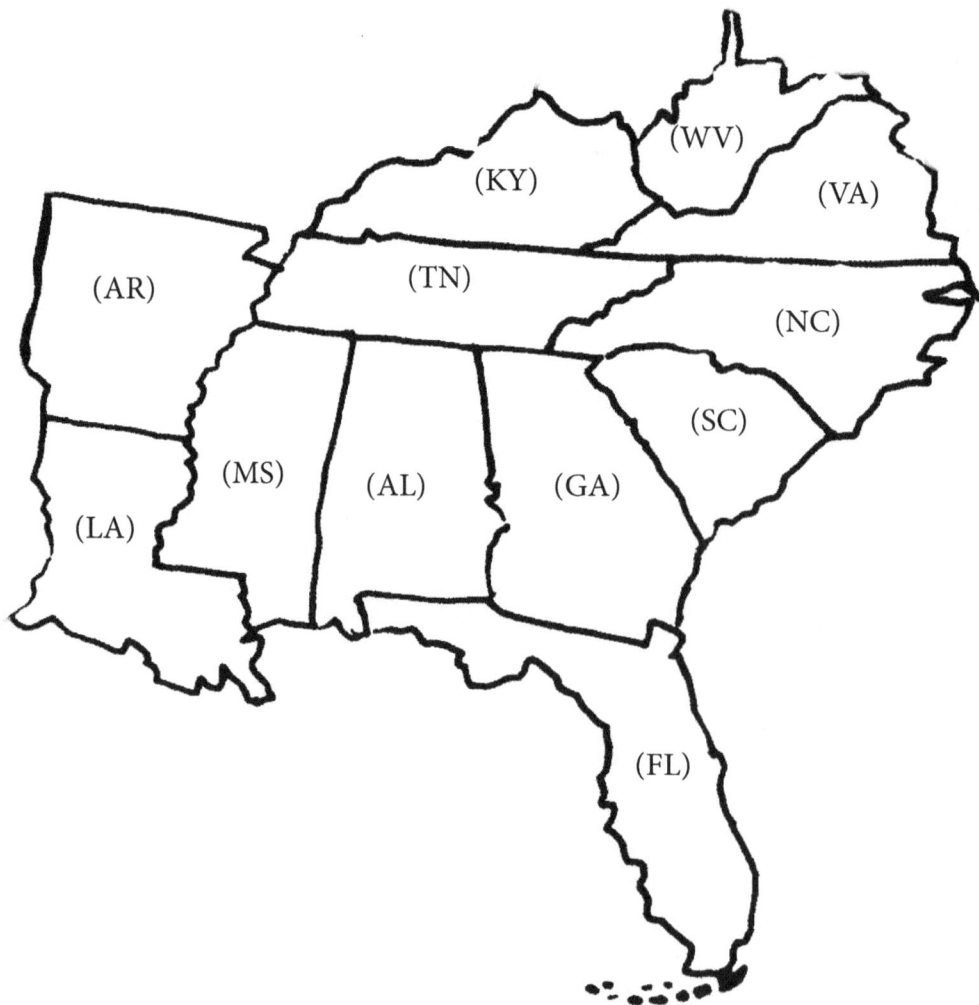

The Northeast Region

PEJETALES©

Each state has been abbreviated, identify and name each state.

1. (CT) _____

2. (DE) _____

3. (ME) _____

4. (MD) _____

5. (MA) _____

6. (NH) _____

7. (NJ) _____

8. (NY) _____

9. (PA) _____

10. (RI) _____

11. (VT) _____

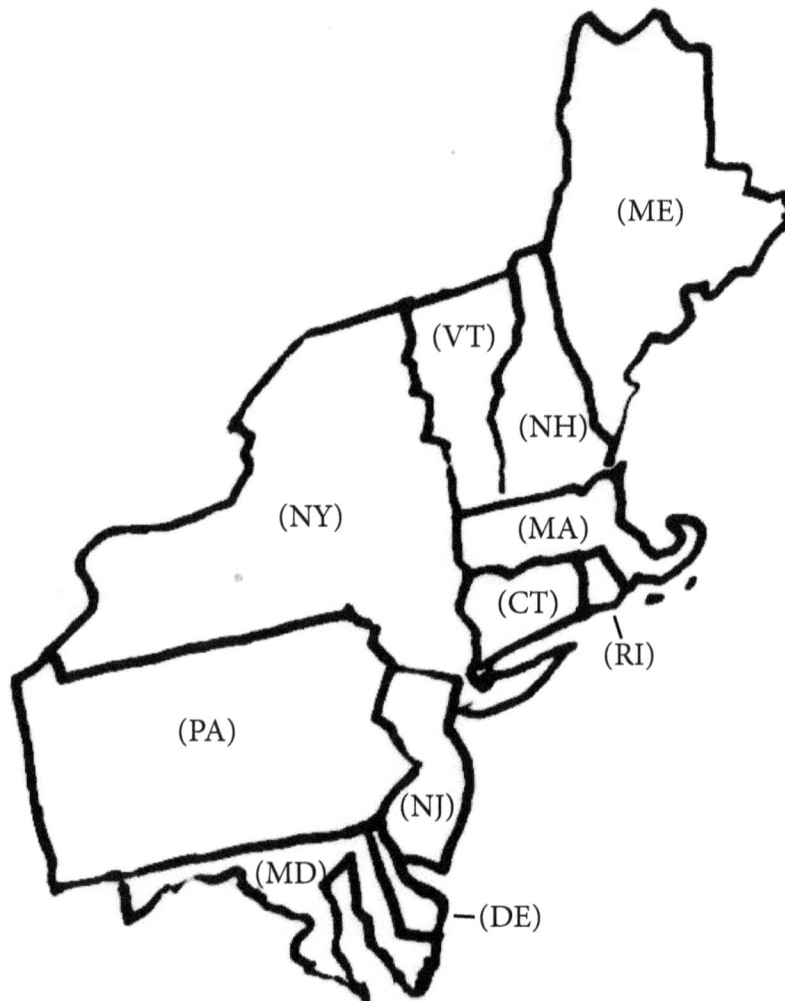

Index

MULTIPLE CHOICE ANSWER KEY

2. Alabama
b) AL
a) Montgomery
c) Yellowhammer State

4. Alaska
c) AK
b) Juneau
a) The Last Frontier

6. Arizona
a) AZ
b) Phoenix
c) The Grand Canyon State

8. Arkansas
c) AR
b) Little Rock
c) The Natural State

10. California
c) CA
a) Sacramento
b) The Golden State

12. Colorado
b) CO
c) Denver
a) Centennial State

14. Connecticut
a) CT
c) Hartford
b) Constitution State

16. Delaware
a) DE
b) Dover
a) Diamond; First State

18. Florida
c) FL
c) Tallahassee
b) Sunshine State

20. Georgia
b) GA
b) Atlanta
c) Peach State

22. Hawaii
a) HI
a) Honolulu
a) Aloha State

24. Idaho
b) ID
c) Boise
a) Gem State

26. Illinois
c) IL
b) Springfield
a) Prairie State

28. Indiana
b) IN
c) Indianapolis
b) Hoosier State

30. Iowa
a) IA
c) Des Moines
b) Hawkeye State

32. Kansas
c) KS
c) Topeka
a) Sunflower State

34. Kentucky
a) KY
b) Frankfort
b) Bluegrass State

36. Louisiana
b) LA
a) Baton Rouge
b) Pelican State

38. Maine
b) ME
b) Augusta
a) Pine Tree State

40. Maryland
a) MD
a) Annapolis
b) Free State; Old Line State

42. Massachusetts
a) MA
b) Boston
a) Bay State

44. Michigan
c) MI
b) Lansing
c) Wolverine State

46. Minnesota
b) MN
b) St. Paul
b) North Star State; Gopher State;
  Land of 10,000 Lakes State

48. Mississippi
c) MS
a) Jackson
b) Magnolia State

50. Missouri
c) MO
b) Jefferson City
a) Show-Me-State

52. Montana
b) MT
a) Helena
c) Treasure State

54. Nebraska
a) NE
c) Lincoln
b) Cornhusker State

56. Nevada
a) NV
b) Carson City
c) Silver State; Sagebrush State;
  Battle Born State

58. New Hampshire
b) NH
b) Concord
c) Granite State

50 STATE ACTIVITY GUIDE

MULTIPLE CHOICE ANSWER KEY

60. New Jersey
c) NJ
b) Trenton
c) Garden State

62. New Mexico
b) NM
c) Santa Fe
b) Land of Enchantment

64. New York
a) NY
b) Albany
b) Empire State

66. North Carolina
a) NC
a) Raleigh
a) Tar Heel State

68. North Dakota
b) ND
c) Bismarck
a) Peace Garden State; Sioux State;
Flickertail State; Rough Rider State

70. Ohio
a) OH
c) Columbus
b) Buckeye State

72. Oklahoma
c) OK
c) Oklahoma City
c) Sooner State

74. Oregon
b) OR
a) Salem
b) Beaver State

76. Pennsylvania
b) PA
a) Harrisburg
c) Keystone State

78. Rhode Island
a) RI
a) Providence
b) The Ocean State

80. South Carolina
c) SC
a) Columbia
c) Palmetto State

82. South Dakota
a) SD
b) Pierre
a) Mount Rushmore State;
Coyote State

84. Tennessee
c) TN
b) Nashville
c) Volunteer State

86. Texas
c) TX
a) Austin
a) Lone Star State

88. Utah
a) UT
a) Salt Lake City
b) Beehive State

90. Vermont
b) VT
b) Montpelier
b) Green Mountain State

92. Virginia
a) VA
c) Richmond
b) The Old Dominion;
Mother of Presidents

94. Washington
c) WA
c) Olympia
a) Evergreen State

96. West Virginia
b) WV
a) Charleston
c) Mountain State

98. Wisconsin
b) WI
a) Madison
a) Badger State

100. Wyoming
b) WY
b) Cheyenne
b) Equality State

STATE ABBREVIATION MAP ANSWER KEY (PAGE 103)

1.	(WA)		26.	(IL)
2.	(OR)		27.	(WI)
3.	(CA)		28.	(MI)
4.	(AK)		29.	(IN)
5.	(AZ)		30.	(OH)
6.	(NV)		31.	(KY)
7.	(UT)		32.	(TN)
8.	(ID)		33.	(AL)
9.	(MT)		34.	(FL)
10.	(WY)		35.	(GA)
11.	(CO)		36.	(SC)
12.	(NM)		37.	(NC)
13.	(HI)		38.	(VA)
14.	(TX)		39.	(WV)
15.	(OK)		40.	(MD)
16.	(KS)		41.	(DE)
17.	(NE)		42.	(NJ)
18.	(SD)		43.	(PA)
19.	(ND)		44.	(NY)
20.	(MN)		45.	(CT)
21.	(IA)		46.	(RI)
22.	(MO)		47.	(MA)
23.	(AR)		48.	(NH)
24.	(LA)		49.	(VT)
25.	(MS)		50.	(ME)

REGION ANSWER KEY

105. The West Region
1. Alaska
2. California
3. Colorado
4. Hawaii
5. Idaho
6. Montana
7. Nevada
8. Oregon
9. Utah
10. Washington
11. Wyoming

107. The Southwest Region
1. Arizona
2. New Mexico
3. Oklahoma
4. Texas

109. The Midwest Region
1. Illinois
2. Indiana
3. Iowa
4. Kansas
5. Michigan
6. Minnesota
7. Missouri
8. Nebraska
9. North Dakota
10. Ohio
11. South Dakota
12. Wisconsin

111. The Southeast Region
1. Alabama
2. Arkansas
3. Florida
4. Georgia
5. Kentucky
6. Louisiana
7. Mississippi
8. North Carolina
9. South Carolina
10. Tennessee
11. Virginia
12. West Virginia

113. The Northeast Region
1. Connecticut
2. Delaware
3. Maine
4. Maryland
5. Massachusetts
6. New Hampshire
7. New Jersey
8. New York
9. Pennsylvania
10. Rhode Island
11. Vermont

CONTACT US

If you love this book, do not hesitate to visit the following distributors below to show your support, provide feedback and share your review at:

AMAZON.com
AU-DE-CAN-US-UK
&
BARNES & NOBLE.com

Support via e-mail is welcomed at:
Pejepublishing@gmail.com

Also, do not hesitate to connect with us on:

 ❖ @pejepublishing

www.thelimitiswhenyousaystop.com

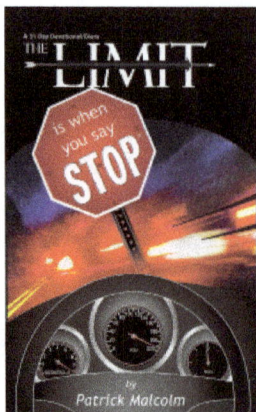

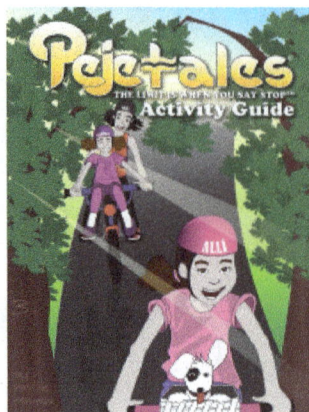

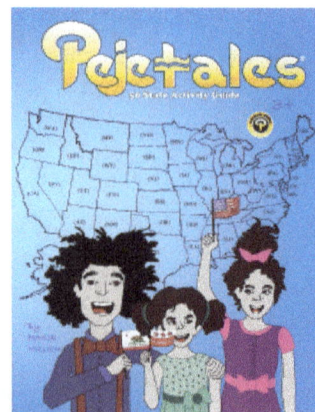

9 780989 023733

SMITHSONIAN ANNALS OF FLIGHT

VOLUME 1 • NUMBER 3

THE LIBERTY ENGINE
1918-1942

PHILIP S. DICKEY III

Lieutenant Colonel, United States Air Force (Retired)

SMITHSONIAN INSTITUTION PRESS • NATIONAL AIR AND SPACE MUSEUM

WASHINGTON, D.C. • 1968

Second Printing, 1970
Third Printing, 1973
Fourth Printing, 1977
Fifth Printing, 1978

For sale by the Superintendent of Documents, U.S. Government Printing Office
Washington, D.C. 20402

Stock Number 047–005–00003–5

Contents

Foreword

In this third number of the *Smithsonian Annals of Flight*, Philip S. Dickey tells the history of America's remarkable contribution to early aviation, the Liberty engine, the original model of which is now in the Smithsonian Institution's National Air and Space Museum.

In delineating the history of the engine from its brilliant conception through its role in World War I to its final production and use in World War II and thereafter, the author draws on a wealth of information contained in letters, memoranda, reports, and personal accounts, most of which have hitherto been unpublished. His accounts are reinforced by statistical tables, charts, detailed photographs, specifications and details of the engine's performance.

S. PAUL JOHNSTON, *Director*
National Air and Space Museum

2 January 1968

Preface

The engines about which this paper is written are called "Liberty." They came in series of 4, 6, 8, and 12 cylinders and were developed for interchangeability of parts and ease of production. Without doubt, the Liberty engine was America's greatest contribution to the Allied cause in World War I and to American aviation during the postwar period. Designed in six days during late May and early June of 1917, the engine was still in active use by the Army Air Service in 1936.

But the name was not always "Liberty." It was originally the U.S.A. Standardized Aircraft engine, but, when the name "Liberty" was suggested by Admiral D. W. Taylor in the early part of the period of production, it immediately caught on,[1] and, though there was already a Liberty truck on the market,[2] no other name would do for the new engine.

The Liberty became a legend in its own time and was known even by some members of a new generation of fighting men in World War II. The author, in fact, in 1945 tested a 45-foot Sparkman and Stevens aircorps rescue boat powered by two 500 hp Vimalert conversions of the famous Liberty engine.

The name "Liberty," as associated with the engine, was given the distinction of being registered as the trademark of the U.S.A. Standardized engines by the United States Government on 17 June 1919, under certificate of registration number 125,853. This is the first instance of the United States Government registering a trademark under its own laws or the laws of any other country.[3]

---

[1] History of the Bureau of Aircraft Production (MS, The United States Air Force Museum, Wright-Patterson Air Force Base, Ohio), vol. 7, p. 1904. Cited hereafter as History of BAP.

[2] McCook Field decimal files (MS, Air Force Records Repository, St. Louis, Mo.), 452.8, letter, Emmons from Heaslet, 20 November 1917. Cited hereafter as McCook files. (McCook Field no longer exists. Located in North Dayton, Ohio, during World War I, it was the heart of the United States' aircraft- and engine-development effort.

[3] History of BAP, vol. 7, p. 1904.

The following examination of the Liberty engine is not intended to be a technical description of the inner workings of an internal combustion engine. It ran the same way a car engine runs. There will be some reference to pistons, horsepower, battery ignition versus magneto ignition, and like subjects, but only to put into proper perspective some of the controversies that revolved around the engine during its testing and production period. There will also be some discussion of the problems of inverting, air-cooling, and gearing the engine. These are brought out to show the versatility of design. The postwar story shows the durability of design and tends to prove that the engine was far ahead of its time.

If it appears that Jesse G. Vincent predominates in the references, the appearance is not deceptive, for Vincent was the engine's codesigner, actively participating in its testing, modification, and production until he left the Air Service after the Armistice. A nonflyer, he entered service, became an expert aviator, and, as commander of McCook Field, flew many hours behind the Liberty engine. As an expert engineer and an inventive genius, he was able to examine the operation of the engine on the dynamometer, the test stand, and in the air. If any one man can be granted primary credit for the success of the Liberty, he is Vincent. He was a prolific and lucid writer, and the McCook Field files during his tenure are filled with his correspondence.

E. J. Hall, the engine's codesigner, was moved from the Liberty project to troubleshoot the DH–4 production early in 1918. It is regrettable that so little evidence is left of his role in the Liberty project.

Ante Bellum

This is the history of an engine, but not just a description of the nuts and bolts that held it together or of the juxtaposition of component parts that caused it to run and produce power. The engine, the principal character in the story, can be properly considered and known only in the context of the times and the people and the circumstances that led to its birth. The Liberty engine was a child of war, and it stands today as a monument to the capacity of a nation to change and, in changing, to move a giant step beyond its peers in the development of an infant technology. The Liberty was an apology for our nation's lack of foresight and for its failure to develop the aircraft born at Kitty Hawk.

In the early days of March 1917 the United States stood uneasily on the threshold of a conflict not of its choosing, soon to learn a harsh lesson in education for world leadership, begun in the closing years of the last century. America, the beautiful, was isolated by the high seas from the lunacy in Europe; America, complacent in the self-hugging warmth of its parochialism, was, in time, to become a disorganized mass of patriotism trying desperately to focus its massive energy on production for war.

Fortunately, the nation had developed and prospered prior to World War I, partly because of an innate ability to organize and a willingness to try something new if given the proper impetus. With the sinking of *Vigilancia*, *State of Illinois*, and *City of Memphis* reported on 18 March 1917, and the subsequent declaration of war on 6 April, the magnitude of the task of war production struck the nation's leaders with stunning force, for the country was totally unprepared.

The United States' lack of preparation for World War I was across the board; the segment of interest for this story, however, is aviation. It should be remembered that the achievements of industry in the production of aircraft and of aircraft engines were accomplished against a backdrop of universal competition for the manpower, equipment, supplies, and resources required to mobilize the nation for participation in the European War.

Before considering the record made by the United States in the design and production of the Liberty engine, the page must be turned back to

1

show the development of the aviation-engine industry in the United States and its condition at the time war was declared.

Until 14 April 1917, the total production of aircraft in the United States had been 666 machines, none of a more complicated type than training planes built for the British Royal Flying Corps.[1] Soon after the United States entered World War I, the National Advisory Committee for Aeronautics requested capability studies from all aircraft companies. The answers showed a disheartening lack of the immense production potential which would be required to place America's name at the forefront of the aviation powers of the world. The government had done nothing to encourage industry or individuals to enter the aircraft or aircraft-engine production field. The government incentives that characterized the development of our early technology were not applied to the furtherance of the aviation industry in the nation that invented the first heavier-than-air machine to lift a man from the ground in sustained, controlled, powered flight. The aircraft developmental work the Wright Brothers carried out almost in secrecy on the Huffman Plain near Dayton, Ohio, was accepted and continued with great energy and enthusiasm in Europe. It was treated as a curiosity, a passing fancy in the armed services of the country of its birth.

At the beginning of 1917 the United States ranked 14th among the nations of the world in aviation. The first Congressional appropriation specifically for aviation was $125,000 on 3 March 1911. From 1908 to 1916 appropriations for aviation had totaled only $930,000.[2] In the same period a total of only 59 aircraft was delivered to the United States Army. During 1916, 83 more were delivered, and, in the first three months of 1917, an additional 82.

The Aviation Section of the Army Signal Corps was established by an act of Congress on 18 July 1914. Our aviation effort in the Mexican punitive expedition amounted to 16 aircraft which, owing to maintenance problems, seldom operated. The total number of aircraft delivered to the Army prior to World War I was 224; and all of these were training aircraft not suitable for fighting, bombing, or observation service.

The personnel complement of the Army's aviation section as the United States entered World War I was 52 officers, 1100 enlisted men, and 200 civilians. Although 139 men had received flight training, only 26 could be

---

[1] History of BAP, vol. 1, pp. ii–iii.

[2] EDGAR S. GORRELL, *The Measure of America's World Aeronautical Effort* (Norwich University, Northfield, Vermont, James Jackson Cabot Professorship Lectures, no. 6), pp. 2–3.

considered qualified pilots, and then only in training craft. The United States was devoid of airports, and there was not enough civil aviation to produce pilots as an emergency back-up capability. Before our entry in the war we had had but two aviation officers in Europe, and only one of them, Colonel George O. Squier, had been permitted to view the aeronautical effort at the front.

Prior to April 1917 only four United States companies had successfully produced aircraft engines. These were: the Hall-Scott Motor Car Company of Berkeley, Calif., the Curtiss Aeroplane and Motor Corporation of Buffalo, N.Y., the Wright-Martin Aircraft Corporation of New Brunswick, N.J., and the General Vehicle Company of Long Island City, N.Y. Because the demand made upon these companies was slight their capacity was extremely limited. Their product was built for durability rather than lightness, and power output was adequate only for training purposes. This was to lead to two requirements: an enormous increase in the manufacture of existing types of engines to meet the needs of a wartime flight training program, and, at the same time, the development here or the adaptation from abroad of a wholly new type of engine for battle work.[3] This was the extent of the United States' preparation to shoulder its share of the battle in the air on 6 April 1917.

From the very first, the program for plane and aircraft-engine production had one thing in its favor: as news of the "derring-do" type of war that was being fought in the skies over France was brought to the States, the public's imagination was aroused, and the desire for an American air fleet, second to none, became almost universal. On 1 June 1917, the joint Army and Navy Technical Board secured approval of the Secretaries of War and of the Navy for a program calling for a total of 22,625 aircraft.[4] The $639,241,258 appropriated for this program included 45,250 aircraft engines and was passed by Congress on 24 July 1917 with almost no discussion and absolutely no hesitation. This appropriation, the largest to that date, provided $125,290,000 for aircraft, $239,850,000 for engines, and the balance for the myriad requirements associated with such a vast program.[5]

Unfortunately, all the money in the world could not, at this point, overcome the problems involved in producing an air arm for our forces. On the home front the adversary was time. Almost insuperable problems

---

[3] ARTHUR SWEETSER, *The American Air Service* (New York: Daniel Appleton and Company, 1919), p. 169.
[4] History of BAP, vol. 7, pp. 1827–1828.
[5] GORRELL, op. cit., pp. 7–8.

had already appeared. Our engineers were behind the "state of the art" of military-plane engines. In the years between the invention of the airplane and its emergence as a prime weapon of war, the United States had neglected its military application. The American aircraft industry required tremendous expansion to produce the numbers of military aircraft needed by the Allies. With only one qualified observer at the war front, the United States knew little of modern fighter and bomber technical requirements and had absolutely no experience that would help build aircraft and engines superior to those of the enemy.

Most American industry was already saturated by the demands of the armed services. Skilled manpower, already involved in war production or in the Armed Forces, was scarce. Vital materials were at a premium, and priority systems were not at first adequate.

Thus the aircraft and aircraft-engine programs presented complicated production problems. The first attack had to be made in the engineering field. The difficulties involved in aircraft and engine engineering were much more complex than had been encountered in the fields of electric, marine, steam or gasoline locomotion. The emphasis on power and reliability with extreme lightness of construction created problems that increased geometrically with the increase of power and the decrease of weight. To make matters worse, the European technicians who had experience and knowledge in these matters were 3000 miles away and endless red tape had to be cut and deadly submarines evaded before their skills could be tapped. Steps were immediately taken to bring them to this country and to send American mechanics and engineers to Europe, but all this took time and thus played into the enemy's hands.

The nucleus of American production experts available to the aviation project centered in the joint Army and Navy Technical Board. These men were successful manufacturers but had little if any experience with aircraft production. There was almost no expert capability in the Army.

Putting all the obstacles together, it was soon apparent that priorities, propaganda, and superhuman effort would be required if the United States was to take a place of importance in the battle for control of the air. In a nation whose every sinew was strained to the war effort, the only answer was government control. So the government bought the manufacturer his land, built his shops, hired his labor, procured his raw materials, parts, and equipment, inspected his work, and audited his books. This kind of control, in turn, spawned a bureaucracy that, when the war was over, consisted of 2064 officers, 31,307 enlisted men, and 8969 civilians organized in 8 divisions with 376 sections. This was the Bureau of Aircraft Production.

4

Missions and Commissions

One of the major problems in getting our production of military aircraft started was our ignorance of which types of aircraft were needed and which engines would be required to power them. The shortest road to this knowledge was to tap the experience our allies had gained in prosecuting the war in Europe. There were two ways to do this: bring missions of allied experts to this country and send commissions of our experts to the battlefields and factories of France, England, and Italy.

Just prior to the closed-door session that produced the initial design of the Liberty engine, E. A. Deeds, of the Aircraft Production Board, called upon the French mission to provide as much information as possible regarding aircraft-engine requirements in battle. Although J. G. Vincent and E. J. Hall, the designers of the Liberty engine, were more than competent in their field, they lacked information concerning the horsepower requirements of engines that would be needed the following year at the front. The French mission was the only source for such information in Washington in May 1917. The mission had arrived in Washington on 24 April 1917, headed by Marshal Joffre on the military side and former Prime Minister Rene Viviani on the diplomatic. It consisted of more than 400 officers and technicians.

The French mission technicians provided full answers to all questions of the American designers. This aviation group was headed by Major Joseph Tulsane. It was initially composed of 25 persons and had expanded to 72 by the war's end. Major Thebault de Channalon, the group's engine specialist, was permanently assigned to McCook Field. On the diplomatic side, the French mission worked out a program with the United States to ship 4500 aircraft to the front by the spring of 1918, to train 5000 pilots, 50,000 mechanics, and to attain a monthly production of 2000 aircraft and 4000 aircraft engines.

The British mission arrived in Washington on 31 May 1917 under the leadership of Lord Northcliffe, a noted publisher. Wing Commander W. Briggs, chief engineer for the Royal Naval Air Service, was attached to the Aircraft Board as technical advisor to the Engineering Division, Bureau of Aircraft Production.

The largest American commission to go to Europe during the war was the Bolling Commission. Raynal Cawthorne Bolling graduated from Harvard Law School in 1902 and, at the time of his entrance into the service, had been the general counsel for United States Steel Corporation. Bolling had been in the New York National Guard since 1907 and had been first lieutenant and then captain in charge of the First Aero Company since 1915. (This was the first such unit to be formed.) Although commissioned in the relatively minor rank of major on 9 June 1917, Bolling was eminently fitted to be the chief of the commission. He was able to observe aviation activities in Europe, translate this information into action to be taken by the United States, and enter into negotiations with the Allies for the mutual benefit of all. He was probably the only individual in the country at that time who combined a knowledge of the infant art of flying and its equipment with the legal background necessary to the successful negotiation of international agreements.

Bolling carried both military and civilian credentials, to be used as conditions warranted. He was to secure, if possible:

1. Reciprocal patent agreements between the United States and the Allied powers in order to preclude exorbitant demands of the European patent owner on the American manufacturer;

2. A plan whereby the United States would concentrate on the manufacture of training planes and the Allies would continue their efforts in the manufacture of combat service planes, since the United States had absolutely no experience in this field;

3. A plan whereby the United States would rush quantity production of aircraft engines for the Allies, whose "choke point" had always been in this area.

Members of the commission sailed from New York on the *SS Adriatic* on 17 June 1917 and arrived in Liverpool, England, on 26 June. They stayed in England until 2 July, in France until 15 July, in Italy until 27 July, and then returned to Paris. About mid-August 1917 the commission broke up; each member submitted a report on his specialty. Bolling's final report was the guide for the beginning of American aircraft production, but the decision to proceed with an American-designed series of standard aircraft engines had been implemented prior to his report. In fact, the decision had been made, the 8-cylinder engine was tested, and the 12-cylinder engine was in final test stages before the Bolling commission disbanded.

Birth of a Concept

Mass production and standardization of parts were not new in the United States in 1917. Eli Whitney, Henry Ford, and others had pioneered the use of standard parts to mass produce arms, automobiles, and other commodities. These techniques, however, had not fully penetrated the aviation field; in the period prior to World War I there was no requirement for standardization and mass production principles in the manufacture of aircraft engines because so few were produced. When the necessity arose, the industry of the country had to build machine tools and other mass production accouterments before it could translate to moving metal and power the genius of the design engineers.

American aircraft engines at this period were of four basic types:

1. Radial: Had a fan-type arrangement of cylinders extending above the horizontal to preclude excessive gravity lubrication. When the forced, metered feeding of oil was developed, it was possible to extend the fan into a circle around the crankshaft and to add individual cylinders or banks of cylinders to increase power. In this engine the cylinders remained stationary, and the crankshaft revolved. This was a very difficult engine to water-cool, so most were of the air-cooled variety. The bulk of the engine caused great head resistance; however, a compact, light-weight engine resulted from this cylinder configuration.

2. Rotary: Similar to the radial in that the cylinders formed a circle around the crankshaft. The crankshaft, however, was fixed and the cylinders whirled around it. The engine was light and easily air-cooled, but the resistance of the air to the rapid rotation of the cylinders, while it provided ample cooling, absorbed up to 10 percent or more of the engine's power. To solve the lubrication problem an oil-gasoline mixture was used, with consequent excessive oil consumption. Cylinder size was limited (normally five-inch bore) due to cooling problems. As in the radial type, power was increased by adding cylinders with a commensurate increase in complexity and maintenance difficulty.

3. Vertical inline: The cylinders stand in a row directly above the crankshaft, as in the ordinary four- or six-cylinder automobile engine. It

7

was inevitable that this engine would be prominent in the development of aircraft engines. The 1912 Graham Clark list of 112 aero engines included 42 vertical types. Most aviators did not like the four-cylinder vertical because of its vibration, and, as the air war developed, it proved inadequate for combat flying. The six-cylinder engine was brought to a high degree of perfection in Germany by Mercedes and Benz. Of the 34 German aircraft listed in the summer of 1914, 31 were propelled by vertical aircraft engines (17 were six-cylinder and 14 were four-cylinder). This type of engine, however, was not a strong contender in the United States.

4. V-type inline: The cylinders extend upward at an angle from the crankshaft in two banks. Although the radials and rotaries were lighter than the inlines because of their compact crankshafts and crankcases and their air-cooling features, they could not develop sufficient power for military applications due to limited cooling capacity and speed of rotation. The V-type inline was, therefore, the most satisfactory military engine from a power-to-weight ratio. This was the basic design of the Liberty engine.[1]

With the declaration of war came the need for immediate and far-reaching decisions if the United States was to pull its share of the load in the conflict. The country was faced with the double requirement of producing aircraft engines in unheard of quantities and in horsepower ratings never before achieved. Two basic courses of action were open: to reproduce the most effective of the European engines, or to design and build a completely American engine.

Examination showed that the Allies were developing or manufacturing 60 different engines, while the Germans, concentrating on no more than 5 varieties, were outproducing the Allies. Allied production potential was not realized because an excessive effort was spent on design. The American solution was to place production under government control, allowing the pooling of all available foreign and domestic experience for use of participating engine designers.

The production of European engines in American facilities was difficult because the foreign engines were handmade, their parts were not interchangeable, and the metric system of measurement was used on all technical drawings.[2] The Wright-Martin Company had spent nearly two years and $3,000,000 on the production of the Hispano-Suiza engine, and by 1917 had attained only limited production. The same results had been experi-

---

[1] History of BAP, vol. 7, pp. 1823–1826.
[2] SWEETSER, op. cit., p. 175.

enced with production of the Le Rhone, the Gnome, and the Bugatti.[3] The difficult logistics involved in repair and supply of engines 3000 miles from home would be minimized by the use of standardized engines with interchangeable parts. The tremendous expense and technical problems involved in achieving engines of 400 to 500 horsepower could be met only by pooling all the United States' resources into one supreme effort.

It was concluded that the United States should design and build an American engine that would lend itself to quantity production and achieve greater horsepower than any contemporary engine. The major requirements of the engine to be designed and produced were: maximum power and efficiency with minimum weight; capability of running at maximum power and speed during a large percentage of its operating time; economical fuel and oil consumption; and, in order to assure a workable engine in the shortest possible time, no device that had not already been tested and proved in existing engines was to be included in the design of the new engine.[4]

---

[3] ISAAC F. MARCOSSON, *Colonel Deeds: Industrial Builder* (New York: Dodd, Mead, and Company, 1948), pp. 234–235.

[4] Ibid., pp. 236–238.

To Design an Engine

Edward A. Deeds, an engineer and industrialist, put the facts together, arrived at a decision, and proved it right to the government's decision-makers. He was appointed to the Aircraft Production Board on 17 May 1917, after service on the Munitions Standards Board, and brought great talent and experience to the problem of organization for aircraft production. On 2 August 1917 he was appointed Acting Chief of the Equipment Division of the Signal Corps, and became Chief of the division after his commissioning as a colonel in the regular Army on 24 August. In January 1918 he was made Industrial Executive in the Office of the Chief Signal Officer. On 24 May 1918 Deeds was relieved of duty in the Equipment Division and ordered to cooperate in the Hughes aviation investigation, in which he became the principal figure and was condemned for unjustified delay in the aircraft-production program and for waste and mismanagement of the program.[1]

It is not the intention of this paper to discuss the several armament investigations that were launched during the last year of World War I. A dispassionate examination of those investigations connected with aircraft production shows that achievements outweighed shortcomings, and proper credit is owing to the men who organized and guided production through its first months of hectic growth.

Edward Deeds was the catalyst in the decision-making process. Two other men provided the ability, experience, and knowledge needed to make the vital engineering decisions. They were Elbert John Hall and Jesse G. Vincent.

Hall was born in San José, California, 8 April 1882. After educating himself by courses from a correspondence school and by night courses in San Francisco, he was employed by the I. L. Benton Machine Works in San Francisco as a steam engineer at the age of 16. Within four years he was made half owner in the company, and during this period he gained experience in the design of marine, hoisting, and gasoline engines. In 1903

---

[1] Marcosson, op. cit., pp. 217–233.

the company started to build auto engines, and by 1905 Hall was working with the Heine-Velox Company making complete autos. Both companies were wiped out in the 1906 earthquake.

In 1910, after a period of building the "Comet," an auto of his own design, he joined with Bert C. Scott in the Hall-Scott Motor Car Company to manufacture industrial locomotives, gas-driven railway coaches, interurban car bodies for electric railroads, and auto and aviation engines. By 1913 aircraft equipped with Hall-Scott four- and six-cylinder aviation engines were being flown by the best known aviators in America. In 1915 the Hall-Scott six-cylinder A–5 was being sold as a military engine to the governments of Russia, China, Japan, Holland, Norway, Australia, England, and the United States.

Hall was commissioned a major in the Signal Corps in October 1917 and was promoted to lieutenant colonel in April 1918. In addition to his co-design of the Liberty engine, Hall adapted the Le Rhone engine to American methods of production, was a troubleshooter in starting U.S. production of the DeHaviland-4 aircraft, and was sent to France at the request of General Pershing. There, in October 1918, he became chief of the Air Service Technical Section. He received the Distinguished Service Medal for his wartime service.[2]

Vincent was born on 10 February 1880 at Charleston, Arkansas. His formal education was limited to attendance at a country school near Pana, Illinois, and the Cote Brilliant Grammar School, St. Louis, Missouri. His engineering education was acquired through correspondence courses.

From 1897 to 1898 he was with Smith, Vincent and Company, commission merchants in St. Louis. From there he worked as a machinist and toolmaker in St. Louis until 1902, and in 1903 he became superintendent of inventions for the Burroughs Adding Machine Company. He remained with the Burroughs Company until 1910. His patents up to this time fill a volume more than an inch thick.

From 1910 to 1912 he was chief engineer of the Hudson Motor Car Company, and from 29 July 1912 to 10 August 1917 he was vice president for engineering for the Packard Motor Car Company. His patents of this period fill a book more than two inches thick.

Vincent was commissioned a major in the Signal Corps on 15 August 1917, and was honorably discharged as a lieutenant colonel on 30 November 1918. He returned to Packard in his former position on 1 January 1919,

---

[2] *Elbert John Hall* (New York: James T. White & Co., 1924), pp. 1–7.

11

and was promoted to colonel in the Signal Corps Reserve 19 August 1919.[3]

Although Jesse Vincent was the prime mover in the success of the Liberty engine, he was accused by the Hughes investigation of having authorized government payments to the Packard Company while he was still a stockholder.[4] This charge was technically correct, but its pettiness is apparent in a letter to Vincent from Alvan McCauley, president of the Packard Company. McCauley points out that the contract in question amounted to $249,159.10. This was a cost plus 12.5 percent contract, and the profit would have been $27,684.35. A federal tax of 50.2 percent would equal $13,796.81, for a net profit of 6.2 percent. On 31 August 1918 there were 118,159 shares of Packard stock, of which Vincent owned 429, or 0.4 percent. He would have made $55.14 on the contract.[5] For this, the Hughes report recommended criminal prosecution, giving no consideration to Vincent's tremendous contribution to the war effort in the design and development of the Liberty engine. Editorial comment in the Detroit newspapers of the period was fiercely loyal to Vincent.[6]

Although Vincent was never prosecuted, he was pardoned by President Wilson on 3 December 1918 and was recommended for the Distinguished Service Medal on 16 January 1919. Despite further invaluable World War II service to the Air Force and Navy in the design and development of engines for fighter aircraft (e.g., P–51) and marine engines for PT and crash rescue boats, this honor was never accorded him because of his involvement in the controversy.[7]

From these two biographical sketches it is obvious that Deeds had in Hall and Vincent the most qualified Americans available to design a series of standardized eng. es. In the two years prior to 1917 Vincent had been experimenting with several types of 12-cylinder aircraft engines of approximately 225 hp. Although these engines were too heavy for military use, Vincent had amassed a great deal of information and experience, and he had built up an extremely efficient experimental-engineering section which played a most important part in the development of the Liberty engine.[8]

In the first months of 1917, Hall completed an experimental 12-cylinder engine, called the A–8, designed to produce 450 hp. This engine was ready

---

[3] Jesse G. Vincent files (MSS, The United States Air Force Museum, Wright-Patterson Air Force Base, Ohio), biographical notes. Cited hereafter as Vincent MSS.

[4] *Dayton Journal*, 1 November 1918, p. 13.

[5] Vincent MSS, letter, Vincent from McCauley, 6 November 1918.

[6] *Detroit Free Press*, 5 November 1918, p. 4; *Detroit News*, 2 November 1918, p. 4.

[7] Vincent MSS, biographical notes.

[8] History of BAP, vol. 7, p. 1894.

for final testing when Hall was summoned to Washington in May 1917 on official business with the Navy Department.[9] About this same time, a combined French and British mission was surveying the great industries located in Detroit. On 26 May they visited the Packard plant. Vincent spent considerable time with them, asked innumerable questions, and gained a good idea of the latest developments in European aircraft. The visitors were impressed with the quality of Vincent's experimental 12-cylinder engine, but informed him that the weight per horsepower was too great for combat use.[10]

The next morning, while reading the latest issue of *Automobile*, Vincent saw an article by a Mr. Bradley which discussed the multiplicity of engines being produced by the Allies. Bradley pointed out that this led to high cost, low production, and a serious shortage of parts in the field. This article, added to the previous day's discussions with the French and British, determined Vincent on a course of action that had been forming in his mind for some time.

He realized that if immediate and strong action was not taken, the United States would find itself in the same position as its allies. Even though it was Sunday morning (27 May 1917) Vincent went to see the Packard Company's president, Alvan McCauley, and explained his fears. Quick to realize the danger, McCauley agreed that Vincent should go to Washington, D.C., at once to discuss the establishment of a standardized line of aircraft engines with Howard Coffin, chairman of the Aircraft Production Board.

On the morning of 28 May 1917 Vincent conferred in Washington with Coffin, Deeds, and Sidney Waldon at the Lafayette Hotel. Vincent discussed his line of reasoning with the Aircraft Production Board members; the Bradley article and the information he had received from the European mission indicated the need for a lighter and more powerful standardized line of engines. Vincent said he was convinced that some of the Packard engine's great weight—occasioned by safety factors—could be reduced without sacrificing reliability.[11]

---

[9] *Pertinent Facts About the Liberty Motor* (San Francisco: Hall-Scott Motor Car Company, n. d.) Cited hereafter as *Pertinent Facts*. History of BAP, loc. cit., indicates this engine was 300 h p and too heavy for military use.

[10] McCook files, letter, Emmons from Vincent, 4 December 1918. This letter predates the Vincent report to the Society of Automotive Engineers in February 1919, from which he is most often quoted.

[11] Ibid.; MARCOSSON, op. cit., p. 238, however, gives Deeds complete credit for the standardized-engine idea. He does not mention the 28 May meeting and indicates that Hall and Vincent were called in on the 29th and that their participation in the project

Deeds had been thinking along the lines that Vincent explained in his discussions with the board members. He believed that an engine had to be developed for maximum power and efficiency with minimum weight; it must be capable of maximum power and speed during a large percentage of its operational time; and it must be economical in the consumption of fuel and oil.[12] His conversations with Vincent solidified his thinking, and he asked Vincent to work with E. J. Hall on the design of a standardized engine. Hall was stopped at Cleveland on his way back to California and agreed to return to Washington.

Both Vincent and Hall had come to Washington to sell their own products, but Deeds, from his more objective position, could see that the force of the United States Government must be the driving power of the project, since the number of engines required would tax the capability of the entire industry.

Hall returned to Washington on the morning of 29 May and early in the afternoon of the same day met with Vincent, Deeds, and Waldon in Deeds' suite at the new Willard Hotel. Hall and Vincent knew each other only by reputation.[13] They got down to business immediately and by midafternoon were laying down two views of a proposed eight-cylinder aircraft engine.[14] Deeds impressed them with the need for speed and, to assure as rapid production as possible, cautioned them to use no untried devices or designs in the new engine.[15]

Vincent called the chief of the Washington branch of the Society of Automotive Engineers, a Mr. Zimmershied, to obtain drafting materials and draftsmen but was able to get only some tools. Vincent and Hall bought the necessary drafting tables and paper.[16] Vincent called Dr. Stratton of the Bureau of Standards at midnight to get the latest data on British and French engines. Stratton had the information for them by the morning of 1 June.[17]

On the evening of 29 May, Deeds called a session in his suite at which

was completely unexpected. History of BAP, loc. cit., pp. 1891–1892, indicates that Deeds had made the decision and discussed it with Waldon before Vincent came to Washington. It is probable that both versions of the story are true, as the facts were evident and both Deeds and Vincent had access to them.

[12] MARCOSSON, op. cit., pp. 236–237.

[13] McCook files, loc. cit. (footnote 10).

[14] Ibid.

[15] MARCOSSON, op. cit., p. 238.

[16] McCook files, loc. cit. MARCOSSON, loc. cit., stated that Deeds and Waldon went out and bought the required materials.

[17] MARCOSSON, op. cit., p. 239.

members of the French mission were present. The French, closely questioned by Vincent and Hall, were able to produce a great deal of up-to-date information.[18] The next morning Zimmershied provided Vincent and Hall with a volunteer, J. M. Schoonmaker, who, though he had done no drafting for many years, took over the task of drawing so that Vincent could dictate the report he and Hall had prepared the night before.[19] By the afternoon of 31 May 1917, the report was finished, and the drawings were fairly well blocked out. At about 3:00 pm, Waldon called, asking that the report and drawings be brought to the office of George Squier (later Chief Signal Officer) for presentation to a joint meeting of the Army-Navy Aircraft Production Board. Waldon read the report, and Vincent and Hall explained the drawings. The Board gave approval to go ahead with complete drawings.

On 1 June, two capable layout men came in from Detroit and worked on layouts of the construction features being completed by Vincent, Hall, and Schoonmaker. The five men worked straight through until Monday afternoon, 4 June.[20] At this point layouts had been completed of the longitudinal, transverse, rear-elevation, and camshaft-assembly views of the eight-cylinder engine. At midnight on the 4th, Hall and Vincent appeared before the joint committee of the Army-Navy Aircraft Production Board, showed the finished drawings, and further detailed their plans for the engine. The Board approved the building of five 8-cylinder and five 12-cylinder engines and asked that the first 8-cylinder engine be produced as soon as possible. Deeds promised it in seven weeks. Vincent sent the layout men to Detroit to work on detailed drawings of "long time parts" such as cylinders and crankcases.[21]

Hall then proceeded to Indianapolis and Vincent to New York, where he met McCauley on the morning of 5 June 1917. The next day they returned to Washington and met with Deeds and Waldon. McCauley agreed that Packard would pioneer the standardized engine and finance it until reimbursement could be made. He also agreed to loan Vincent to the government for three months and to give top priority to the engine project in the Packard plant. This truly was the day on which the U.S. Standardized

---

[18] Ibid. MARCOSSON does not mention this meeting.

[19] Ibid. MARCOSSON, op. cit., p. 238, stated that Deeds and Waldon met Schoonmaker while they were buying drafting materials and shanghaied him into assisting with the drafting. Vincent's version is more plausible.

[20] Ibid.

[21] Ibid. Although Vincent did not say the layout men took the drawings with them, it seems logical that they would. MARCOSSON, op. cit., p. 239, stated that the drawings were sent to the Packard plant in Detroit as soon as each was completed and approved by Deeds. Vincent's version is more logical.

Aircraft engine idea became a fact.[22] On this same day Vincent requested $250,000 from the Aircraft Production Board to continue the design and layout work that was necessary before construction could begin.[23]

Vincent and Hall left Washington for Detroit Thursday noon, 7 June 1917, to supervise the job of producing the experimental engines at the Packard plant. It was decided that the series would include 4-, 6-, 8-, and 12-cylinder engines, each having a five-inch bore and a seven-inch stroke with a maximum of interchangeable parts. The 8-cylinder engine, rated at 225 hp, was designed to anticipate the requirements at the front for the spring of 1918, and the 12-cylinder, rated at 330 hp, was to be the engine for 1919 and 1920. It is important to note that every foreign aircraft expert in Washington at that time agreed that the 225-hp 8-cylinder engine was adequate for 1918. Despite this unanimity, in May 1917—within 90 days— it was clear, and all were equally unanimous, that the 12-cylinder engine must be rushed to fill the need in the spring of 1918. Such was the rapidity of developments in the air war.[24]

Upon arrival in Detroit at 8:00 am, 8 June, Hall and Vincent went directly to the Packard plant to get things "cranked up." O. E. Hunt, the chief engineer, had already procured some billets of steel for cylinders. Hall left for Cleveland to get crankshaft forgings made up; he authorized the Parke Drop Forge Company to "dig out" his dies for the Hall-Scott engine so that the job could be done faster: it was completed in three days. Vincent called for volunteers for weekend work in the drafting department, and every draftsman volunteered.[25] This workforce amounted to 150 men. About 86 percent of the detailed drafting was completed during this period. These were paper drawings and only of the 8-cylinder engine. Almost the entire Packard drafting force worked on the job the following week and finished the remaining paper drawings for the 8-cylinder engine. The job was then transferred to Washington, and Vincent took about 25 draftsmen from Detroit and Buffalo furnished by Dodge Brothers, Packard, Cadillac, and Pierce Arrow. When all paper drawings for the 8-cylinder and the 12-cylinder engines had been completed, they were sent out to various

---

[22] Ibid. In this letter Vincent showed the meeting with Waldon and Deeds to have taken place on the morning of 5 June. The February 1919 report to the SAE is dated the 6th. This was a typographical error in the typescript of the letter, as he could not have met McCauley in New York on the morning of the 5th and have conferred in Washington at the same time. The rest of the chronology of Vincent's movements during this period supports the date of the 6th.

[23] SWEETSER, op. cit., p. 176.

[24] History of BAP, vol. 7, pp. 1892–1893.

[25] McCook files, loc. cit. (footnote 10).

automobile concerns to have tracings made from the paper drawings. During the week required to complete the tracings, at least 300 draftsmen were working on the job at various plants. All drafting work was completed by 15 June.

Meanwhile, patterns and a wood model were under construction. The wood model was completed and shipped to the Bureau of Standards on 16 June. Parts had also been ordered for the first 8-cylinder engine as follows: bronze-back, babbit-lined bearings and aluminum castings from General Aluminum and Brass Company, Detroit; connecting rods, connecting-rod upper-end bushings, connecting-rod bolts, and rocker-arm assemblies from Cadillac Company; camshafts from L. O. Gordon Manufacturing Company, Muskegon; crankshafts from Parke Drop Forge Company, Cleveland; all bevel gears from Hall-Scott Company, San Francisco; ball bearings from Hess-Bright Manufacturing Company, Philadelphia; piston rings from Bord High Compression Ring Company, Rockford; pistons from Aluminum Casting Company, Cleveland; valves from Rich Tool Company, Detroit; springs from the Gibson Company, Muskegon; and all patterns, many dies, and the production of all other parts provided by the Packard Company. Assembly and testing was accomplished in the Packard plant.

The first sample 8-cylinder engine was delivered to the Bureau of Standards on 3 July 1917, just over a month from its conception. During this period, while the engine was being rushed to completion, Deeds had the design submitted to such well-known engineers as H. M. Crane, chief engineer of the Wright-Martin Company; David Fergusson, of the Pierce Arrow Company; a Mr. Fekete, of the Hudson Company, and D. McCall White, of Cadillac, who had designed the Napier. Deeds also had a committee of machine-tool makers approve the design to assure no trouble in tooling up, and a group of manufacturers (e.g., H. M. Leland, C. Harold Wills, of Ford, F. F. Beall, of Packard, and Walter Chrysler, then of Buick) to give their blessing from the production standpoint. All were well satisfied with the design.[26]

In this way the Liberty series of engines was launched. Although the elapsed time from the initial design conference to a completed engine was phenomenally short, there were adequate safeguards against an inferior product. The engine was designed in six days, but this was the culmination of years of thought and experimentation on the part of Hall and Vincent, and the product proved the quality of their effort.

---

[26] MARCOSSON, op. cit., p. 240.

The Engines

In discussing the Liberty engine as a child of American technology, it must be remembered that it was designed as a series of engines—4, 6, 8, and 12 cylinders—with standardized, interchangeable, mass-produced parts. This was the most important basic premise on which its designers worked. The fact that only the 12-cylinder engine was used extensively should not detract from the soundness of the series principle. The exigencies of the war situation relegated the smaller engines to the role of curiosities. All were sound engines, however, with the exception of the L–8, which was taken from production because it vibrated excessively.

Total production of the different sizes varied considerably. Of the 4-cylinder engines, only 2 were built[1]; there were 52 6-cylinder engines[2]; 15 of the 8-cylinder,[3] and, overshadowing its smaller sisters, a total of 20,478 12-cylinder engines was produced.[4] The 12-cylinder power plant was used experimentally as a 24-cylinder X type, as a double-crankshaft type, with spur-gear or epicyclic reduction, and inverted and air-cooled.

So few of the smaller engines were built that only brief reference will be made to them. Because the basic premise of the Liberty design was interchangeability of parts, all engines used the same cylinders, pistons, and

[1] McCook files, letter, Bureau of Steam Engineering (Navy) from Vincent, 14 March 1918. This reference stated flatly that, as of that date at least, only two had been built. In a letter to G. H. Bordel of the Packard Company, 3 November 1917, Vincent directed that an L–8 be rebuilt into two L–4s. These L–4s were to be built by the Hudson Motor Car Company, whereas the first two were built from "scratch" by Nordyke and Marmon. There is no evidence, however, that the latter were actually built. There is no other indication of any others being built.

[2] Ibid., Chief, Engineering Division, from Chief, Air Service, 8 March 1924. This information is not precise. The reference stated that 52 engines were stored at Fairfield Air Depot, Ohio, but did not indicate this as the total produced.

[3] History of BAP, vol. 7, p. 1889.

[4] Ibid. This figure was also used in a letter to the *Aviation and Aeronautical Engineering* magazine from the Chief, Information Group, Air Service, 18 September 1919. GORRELL, op. cit., gave a total of 13,574, but did not include engines produced after 11 November 1918.

numerous other parts such as crankshafts and crankcases; other parts affected by the number of cylinders, however, were individual to each size of engine.

The 4-cylinder (L–4) weighed 398 pounds and developed 102 hp at 1400 rpm with a makeshift carburetor. With proper carburetion this power would have improved., The L–4 was strictly experimental, and it was not put into production since it could be useful only for training aircraft and there was already an ample supply of tested engines for this purpose (Curtiss, Hall-Scott, Hispano-Suiza).

The 6-cylinder (L–6) weighed 540 to 560 pounds and developed 200 to 215 hp. This power could have been increased to 230 to 240 hp, with refinement. The L–6 did not get into production, however, because it was too large for training planes, and there were already good, tested engines available for single-seat fighters. L–6s were built by Thomas Morse and Wright and were considered for installation in the Caproni triplane, light bombers (one or two engines), Navy Amphibians, air ships (blimps), Air Mail aircraft, BUL–12s, Fokker D–VIIs, and a night fighter.

Most of the interest in the L–6 came after the war; however, the McCook files do not show the final disposition of the 52 engines. On 8 March 1924 the Chief, Engineering Division, McCook Field, was asked by the Chief,

Figure 1.—L–4, 1918. (Smithsonian photo A1745)   Air Force Museum

20

Figure 2.—L–6, 1918.   (Smithsonian photo A1746)   Air Force Museum

Air Service, about his retention desires. The answer, 17 March, was that the engines were not required in the McCook Field program and should not be retained by the Air Service. On 20 August 1924, the Chief, Air Service, telegraphed the Chief, Engineering Division, that he understood McCook now wanted to retain the engines. The Chief, Engineering Division, wired back on 21 August that he wanted to retain the Wright and Thomas-Morse L–6s, but that the Hall-Scott L–6s were not desired.[5] Following this exchange, the files are silent.

The Liberty 8-cylinder (L–8) was manufactured by General Motors at a cost of $3000 each. It was a 45°-angle V-type, weighed 575 pounds, developed 270 hp at 1850 rpm, weighed 2.12 pounds per horsepower, averaged fuel consumption of .547 pounds per horsepower hour and oil consumption of .050 pounds per horsepower hour. Fitted with improved intake headers and carburetors, the L–8 generated 330 hp at 1950 rpm.

Like the L–4 and L–6, the L–8 was a victim of competition with a tried and proved engine, in this case the Hispano-Suiza–300. The L–8 was also

---

[5] McCook files, letter, Hallett from Clark, 18 December 1918. The Hall-Scotts were not true Liberty engines. They were called "Liberty" by the company but did not use parts that were interchangeable with the Liberty series.

21

NASM specimen

Figure 3.—L–8, 1917. First Liberty Engine. (Smithsonian photo A54391)

the victim of a more serious problem: vibration. This was so serious that production was stopped at the Buick plant when a total of 15 had been built. In January 1918 six L–8s had been produced and were located as follows: number 1 engine at McCook, number 2 in Detroit (Packard plant), one at the LWF plant, College Point, N.Y., one at the Bureau of Standards, one at Delco, Dayton, Ohio, and one at the Hudson Motor Car Company in Detroit.

The L–8 was the first of the Liberty series to be built. Recognizing the historical significance of this fact, Dr. Stratton, of the Bureau of Standards, requested that one of the original Liberty engines be shipped to him for a historical collection. Vincent was quick to agree and ordered the first Liberty to be carefully "pickled" in castor oil, crated, and shipped to the Bureau of Standards.[6] This was the engine that had been built in 21 days,

---

[6] Ibid., **Marmon** from Vincent, 24 June 1918.

22

Figure 4.—L–12, 1918. Also known as Model A Buick, from NASM's Fokker T–2 Airplane. First coast to coast flight, 1923. (Smithsonian photo A4870 D)

and it was first received at the Bureau of Standards on 3 July 1917. This engine, which had been sent to McCook Field from the Bureau of Standards for further testing, arrived at the Bureau for the second time about the middle of July 1918 for permanent display.

The Liberty twelve (L–12) is the engine referred to as "the Liberty Engine." Its vital statistics were:

Type:	V 45°	Weight per hp:	2.11 lbs
Cylinders:	12	Fuel per hp hour:	.509 lbs
Horsepower:	400	Oil per hp hour:	.037 lbs
RPM:	1800	Average cost:	$4000
Bore and stroke:	5″ x 7″		

The weight of the engine varied according to its accessories and equipment. The basic engine—dry and without radiator—weighed as little as 786 pounds, but fully equipped for flight it would weigh in excess of 900 pounds.

23

As will be seen in "The Critics," pp. 45–54, there was much controversy about some of the L–12's design features. Probably the most accurate criticism was against the scupper oiling system in the original L–12. When it became necessary to increase the horsepower of the engine to the 450 to 500 range in order to stay abreast of German developments, a forced-feed system had to be used. Engineers such as H. M. Crane and D. McCall White consulted with O. E. Hunt and E. J. Hall to effect this and to make changes necessitated by the "beef-up" of the engine to bearings, crankshaft, and other parts.[7] It should not be implied, however, that these changes, with the exception of the oiling system, were design changes in the same sense of redesigning a basically poor engine. The many tests to which the original L–12 was subjected all gave the same result; the 350-hp L–12 was a fine, economical, dependable engine.

The Liberty engine was the product of the thought and experience of many men. Although Vincent and Hall had put it on paper, they drew heavily from their own proved designs as well as from the designs of other manufacturers to assure the best product possible.

Vincent pointed out that:

Every feature going into the Liberty motor had been thoroughly proved out in Europe and also by experimental work in this country. I had personally spent two years at the Packard Factory developing the improved type of valve action which was used in the Liberty motor, as well as light steel cylinders, the water jacketed intake headers, the two part box-section crankcase, and so on through the list of features, which are now well-known as being important features of the Liberty motor.[8]

In another letter he lists the proved design features he had contributed:

On account of the experience which I had gained at the expense of the Packard Company, I was able to contribute the following major features of design:

(A) Crankcase construction split on the center line with the bearings carried between the two halves and through bolts running from top to bottom;

(B) Steel cylinders of the Mercedes type of construction, but designed for rapid production;

(C) Camshaft and valve rocker arm construction;

(D) Intake Header and Carburetor arrangement including means for heating intake header;

_____

[7] GROVER CLEVELAND LOENING, *Our Wings Grow Faster* (Garden City, N.Y.: Doubleday, Doran and Co., Inc., 1935), p. 81. Here Loening says that the engine was redesigned by Crane, White, and others. This does not agree with the story as told by Vincent and others.

[8] McCook files, letter, Emmons from Vincent, 4 December 1918.

24

Air Force Museum
Figure 5.—L–12 with spur reduction gearing, 1918. (Smithsonian photo A693–C)

(E) 45 degree included angle of cylinders;

(F) Water pump design, location and drive, including self-takeup on the stuffing box;

(G) Connecting rods and bearings;

(H) Oiling system as finally adopted including full pressure feed, no grooves in the bearings and tripple oil pump to accomplish dry crankcase.[9]

The Hall-Scott Company, in submitting an accounting of their connection with the Liberty to the Bureau of Aircraft Production, showed that many of E. J. Hall's design features were also used in the Liberty:

It is a noteworthy fact that the experience obtained from the manufacture and production of the A–5, A–7, A–5a, and A–7a engines brought out many features and principles embodied by our Mr. Hall in the Liberty engine. Several of these were as follows:

a. The special heavy duty type aluminum pistons. This design was never used before to our knowledge in any aviation engine.

---

[9] Ibid., Potter from Vincent, 9 May 1918.

25

Figure 6.—Allison V.G. 1410 (Air cooled Inverted Liberty L–12). Geared super-charger and Allison epicyclic propeller reduction gearing. (Smithsonian photo A1042 D)

b. The method of camshaft drive, which resembled in a great many ways the Mercedes drive, excepting that the camshaft was entirely enclosed, which at the time the Mercedes was not.

c. The special method of drawing water from the exhaust valve side of the cylinder, which tends to equalize the heat distribution of the cylinder. This is clearly a Hall-Scott feature and was one of the things that lead [sic] to the success of the Liberty cylinder.

d. The propeller flange drive was designed and manufactured solely by Hall-Scott and was similar upon all types of our engine. This flange as a unit was adopted upon the Liberty engine and was an entire success.

e. The Hall-Scott crankshaft was used throughout all of our engines and the bearing diameter etc., proportioned as to the horsepower carried on the various types. It was a noteworthy fact that this same shaft with correct pro-portions to the horsepower carried by the Liberty engine was installed in that

26

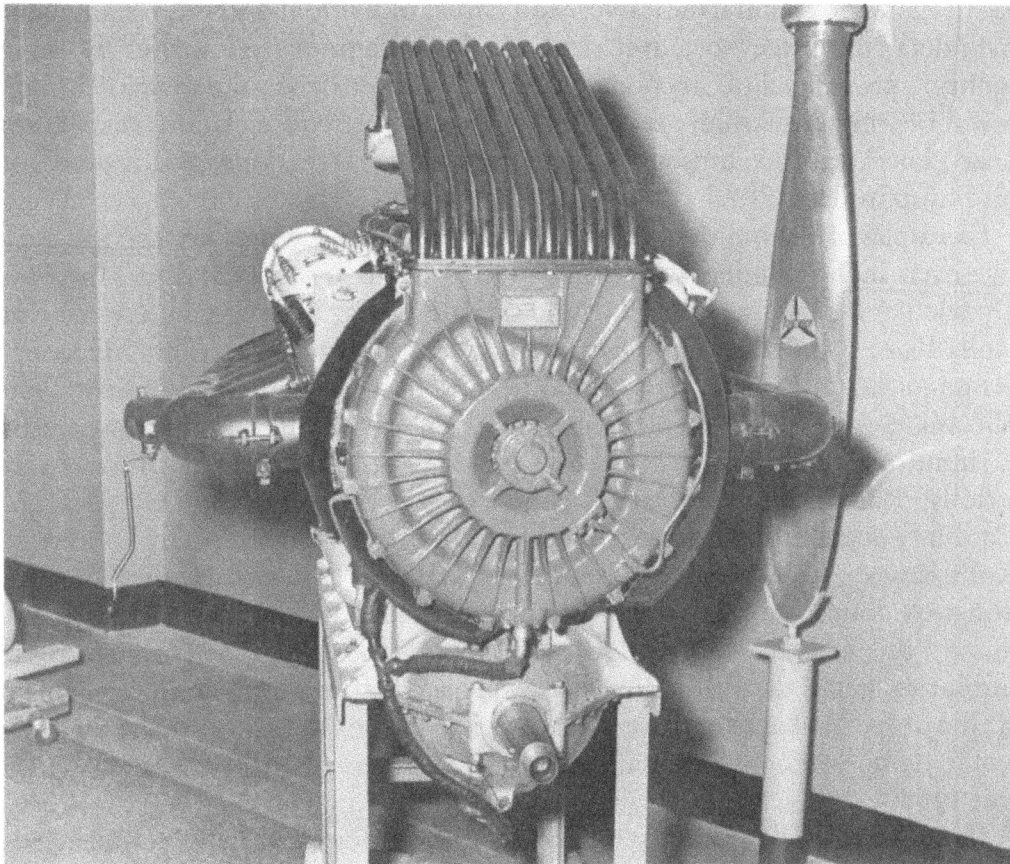

Figure 7.—L–12 with General Electric supercharger installed in 1922. (Smithsonian photo A1099)

engine. In fact all the Hall-Scott dies were used in producing the first Liberty engine . . . . The direct drive feature of the Liberty engine was one of the greatest reasons of the success of the Liberty engine . . . . This design was insisted upon by our Mr. Hall at the time of designing the Liberty engine and approved by Mr. Vincent only after Mr. Hall had agreed to take the entire responsibility in the event the directly driven job should fail.[10]

A further indication of Hall's contribution to the Liberty is contained in a booklet published by the Hall-Scott Company after the war. It pointed out that, prior to 1 May 1917, the Hall-Scott Company had a 12-cylinder design called the A–8 which was designed for 450 hp. This engine was ready for test when Hall went to Washington on official business with the Navy and was pulled into the Liberty project by Deeds. The A–8 and the

---

[10] History of BAP, loc. cit., pp. 1848–1849.

27

L–12 had many similarities: overhead cams; individual and interchangeable cylinders; the same bore and stroke in both engines (five inches by seven inches); propeller hub and bolts the same; direct drive, nongeared timing; seven bearing crankshaft; crank throw bearing centers; ignition; distributor head; bevel gear on camshaft driveshaft; piston rod sections; and submerged oil pump in sump.[11]

Examples of proved design features used in other engines are the five inch by seven inch cylinder, which had been proved by Curtiss and Lorraine-Dietrich as well as by Hall-Scott; the cylinder design was based on Mercedes, Rolls-Royce, and Lorraine-Dietrich; the camshaft was based on Mercedes, Hispano-Suiza, Rolls-Royce, Renault, and Fiat, as well as Hall-Scott; the 45° angle was used by Renault as well as Packard; Delco ignition was used in hundreds of thousands of autos; die-cast, aluminum-alloy pistons were strictly Hall-Scott; the forked connecting rods were used by DeDion, Cadillac, and Hispano-Suiza; the crankshaft design was used by Mercedes, Rolls-Royce, Curtiss, and Renault, as well as Hall-Scott; the Vincent-designed crankcase was very close to that used by Mercedes and Hispano-Suiza; the original lubrication system and the redesigned system were similar to that of the Rolls-Royce, as well as to features of the Hispano-Suiza; Hall's propeller-hub design was very similar to the Mercedes; the centrifugal water pump was conventional; and an established Zenith carburetor design was used.[12]

The inversion of a Liberty engine was first attempted in December 1918 in an experimental 24-cylinder X-type engine.[13] This engine was a combination of two L-12s, the cylinders of one standing in an upright position and the other pointing downward or inverted. The junction between the two was specially designed. The engine failed on 6 December 1918, however, when a connecting rod broke. There is no further mention of this engine in the McCook files. Further experimentation was probably dropped, as Vincent, who had sponsored the development of the engine, left government service on 30 November 1918.

Although there is no indication that the X-type engine was perfected or even tested further, the interest in inverting a Liberty engine did not cease. There were some definite advantages in inversion. By shifting the weight of the installed engine, the thrust line could be made to coincide with the airplane's center of gravity. This allowed the mechanic to work on the

---

[11] *Pertinent Facts.* This is a summary of the similar items that were listed by the Hall-Scott Company.

[12] History of BAP, loc. cit., pp. 1896–1898.

[13] McCook files, letter, Curry from Ridenour, 9 May 1925.

Figure 8.—24 Cylinder Liberty "X", 1918.   (Smithsonian photo A1747)

engine from the ground instead of from a maintenance stand. The relocation of the cylinder under the engine provided maximum visibility for the pilot, and, when the inverted engine was air-cooled, the air scoops did not interfere with visibility. Inversion increased the weight of the engine but also gave a slight increase in power.

The next inversion test was made between 5 and 7 February 1919. The test showed that inversion was feasible if the problems of oil scavenging and water flow could be solved. Four years went by before another serious attempt to solve the inversion problem was made, but this time the job was done correctly.

After the modifications were made, tests proved to be very successful, except that the oil had a tendency to overheat. The inverted engine developed 422 hp at full throttle, with a fuel consumption of .499 pounds per horsepower hour. At 90 percent of normal speed under a propeller load, oil consumption was 8.7 pounds per engine hour. This engine, L–12 #E0501121, weighed 915 pounds, including generator but less starter, air intake pipe, and exhaust pipe. It was shipped to Grover Loening in 1924 for installation in one of his designs, although it had initially been tested in a DH–4B. The first flight, of 14-minute duration, was made on 5 September 1923 by Lieutenant James Doolittle. Flight Officer Carroll made a cross-country flight to Toledo on 9 September and in October flew in the Pulitzer races to St. Louis and return. The first flight of an inverted Liberty engine in an amphibian was on 7 June 1923, but in this flight the aircraft was wrecked on landing when it struck an obstacle in the water. The next tests in the amphibian occurred in January 1925 when, on the 8th, the amphibian was flown from Mitchell Field to Bolling Field, on 2 February 1925 from Bolling to Langley, and on 13 February from Langley to McCook.

Grover Loening was quite interested in the inverted Liberty engine. He made "numerous visits" to McCook, and on 20 April 1923 made a statement to the press that he had tried to interest the Air Service in inverted Liberty engines "five years ago." He had also pointed out in lectures right after World War I that inversion would provide better propeller clearance and visibility. When inversion finally came, Loening designed his amphibian for it. Twenty inverted Liberty engines were built for the Loening Amphibian (COA–1) in the Air Service inventory. This was the total production of inverted Liberty engines through fiscal year 1925; the programmed 30 engines for that fiscal year were reduced to 20. The program had been for 5 engines up to February 1924 and 20 through the balance of the year. The total in the program for 1926 was 15, 10 for the Air Service and 5 for the Coast Guard. The Allison Company of Indianapolis, Indiana, was the contractor for conversion; the price per converted engine was $1472. After 1926 the McCook files do not indicate additional conversions of Liberty engines to the inverted configuration.

In January 1918 work started on gearing the propeller of the Liberty engine to provide more power. The engines produced for the war in Europe were direct drive; this method of propulsion was cheaper to produce and lighter and easier to maintain than a geared method. The prime Liberty-equipped aircraft for use in France by the United States was the DH–4; the direct drive L–12 was more than adequate for this aircraft. Its use in larger, multi-engined aircraft and flying boats, however, would require more power so that a geared engine was necessary. (Gearing provides higher engine rpm, which increases power, and lower propeller rpm, which increases efficiency.)

Vincent, after study, chose an epicyclic gear-reduction design as the most promising because it made use of only known and successful construction, and, as Vincent put it, "... if there ever was a clean piece of design in the world that could be banked on this is the one."[14]

Vincent had studied the Rolls-Royce epicyclic gear and had made "a tremendous simplification" of it. His new design would weigh 50 to 75 pounds less than the spur gear, "with all its advantages and none of its disadvantages."[15] After a series of tests in which considerable trouble was encountered due to faulty lubrication and improperly set bearings, a "fix" was finally achieved and the assembly went through a 20-hour test at 1800 rpm giving no sign of distress and every indication that it would continue for another 80 hours with no trouble. In October 1918 an assembled reduction gear finished a 30-hour test at 1800 rpm. At this time six sets of gears were being made at Allison Experimental Engineering Company, and six sets had been completed.

The Navy was particularly interested in the epicyclic-geared engine. In August 1918 they had requested 2000 but Vincent was concerned that too much production emphasis on the geared engine would hold up production on the direct drive type. The Navy could not understand why the Air Service had trouble in recognizing its need for the geared engine. The Navy felt that the end of development had been reached on the direct drive and pointed out that "... our plane development is restricted by the inability of the engine to get the larger boats into the air ... the Navy wants the geared Liberty engine and wants it badly."[16] The reason the Navy was so interested is evident in a report of a flight test of the F-5 flying boat equipped with two geared Liberty engines. Even with a strong side wind and improper propellers the boat got into the air in 23 seconds, whereas the average was 35 seconds.

By February 1925, however, there was a surplus of the geared engines in the Navy inventory. The Allison Company had built 250 of the epicyclic type for the Navy, but only a few had been used. The Air Service was now the interested agency and sought to procure some from the Navy, since that department was willing to reduce its inventory without transfer of funds. A year was to pass, however, before arrangements were made. The Air Service requisitioned 100 geared engines from the Navy on 9 February 1926, and the requisition was approved on 1 March. The Air Service intended to air-cool the engines and to use them for transports and multi-engined bombers.

The final transaction on epicyclic-geared engines in the McCook files

[14] Ibid., Potter from Vincent, 25 April 1918.
[15] Ibid., 22 April 1918.
[16] Ibid., Vincent from Atkins, 21 October 1918.

Figure 9.—Air cooled L–12 with geared supercharger, circa 1925. (Smithsonian photo A1042 C)

concerns an engine that had been in stock for a number of years and that was made available to the Army Aeronautical Museum on 1 January 1936.

The development of the air-cooled L–12 began in August 1923 when specifications were sent to contractors. Air cooling improved flying qualities through reduction of weight, streamlining and pilot vision, reduced noise, cleaner and smoother operation, reduced cost, and improved maintainability.

The air cooling of a Liberty engine reduced its basic weight by 141 pounds, and it pulled 436 hp at full throttle. The power was as good or better than the water-cooled engine, so the weight advantage was significant. Production in fiscal year 1924 was five to seven engines, and in fiscal year 1925 another five for use in a ground-attack plane. This number was subsequently reduced to two. The cost of these engines, geared and inverted, was more than $8500 apiece, about twice the cost estimated per engine in 100-engine lots. There is no indication that this type of engine, regardless of its advantages, was ever produced in more than two- to five-engine lots.

Ground Tests

During the first part of July 1917 the work of consolidating and numbering the drawings and of checking and correcting tracings, bills of material, limits, and the like was completed. On Saturday, 21 July, O. E. Hunt, at the Packard plant, informed Vincent that the first standard 8-cylinder engine would be ready to run on 23 July.[1] Vincent could not leave Washington just then and so told Hunt to "work the engine in" immediately.[2]

Hall arrived in Detroit on 21 July, and on the following day he and Hunt ran the engine under its own power. Vincent arrived at the Packard plant on 25 July and started testing.

> I was very anxious to test the motor for smoothness and immediately pulled some tests from low speed up to 2000 RPM under full throttle conditions and also under light throttle conditions. I quickly found that the motor was very smooth, and that up to 2000 RPM at least, there was not even a suggestion of a period of vibration. This was, indeed, gratifying as it thoroughly proved out my contention that even a large bore eight cylinder motor could be made smooth by setting the cylinders at an included angle of 45 degrees.[3]

Hall and Hunt had run the engine about eight hours the day before and had found no problems. They had even cut the intake water to bring the temperature to boiling, but no steam pockets had developed.

On 26 July and the morning of the 27th the engine was mounted on a truck and fitted with a propeller. In the afternoon of 27 July 1917, H. M. Leland, W. C. Leland, Charles King, Glen Martin, H. B. Joy, and Alvan

---

[1] Vincent MSS, "History of the Development of the USA Standardized Aircraft Engines" (proposed report). This first standard L–8 should not be confused with the L–8 which was delivered to Washington on 3 July 1917. The Washington engine was not built to run but to show that an engine had been developed.

[2] Ibid. The "working in" was accomplished by powering the engine from an external source.

[3] Ibid. The 45° included angle was criticized by a number of people as being experimental. The pros and cons of this controversy will be discussed below. No explanation was found as to why there was no vibration during the test of the L–8, and yet production was later canceled because of excessive vibration. It is probable that the more solid base of a test platform may have tended to dampen vibration.

33

McCauley came out to see the run. The engine started on the first pull of the propeller but had to be stopped since the oil pressure line had not been connected. The second start required more time because the operators were not familiar with the new engine and overprimed it. After the second start, it ran for an hour and a half with no trouble. The first hour was at nine-tenths power, and the last half hour at full power. After the run, the oil temperature in the crankcase was 127°F and less than half a gallon of oil had been used. Glen Martin, one of the few aircraft producers in America at the time, was very pleased with the design and the test. Vincent, also pleased with the test, said: "I was very much pleased with the ignition because I had found it to be lighter than magnetos, probably more reliable, and best of all, . . . it made for easy starting." [4]

With the successful conclusion of the first tests, Vincent called Deeds for permission to ship the truck and engine to Washington. Deeds agreed, and on 28 July preparations were made. On the 29th the unit was shipped, arriving in Washington on the 30th. Vincent and Hall also arrived in Washington on the 30th and supervised the unloading and preparation for run at the Bureau of Standards on the 31st. The engine was ready by 8:00 pm, and Hall, Vincent, and Frank Trego, of Trego Motors, ran some short tests.

Wednesday afternoon, 1 August 1917, Waldon and Deeds arranged for a test before the joint technical committee of the Army and Navy. The test started at 4:30 pm and continued until 6:00 pm. The engine ran perfectly without attention or adjustments and used only one quart of oil. Vincent told the committee he recommended immediate manufacture of the engine, although he assured them that exhaustive tests would also be conducted. There was no dissent to his recommendation. [5] The committee was also shown the disassembled parts of the original engine that had arrived in Washington on 3 July 1917.

More tests were run on 2 and 3 August for members of the French commission and Mr. Riker of the Locomobile Company. On 4 August a final exhibition run was made for members of the Committee on Military Affairs of the House and Senate. Again the engine ran perfectly without attention. On 6 August 1917, the test engine was dismantled, and the parts were minutely examined and found to be in excellent shape. Higher pressure

---

[4] Ibid. This ignition, another controversial point of design, will be discussed below.

[5] Ibid. This appears to be the first time that the technique of "concurrency" of test and manufacture had been suggested. This technique was not used again for many years, but is now an accepted production method.

pistons had been ordered, but these proved to be unusable when they arrived. The engine was then reassembled and shipped back to Detroit. The test truck was shipped to Colorado Springs for the altitude tests, which were to be held on Pike's Peak at a later date. Up to this time the test engine had run 15 hours under wide-open throttle without a single change or adjustment.

As of 4 August 1917, 68 days from conception, the standard-detail drawings for the L–8 and the L–12 were completed; the standard bills of material and the standard material specifications for the L–8 and the L–12 were completed; the final construction drawings for both engines were within two weeks of completion; the general designs were approved for manufacture; and the first L–12 was within one week of being tested.

On 13 August 1917 the first L–12 started its preliminary tests. It was run under its own power, pulling a light dynamometer load most of the day. The engine was equipped with the low-compression pistons (clearance volume of 20.5 percent of the total) designed mainly for the Navy. On 14 August power curves were started, but they were delayed by a defective carburetor. Although this carburetor was replaced, the engine continued to "spit back." After adjustment, 230 hp was obtained at 1600 rpm. That night, higher compression pistons (18.9 percent clearance volume) were installed. On 15, 16, and 17 August different carburetor settings were tried. The best results were obtained with number 30 chokes, number 145 jets, and number 160 compensators. A one-inch hole had to be drilled through the intake-header partition to equalize the mixture. These adjustments resulted in 346 hp at 1700 and 1800 rpm.

At this point the engine was removed from the dynamometer and placed on a test cradle in a shed, and a test propeller, or "club," was installed. A two-hour run was made in the evening of 18 August. The next morning a five-hour run was started, but was stopped after two hours so that the carburetor jets could be changed to "lean down" the mixture. The run was then finished with an average of 200 hp at 1500 rpm.

On the morning of 20 August it was decided to put back the lower compression pistons ". . . as this would remove the human element and give the engine a consistent hard test, considerably more sure than could be obtained under flying conditions."[6] All dimensions were also measured for record purposes prior to the fifty-hour government acceptance test. The measurements took all day Monday and continued well into the night, but the engine was ready to run early Tuesday morning, 21 August 1917.

---

[6] Ibid.

After preliminary runs, number 29 chokes had to be made and installed; accordingly, the engine was not ready for the 50-hour test until 3:00 pm, 22 August. A variance was found in the carburetors that could not be adjusted out, but, even though gas economy would be poor, it was decided to make the test rather than wait for new intake headers.

At 5:00 pm, 22 August, the engine was started, and, after a warm-up and adjustment, the official 50-hour test run was begun at 5:20 pm. A nonstop run of five hours (until 10:20 pm) was made. There had been some backfire through the carburetor on the first 5-hour run so 2 hours and 35 minutes were expended clearing the fuel system, the primary problem having been air-bound water traps. The second five-hour run began at 12:55 am, 23 August, and was completed at 5:55 am. No problems were encountered during this run; the engine performed beautifully throughout. After a 10-minute shutdown, the third five-hour run was started at 6:06 am and completed at 11:05 am. The oil was changed and a 10-hour run was begun at 11:50 am, 23 August. At 9:50 pm, the engine was again stopped and carefully examined. Nothing was found wrong. The next run commenced at 11:00 pm and was completed 10 hours later at 9:00 am, 24 August 1917. Again the engine performed superbly, and examination showed no problems. The final run was started at 10:30 am, 24 August, and was completed 15 hours later at 1:30 am, 25 August. During the 50-hour test run, no adjustments had been made; not even a sparkplug was changed. The average rpm was 1584; average horsepower, 315; and average gas consumption, .58 pounds per horsepower.

Upon completion of the 50-hour run, the engine was transferred to the dynamometer, and a power curve was run without change or adjustment to the engine. The curve showed 337 hp at 1700 rpm and 346 hp at 1800 rpm. The engine was then disassembled and examined, and all parts were measured under the supervision of the government inspector, Lynn Reynolds. His report showed a maximum variation of 5 percent in rpm with the brake horsepower for the first run averaging 304 minimum, and for the second run averaging 319.5 maximum, an increase of 15.5 hp. This was 6.5 percent in excess of the engine's rated horsepower. The average thermal efficiency of the engine was 23.1 percent; the average oil consumption .0238 pounds per horsepower hour; the average water-outlet temperature was 183°, and the average temperature difference was 20°.

The accessories used, as shown by the report, were: Delco ignition system with battery and two distributors; two duplex Zenith carburetors; and AC Titan spark plugs from the Champion Ignition Company. The engine was fueled by Red Crown gasoline with a Baume gravity test of

58° at 60° F, and lubrication was provided by grade-B Mobil oil combined with 25 percent castor oil.

During the test there was no undue vibration, and, upon completion of the last run, the engine was disassembled for examination of parts. The ensuing inspection showed the valves to be in good condition, with no evidence of warping, overheating, leaking, or scoring and with an acceptable seat surface. The bearing surface on the piston rings and cylinders was within tolerance, and only slight wear was evident. These conditions indicated that the lubrication and cooling systems were adequate and that there was no leakage of lubricating oil.

Reynolds' report suggested that alteration of the intake manifold would increase engine efficiency as would the installation of an auxiliary breather in the vertical-shaft compartment. He also recommended that a new type of babbit bushing be designed for the lower connecting-rod bearings to preclude cracking at high speed.

After this examination, the engine was reassembled and a five-hour run was made for Lieutenant Scofield, U.S. Navy, on 27 August 1917. After this run, the engine was disassembled, checked, reassembled, and shipped to Washington, D.C., on Tuesday, 28 August 1917.

The completion of the 50-hour run in an elapsed time of 55 hours was, in itself, a record; most 50-hour acceptance runs of that period took around five days to complete. Reynolds' foreword to his completed test report bears witness to the competency of the basic design:

> The appended report is a survey of the main phases of the 50-hour endurance test, maximum power curve calibration on the electric dynamometer, and inspection of dismantled parts of the USA twelve Aircraft Engine Number 1, which were made under the supervision of the Equipment Division, Signal Corps at the Packard Factory, Detroit, Michigan, August 22–25, 1917.
>
> A consideration of the data collected, we believe, will show that the fundamental construction is such that very satisfactory service with a long life and a high order of efficiency will be given by this power plant, and the design has passed from the experimental stage into the field of proven engines.[7]

In November 1917, Lieutenant Emmons directed that the no. 5 production engine from Packard be run to destruction at the Packard plant; Captain Heaslet and Mr Reynolds were to conduct the test. "This is for the purpose of avoiding any criticism of Major Hall or Major Vincent, designers of the engine, conducting this essential test."[8] Vincent was upset by being excluded from the tests and voiced his opinion strongly to Colonel

---

[7] Ibid. Vincent quotes from Reynolds' report on the 50-hour test.

[8] McCook files, letter, Heaslet and Hall from Emmons, 1 November 1917.

Deeds. He thought the test was for engineering purposes preliminary to public tests at Dayton and that no engineering information would be obtained ". . . because there will be nobody on the job that really knows the structure in its numerous details." [9] Vincent went on to say:

> These are, of course, orders, and I will be governed accordingly. I want to state, however, that I consider this is being handled in an unnecessarily dangerous way, and I don't believe that the information will be obtained that would have been obtained under the plans which I had laid. You, of course, know that I am the only one that has followed this job in all its details from the first; I am the only one that knows just what moves have been made in order to step up the M. E. P., and I know better than anyone else where the danger points lie.[10]

The above quotation is only one example of the almost jealous interest Vincent continued to have in the Liberty throughout his service career. He was completely dedicated to assuring the success of the engine, reacting immediately and forcefully whenever, in his opinion, this goal was in jeopardy. Deeds was not unaware of Vincent's contribution and knowledge, and so, in the instance in point, quickly took action to insure that Vincent and Hall would not be excluded. He wrote to Vincent with copies to Hall, Heaslet, and the Packard Company modifying the tests so that preliminary runs would be made by Vincent and Hall to elicit whatever engineering information they might desire; a 50-hour test would then be run controlled by Heaslet and Reynolds. The test to destruction would also be controlled by Heaslet and Reynolds, but Hall and Vincent would be present as observers and would be available to help remedy any serious trouble that might develop. Deeds' quick conciliatory action in this case typifies the leadership he exerted during his tenure as the head of production to assure the harmonious cooperation of his subordinates in order to achieve the goal of rapid production of the Liberty engine.

For reasons not now apparent in the McCook Field files, Vincent was not present at the destruction tests. As it turned out, the tests were run on two engines, no. 5 as originally scheduled and no. 12; the latter was a production model, the former an experimental model. These tests had been preceded by a series of 50-hour tests to prove out a "beef-up" of the basic design from 315 to 400 plus hp. This "beef-up" was symptomatic of the requirement for more and more horsepower to support the air war in France. In effect, the war brought on a compression in time of the development of aircraft and aircraft engines. This compression was particularly

---

[9] Ibid. Emmons from Vincent, 3 November 1917.
[10] Ibid.

felt in the United States because of our almost nonexistent research and production prior to World War I. The Liberty engine is a good example. It was thought in May 1917 that a 250-hp eight would be the engine for the spring of 1918. Two months later a 300–350-hp twelve was required, and by September 1917 the horsepower race required 400–450. It is a tribute to the basic design of the 12-cylinder Liberty that this escalation could be absorbed and more than 1000 engines produced within one year of the initial design conference.

The basic changes that raised the horsepower of the L–12 from 315 to 400-plus were an improved intake-header design and increased valve lift. Fifty-hour tests in September and early October, following these changes, but based also on the experience of our Allies in combat, resulted in a modified oil pump and propeller hub. Because of the increase in power, the strength of many of the engine parts—designed for a hundred horsepower less—was questioned. A series of 50-hour tests, started in November and continued into February 1918, dictated changes to connecting rods, the crankshaft, connecting rod bearings, piston-pin retainer, and other details. The oil system was also changed from the scupper to the forced-feed type to provide more positive lubrication. These tests and the resulting changes were the responsibility of Major Hall and O. E. Hunt of the Packard Company. Other than his participation in the design of the engine, this was E. J. Hall's major contribution to its success, since the changes he and Hunt worked out remained valid, for the most part, for the duration of the war. Shortly after the breakdown tests of the nos. 5 and 12 engines, Hall was relieved from further contact with the engine program and was sent to Dayton to assist in getting the American-built DH–4 into production.[11]

The tests of the two engines were the culmination and proof of the "beefed-up" engine. The first test of no. 5, equipped with low-compression pistons, was of 29-hour duration, 20 hours at full throttle. Although oil consumption was low, the test resulted in excessive ring wear, gave evidence of valve overheating, and showed that the connecting-rod bearings had suffered from insufficient lubrication. The engine was pulled down and reassembled with new rings, the valves were ground, and the main and connecting-rod bearings were grooved to provide more oil to their surfaces. The next run had lasted four hours when a connecting rod broke; examination proved the connecting-rod bearings had been too tight. The engine was reassembled, allowing more clearance, and an experimental high-chrome exhaust valve was installed.

---

[11] History of BAP, vol. 7, pp. 1937–1938, letter, Ingoldsley from Hunt, 5 March 1919 (quoted in full).

The next run lasted five hours, when an exhaust valve burned out. Thirty-eight hours, 25 at full throttle, had been run at this point at an average horsepower of 404.9. Back in test the engine ran 11.5 more hours (9.5 at full power) and broke the crankshaft (this was the light shaft designed for the 315-hp engine); the chrome exhaust valve held up well. The engine was reassembled with the redesigned heavy crankshaft and other improvements and was run wide-open for nine hours; this time stoppage was caused by a broken piston pin. The total run was 63.5 hours, 43.5 at full throttle. The average horsepower was 412.48.

The no. 12 engine was set up for test with the heavy connecting-rod bearings, the high-chrome exhaust valve from the no. 5 engine, and with updated parts that had been developed in the series of 50-hour tests run from November through January. The first run was for 27.21 hours, 21.21 hours wide open. The average horsepower was 407.87. When the engine was torn down, it was found to be slightly underlubricated; some valve springs were broken, and all the connecting-rod bearings were slightly cracked. The timing was 10° late. The engine was rebuilt with special grooved connecting-rod bearings, and grooves were scored in the main bearings. The next run was of 31.35 hours' duration, 24.35 hours at full power. The average horsepower was 399.48. Teardown after this run showed the connecting-rod bearings cracked and four valve springs broken but lubrication was good. Reassembly was accomplished with stock connecting-rod bearings and valve springs. After a short run, the engine lost 200 horsepower, and it was found that the connecting rod bearings were too tight.

Special Ford connecting-rod bearings were now installed, and the engine was run to a total of 108.91 hours, 85.41 wide open. Average horsepower to this point was 403.74. Shutdown was required only for new spark plugs. The next run was terminated after 19 hours, when the timing gear broke. Examination of the Ford bearings showed them to be at least 50 percent better than any others previously tested. After replacement of the timing gear, a 12-hour run was terminated because of a cracked cylinder. This failure was not the fault of design, but rather owing to improper design specifications for the cylinder. After replacement, a final run of 30 hours was made with no more trouble. Teardown proved the parts, including the experimental chrome exhaust valve, to be within tolerance. Total test was 156.66 hours, 128.16 wide open.[12]

Following these tests a committee of manufacturers was appointed to assist in design matters from a production standpoint. O. E. Hunt was a

---

[12] McCook files, letter, Vincent from Hunt, 6 February 1918.

member, as well as such men as Henry Crane, D. McCall White, and others of equal experience and ability. During March, April, and May 1918 the tremendous effort of the preceding year bore fruit, and by June 1918 the Liberty engine was acknowledged a success.

Flight Tests

The first flight of a Liberty engine was made on 29 August 1917 at Buffalo, New York, in an LWF airplane. L–8 no. 3 was the engine tested.

The plane was pulled out on the field at 3:15 pm, and ". . . promptly at 3:30 Aviator Blakely pulled the throttle wide open and left the ground in exactly 3 seconds."[1] Blakely made a 20-minute flight. Three more flights were made after which Vincent—who was observing with Mr. Flint of the LWF Company and Mr. Crane of the Crane-Simplex Company—noted that the cooling was perfect with an average temperature of 85°F. Lubrication and ignition were also perfect; carburetion, however, was only fair. The carburetion problem was investigated, and it was found that a rubber fuel line had collapsed and some jets had been installed that were a quarter inch too short. When these faults were corrected, the engine ran well through subsequent tests, although still a little rich. On 30 August more flights were made, and speeds up to 104 mph and 17,000 feet altitude were recorded. The first Army officer to fly a Liberty engine, Major Kilner, of the Air Service, made two short flights and reported that this was the first aircraft he had flown that seemed to have a surplus of power. This eight-cylinder engine installed in the LWF later broke the American altitude record.

The flight testing of the L–12s began in October 1917. The first was made on the 21st in a Curtiss HS–1 flying boat. This was a Navy test at the Curtiss plant in Buffalo, New York. The flight was successful, and a speed of 95 mph was reached at 1680 rpm. The boat climbed 4000 feet in 10 minutes with a useful load of 1500 pounds. It was powered by the no. 3 experimental engine.

On 28 October the first flight in an American-built DH–4 was made. It also did well.

There were, of course, hundreds of test flights of the L–12 in various aircraft prior to its entry into combat in France. Two more examples follow to give an indication of the flying methods and flight conditions encountered during this period of American aviation history.

---

[1] Vincent MSS, "History of the Development of the USA Standardized Engine."

In December 1917 the no. 2 production L–12 was shipped to the LWF Company for installation in an experimental aircraft. On 18 January 1918, Vincent queried A. H. Flint, Vice President of LWF, by telegram as to the progress of the flight-test program, suggesting that he ". . . consider advisability of having Blake [Aviator Blakeley] fly from New York to Washington and Washing [sic] to Dayton as soon as weather moderates . . . ."[2]

Flint's shocking telegraphic reply to this request was: "Impossible to make flight. Blakeley killed in accident." [3] This laconic response was followed by a letter which related, in part:

> Blake left here on the afternoon of the 16th, while I was in Washington. He took Higgins, our purchasing agent with him. The engine [L–12, high compression, number two production] was working beautifully. He left the ground and instead of his customary little run of fifty to a hundred feet pulled her right square off the ground, using the same blade [propeller] that we had when you were here, the 9'6'', eight pitch. The new blades were not ready and there was no special object in making the flight except to make it as near daily as possible. His trip thru the air was the craziest flight that Blake had ever made. He was only a short way from the ground when he started to loop. He made seventeen loops in succession, gaining all the time. He did the most erratic flying when he was up to altitude that any of the boys had ever seen and they watched him throughout the entire flight on account of his peculiar get away. He started on a right hand tail spin, pulled her out and then went into a left hand. All of a sudden he came straight down, never making the slightest attempt to pull her out. The whole flight was so wild that investigation was started before I got home. The Army Intelligence Bureau are handling the whole matter and have some very interesting facts. I shall probably know more of it before the end of this week. The impression of everyone is that Blake was doped and they find that one of the men down there, without mentioning any name, you have met him, should not have been there. The man has been placed under arrest, but I doubt if they can hold him on the information they now have. But one thing sure is that this man has all the data on the performance of the Liberty engine in this plane. It looks as though it was decided to put this model out of business so that it would not be used this year.[4]

Vincent was not too receptive to Flint's sabotage theory since his mechanic at LWF had told him, ". . . Blakeley asked me to go up with him but I told him that I wanted to get some lunch first. He said: 'All right I will take Mr. Higgins up and see if I can scare him a little, because he has been

---

[2] McCook files, telegram, Westervelt to Marmon, 29 October 1917.

[3] Ibid., letter, Vincent from Flint, 18 January 1918.

[4] Ibid., 21 January 1918.

43

asking me for a ride for the last week.' " [5] On the basis of this information, Vincent recommended against the government's footing the bill for the crash; he was subsequently overruled by Colonel Deeds.

On 29 May 1918, a cross-country flight test started that was to have a much happier ending than Blakeley's last flight. This was a flight test of a typical-production L–12 in a typical-production DH–4. The test was authorized by Special Orders 124, 9 May 1918, Headquarters Signal Corps Aviation School, Wilbur Wright Field, Fairfield, Ohio.

> The following is my report of the trip from Wilbur Wright Field to Selfridge Field in the Dehaviland four number 32098 with Major Smith as pilot.
>
> Left Wilbur Wright Field at 10:15 a.m., May 29th. Climbed to an average height of from six to nine thousand feet. Flew north and arrived at Lake Erie over Sandusky, then headed for Toledo and at 12:10, the oil supply was exhausted and a forced landing effected on a farm six miles east of Toledo. At 12:13 p.m. a new tube was inserted in left hand wheel and broken plug in rear cylinder in left hand block was replaced.
>
> Started out at 3:20 for Selfridge Field, encountered low clouds as far as Detroit when we ran into a rain storm, then headed for Mount Clemens, Michigan, and at 4:44 was forced to come down under clouds and fly at an altitude of about two hundred feet to locate the field. After dropping several notes to a farmer asking the direction of the field, found the oil supply was nearly exhausted and made a forced landing on a farm near Richmond, Michigan. Owing to the condition of the field resulting from continuous rain all afternoon, the landing gear settled in the mud and the ship overturned very gently, having lost all its speed before overturning.
>
> On June first left Selfridge Field at 12:12 p.m. and at an average height of about seven thousand feet, flew to Toledo, landed on the golf course of the Toledo Yacht Club. Filled with oil, gas, and water and started at 3:39 p.m. for Wilbur Wright Field. At 4:48 landed on a farm at Wapakoneta, Ohio, and filled with gas, oil, and water and started to Wilbur Wright Field at 6:17 p.m. Landed at Wilbur Wright Field 6:50 p.m. [Signed] S. J. Green. [6]

---

[5] Ibid., Flint from Vincent, 29 January 1918.

[6] Ibid., undated report on flight from Wilbur Wright Field to Selfridge Field and return.

The Critics

The Liberty engine did not enjoy universal praise, and unfortunately some news media emphasized its shortcomings rather than its good points. The furor was initiated by one of the most amazing characters ever produced in America. He was Gutzon Borglum.

Borglum was a very competent sculptor, as his "Mares of Diomedes" in the Metropolitan Museum in New York and his "Lincoln" at Newark, New Jersey, will attest. Unfortunately, he believed himself an inventor, a publicist, and an all-around expert on almost any subject. Based on his friendship with President Wilson, he procured a letter authorizing him as an unofficial investigator of aircraft production. His charges of incompetence and waste in the production of aircraft were, for the most part, completely false, but they served to set up a hue and cry against the aircraft-production effort. As a direct result, investigations were launched in quick succession by H. Snowden Marshal, the Chamberlin Committee of the Senate, and finally the famous Hughes investigation.

Borglum was completely discredited in the end, when it was revealed that he had been trying to form a company to build aircraft during the period of his investigation. To make this fact even more unsavory, he had based his contribution to the company on his friendship with the President and had insisted on keeping his participation secret.[1] (Although discredited in 1918, Borglum is known today as the creator of what must be considered one of the wonders of the modern world, for his genius created the everlasting Mount Rushmore Monument.)

Borglum's press releases served to bring on a rash of criticism against the Liberty engine. The derogatory comments concern eight areas. These criticisms and the rebuttals to them follow:

1. The Liberty engine was not suitable for single-seat fighters: Untrue. It could be used in this type aircraft. The Germans used a Mercedes engine in their single-seat fighters that outweighed the Liberty by 150 pounds and generated 125 less horsepower.[2] Beyond this, however, was the

---

[1] MARCOSSON, op. cit., pp. 255–283.

[2] McCook files, letter, Moscovics from Vincent, 22 April 1918.

fact that the L–12 was never intended for fighter aircraft. The L–8 was developed for this purpose. Not until the L–12 was well into production was the L–8 again considered, since the Allies had a number of engines that were better suited for this type of aircraft.

2. The Liberty engine was not fast:
The Liberty was installed in airplanes that were not designed for great speed. Here again, the exigencies of the air war dictated where the United States should place its weight, and observation and bomber types were most critical. Installed in the DH–4, the Liberty drove that aircraft faster than did any foreign engine.[3]

3. The Liberty engine was hard to cool:
There was evidence to support this criticism. Leon Cammen, one of the most vociferous of the engine's detractors, attributed overheating to poor design. He said that a poor design would throw off more BTUs than a properly designed radiator could handle.[4] A more scientific study was made by Major George E. A. Hallett while assigned to the McCook test section. Hallett observed an L–12 in a DH–4 equipped with the largest radiator designed for this aircraft. He found that, below 5000 feet at full throttle and load, the cooling water would boil within 15 to 20 minutes of level flight and in 2 to 3 minutes if climbing with the outside temperature over 65° F. In all climb tests it was necessary to level off once or twice to prevent boiling until 6000 feet was reached; above 6000 feet there was no trouble. Hallett recommended moving the radiator two inches farther from the engine and cutting louvers in the engine cowling wherever possible to provide free air flow around the engine. He felt a great part of the overheating was caused by preignition as a slight decrease in engine speed from full power was sufficient to cool the water.[5]

Hallett later put his ideas to work and made test flights at full throttle, both climbing and horizontal. In addition to the improvement mentioned, he also installed an expansion tank in the wing above the engine, connecting it with the cooling system by a one-inch brass tube. He found that the water would still boil if the outside air was over 85° or 90°F, but that the expansion tank permitted boiling for a longer period of time without serious loss of water.[6]

[3] Ibid., Emmons from Vincent, 4 December 1918.

[4] Ibid., Senator Frank Broudegee of Connecticut from Leon Cammen (extracted in part from Congressional Record, 13 May 1918, pp. 6925–6926).

[5] Ibid., report, "Observations and Opinion of Liberty 12 in DH–4," Air Service, Technical Section, from Major George E. A. Hallett, 26 May 1918.

[6] Ibid., report, "Cooling of Liberty 12 in DH–4," Commanding Officer, Test Department, from Hallett, 22 July 1918.

There were many other tests, conjectures, and suggestions as to how the cooling problem could be overcome, but Hallett's tests typify the best of them. Strangely, there was little or no trouble at the war front in cooling the engine. First Lieutenant H. C. Herbert, with the AEF in France, reported:

Only a few motors in planes with small radiators seriously overheated even during hottest summer weather. . . . Good climb, full horsepower and good running conditions under normal temperature were obtained with small radiator and it was possible at an elevation over 5,000 feet to get proper temperature control with use of shutters. With present large type radiator, it has been difficult with the additional weight and head resistance to obtain good climbs to altitude and it has been found impossible even in the present summer weather to keep motor hot enough for good running. As this tendency is shown in present weather conditions, it is feared that a great deal of trouble is to be experienced in regulation in the next eight months. . . . It is the consensus of opinion of the engine men in this country that the old type small radiator should be able to given [sic] ample cooling to this motor with its present development of horsepower.[7]

Herbert's findings were borne out by British experience. "No trouble has been experienced with the cooling system on the Liberty engine in the DH–9a on the hottest day on which this machine was climbed at full throttle from the ground." [8]

Vincent believed the engine was easy to cool in proportion to its horsepower. The initial troubles were caused by lack of experience with an engine of the Liberty's power, and lack of up-to-date radiators.[9]

4. The cylinder arrangement of the Liberty engine was wrong: Cammen had several words to say on this. The motor was not the best that could be developed as ". . . in the design of the motor a feature has been introduced which is known to be wrong from an engineering standpoint." The engine was to have embodied proved engineering practices, but the use of a 45° included angle between the cylinders, rather than the conventional 60° was an unwarranted experiment. The War Department claimed the 45° angle lessened head resistance, provided greater crankcase strength, and reduced vibration. Cammen believed that the 45° angle would increase vibration. "From a general knowledge of balancing, it would appear

---

[7] Ibid., undated report, Chief of Production, Department of Military Aeronautics, from First Lieutenant H. C. Herbert, Plane and Maintenance Division, in charge of engine test in fuselage and plane.

[8] Ibid., letter, Bureau of Aircraft Production from British War Ministry, 4 September 1918.

[9] Ibid., Emmons from Vincent, 4 December 1918.

47

vibration would occur at 1450–1550 and again above 2,000." Cammen stated additionally that not a single foreign maker used a 45° angle and that the Liberty was the only engine in existence using this angle.[10]

Mr. Cammen was partially right, but he also had some facts wrong. The L–12 did develop a slight vibration between 1400–1500 rpm, but during the testing of hundreds of them not one failure was attributable to vibration nor were there any flight failures recorded because of this small defect. As to the Liberty's being the only engine using the 45° angle and there being no foreign aircraft of this design, Renault already had more than 2000 engines in combat with this angle.[11]

Vincent's response to this criticism follows:

Before designing the Liberty motor, I had experimented extensively at various angles of cylinders and knew that the 45° arrangement would not be notice-able so far as lack of smooth running was concerned and that it had distinct advantages, not only in that it reduced gear resistance but also that it reduced synchronous vibration of the crankshaft, due to breaking up of the evenly spaced intervals. This latter result is of great value as it allows all the timing gears to be made lighter than would otherwise be the case. It is pretty generally known that saving a pound of gear resistance is equal to saving seven or eight pounds of weight.[12]

5. The ignition of the Liberty engine was a poor system:
Cammen said that the ignition was as great an adventure in engineering as the 45° angle. The angle, according to Cammen, would not admit the use of magnetos, or of any other system but the Delco, and it was the weakest point in the engine.[13]

Vincent did not use a battery system without full knowledge that it would be criticized. It was viciously attacked

. . . by certain people having magnetos to sell and every kind of pressure was brought to bear on me to force me to specify magnetos. I deliberately had the Liberty ignition system designed in spite of the fact I knew I would meet such opposition because I knew that this would be the best ignition system for the Liberty motor.

Vincent had knowledge of magneto problems overseas which he felt would be aggravated as cylinders and horsepower were multiplied. The battery

---

[10] Ibid., lecture, "Criticism of the Liberty Engine," presented by Leon Cammen before the Aeronautical Society of America, 28 May 1918.

[11] Ibid., letter, Senator Charles S. Thomas from O. E. Hunt, 6 June 1918.

[12] Ibid., Emmons from Vincent, 4 December 1918.

[13] Ibid., "Criticism of the Liberty Engine."

system made the engine easy to start ". . . if the propeller is pulled over even so slowly as to equal two revolutions per minute."[14]

Cammen's statement that ignition was the weakest point in the engine does not appear to be based on fact. The McCook files—which contain the bad with the good about the engine—record not one instance of trouble due to ignition failure, nor do the other authorities on which this paper is based. The facts of the matter are that no magnetos were designed for a 12-cylinder engine with a 45° included angle; Vincent was basically an automobile-engine designer and battery ignition had proved eminently successful in Packard autos; the Allies had problems with magnetos overseas; and the Delco system was cheap, light, easy to maintain, and reliable.

Paul D. Wilson, of St. Petersburg, Florida, who worked with Liberty engines at McCook, stated:

> It was pretty generally known that the power plant Section had obtained a slight increase with the magnetos. But the Delco system was doing a satisfactory job and one could start these engines on a cold day. The distributors were up on the top of the rear cylinders where [they were] easy to work on and little skill was required to keep them operating properly. I have never had a failure with a Liberty from ignition trouble. From a cost standpoint, the battery system must have offered a considerable saving.[15]

The Liberty-engine handbook offers these advantages for use of the battery system over the magneto system:

a. Easier starting: a spark of greater intensity was produced in cranking and flying speeds.

b. Reliability: two distinct distributor mechanisms; each uniting all 12 cylinders through separate spark plugs. Each distributor head with two sets of breaker arms and two distinct sources of electrical energy: battery and generator.

c. Safety: the auxiliary breakers prevented the possibility of a backkick.

d. Complete range of spark-timing control: a spark of the same intensity was produced whether advanced or retarded through 360°.

e. Amperage meters: permitted pilot to determine if the system was operating properly.

f. Simplicity: distributor heads were driven directly from the camshafts without the necessity of gears or extra shafts.

g. Long life: the distributor heads ran at slow speeds, half crankshaft speed, so wear was slight.

---

[14] Ibid., letter, Emmons from Vincent, 4 December 1918.
[15] Letter, author from Wilson, 12 August 1964.

h. Timing: as the distributor and breaker were advanced and retarded together, they were always properly timed with relation to one another. Consequently, there was no possibility of preignition because of high-tension current being carried to the wrong plug.

i. Spark intensity: the spark was hot and of short duration so that no crank trouble was experienced. With the magneto, the high-tension impulse tapered off gradually, and the spark was drawn off by the motor brush after it had left the distributor segment.[16]

O. E. Hunt pointed out that the L–12 could have used four 6-cylinder magnetos, the only system available when the engine was designed, but this would have added 30 to 40 pounds to the engine's weight. The essential principles of the Delco system had been successfully and thoroughly proved on the Packard 229-cubic-inch aircraft engine.[17]

Although the Delco system was successful in the Liberty engine, the proponents of magnetos did not give up. On 17 August 1917, Major Southern asked Splitdorf Electric Company of Newark, New Jersey, to design a magneto for the L–8. The resulting magneto was taken to Washington, D.C., on 17 September 1917 and tested on the L–8 at the Bureau of Standards. The engine broke down before a thorough test could be accomplished. On 22 November 1917 a magneto for the L–12 was taken to McCook for testing. The testing personnel waited for six weeks before being allowed to place their equipment on a test engine. On 3 January 1918 a five-hour test was run, and it showed better performance with 7.5° less advance. Ten to sixteen more horsepower was obtained than with the battery system.

Following this test the Splitdorf people were ignored until the latter part of June 1918, when Major Hallett, chief of motor testing at Wilbur Wright Field, requested a set of magnetos and subsequently ran them on test stands and on a DH–4. Water temperature stayed at 85°, fuel consumption was less, more horsepower was developed, 7.5° less advance was required, spark plugs remained clean, the exhaust valves were cooler, and there was very little "loading."[18]

---

[16] B. V. Bassett, *Instructions for the Installation, Inspection and Maintenance of the U.S.A. Standardized Engine* (U.S. Signal Corps, Equipment Division, n.d.).

[17] McCook files, letter, Thomas from Hunt, 6 June 1918.

[18] "Liberty Motors: Sales and Transfers," report, Colonel W. C. Sherman, Operations and Training Section, Department of Military Aeronautics, from Splitdorf Electric Company (Record Group 18 [Army Air Forces], Central Decimal Files [1917–1938] 452.8, Washington, D.C.: National Archives of the United States). Cited hereafter as National Archives files.

Hallett reported that:

> Dixey magnetos have been tried and a gain in revolutions was obtained and the spark plugs were far cleaner than when the Delco System was used and it is believed the plugs would not be able to foul up with this ignition system, but new and improved magnetos are coming and will be thoroughly tried out.[19]

The use of magnetos on the Liberty was slow in coming. In October 1919, testing was still in the preliminary stages; the tests appeared favorable, however, and the magnetos were felt to provide a better safety factor due to the redundancy provided by a dual system. At this time it was recommended that a service test of magneto-equipped aircraft be made under field conditions on the Mexican border. Six aircraft in each squadron would be so equipped.[20]

The Dixie and Berkshire Magneto Company finally developed two magnetos that were suitable for the Liberty engine.

> . . . Both are of the induction type. The Berkshire is a very unusual instrument being similar in appearance to the small fractional horsepower motors in cylindrical form. Four pols [sic] are used being located alternately 67½° and 112½° with one another to accommodate the firing order of the Liberty engine. On opposite ends of the magnetos are two nearly circular magnets the ends of which are nearly in the center of a pair of poles. The coil is stationary. This gives four sparks per revolution. The distributor with radial receptacles for the spark cables is located on the end of the magneto. It is driven at three times camshaft speed by a train of gears.[21]

It appears that criticism of the Liberty for using the Delco battery-ignition system was not warranted. The Delco system was good and the "state of the art" of magneto development had not reached such perfection that magnetos could cope with an engine the size and design of the Liberty.

6. The Liberty engine oil sump cover was dangerous:
Cammen's criticism here was that the oil-drain plug on the Liberty—instead of being a screw-in type—was a ground fitting held in place by a spring wire (like that on a Mason jar). If a piece of dirt were to get into the ground joint, the oil could drain out. Cammen considered it poor engineering safety to have only one spring because he felt that cold and

---

[19] McCook files, "Cooling of Liberty 12 in DH–4."

[20] National Archives files, letter, Bane from Menoher, 23 October 1919.

[21] JOHN S. RATHBUN, *Airplane Engines in Theory and in Practice* (Chicago: Stanton and Van Fliet Co., 1921), p. 247.

vibration could snap the single spring.[22] Hunt replied that, up to 1 June 1918, 1286 engines had been shipped and no trouble had been experienced either on the test stand or in flight.[23] Vincent said only that the spring fastener was a well-known device used for similar purposes for years.[24]

7. The Liberty engine used excessive fuel:

This was a common criticism of the Liberty during World War I and even today. During the June 1964 reunion of the 20th Aero Squadron some of the former members of the Squadron, which was equipped with Liberties in DH–4s in France, were interviewed. The consensus was that the engine was a "gas hog."

Vincent says:

> All well known aircraft motors at the present time have about the same consumption per horsepower hour. This runs from .48 pounds of fuel per horsepower hour to .56 pounds, depending on conditions. In this respect, the Liberty motor is no better and no worse than other well known designs.

He went on to say that at 410 hp at or near sea level the L–12 would have a gasoline consumption of .52 pounds per horsepower hour which would be 213.2 pounds, or 35.5 gallons, per hour. At 15,000 feet at 295 hp usage would be 153 pounds, or 25.5 gallons, per hour.[25]

This difference of opinion results from the fact that Vincent compared the Liberty with other engines on a horsepower-to-horsepower basis which is the proper method. The critics, however, saw only that, when a Liberty was mounted in a DH–4, it used more fuel than a lower-powered British engine in the same make of aircraft. Increased speed and performance were not considered.

8. The Liberty engine's oil consumption was excessive:

Again, this was a general criticism. Examination seems to prove that the fault lay with the quality of the mineral oil that was initially used (prior to the development of "Liberty Aero Oil") rather than with the design of the engine.

Vincent said that oil consumption was bound to vary with the kind of work being done and the kind of oil being used. The Liberty averaged .03 pounds per horsepower hour. He continued:

> On account of the shortage of castor oil, it has been necessary to run the Liberty motor on mineral oil and some engineers claim that a mineral oil

---

[22] McCook files, "Criticism of the Liberty Engine."
[23] Ibid., letter, Thomas from Hunt, 6 June 1918.
[24] Ibid., Emmons from Vincent, 4 December 1918.
[25] Ibid.

can be made which will be just as good as Castor. After very careful investigation and after many hours in the air with the Liberty motor, I do not believe that this is so and unqualifiedly recommend castor oil.[26]

Until the United States entered World War I, castor oil had been used for high-powered internal-combustion engines, and as the indispensable lubricant for rotary engines because of its greater viscosity, high flash-and-fire tests, and greater penetrative qualities. It was the only satisfactory lubricant for the Liberty until the development of Liberty Aero Oil (mineral).

In the fall of 1917, an immense engine-production program was shaping up in the United States, a country which grew almost no castor beans. On 8 October 1917 a "Castor Oil Board" was appointed. After some research, it was found that:

a. An aircraft program calling for the production of 5749 rotary engines to be in operation by 30 June 1918 had been approved. It was estimated that the flying program for these engines would require 2,702,110 gallons of castor oil.

b. Annual United States consumption was 2,000,000 gallons.

c. Canada had requested 1200 gallons a month.

d. France wanted 2000 tons up to 1 July 1918.

e. 6,000,000 gallons were required for the period 1 July 1918 to 1 July 1919.

f. A planting-and-growth program was required.

g. A shortage of 1,500,000 gallons was apparent from November 1917 to July 1918.

h. Britain offered to supply our overseas commitments up to 3,000,000 gallons, which left a requirement of a like amount to be supplied by the United States.

Detailed plans were laid for the growth program. Publicity was developed, sectors laid out, incentives offered, and seed distributed. Owing, however, to ignorance, lateness in planting, poor seed, inferior harvesting and hulling machinery, adverse publicity, indifference, drought, lack of labor, army worm, and graymold, the expectation of 1,000,000 bushels turned out to be 183,816. Nevertheless, the importation of 638,248 bushels of beans and 1,097,544 gallons of oil provided an abundance for the aircraft program.[27]

During this same period the development of an acceptable mineral oil was given priority second only to the development of the Liberty engine. A committee was appointed to find the solution, and after months of

---

[26] Ibid.

[27] History of BAP, vol. 6, pp. 1575–1596.

intensive experimentation the lubricant known as Liberty Aero Oil was produced. This oil stood up perfectly under the high temperatures and bearing pressures of the Liberty 12 and could be produced at a cost of only 75 cents per gallon.[28]

The production of the new oil did not necessarily solve the problem:

> Much opposition was experienced at first and the department was obliged to resort to scheming. Whenever the flier or motor maker refused to believe that Liberty Aero Oil was equal to or better than his favorite brand, this oil was put into containers from which he supposedly drew his pet supply. The flier would be requested to state the efficiency of his lubricant at the end of the flight and when his unqualified praise was given, he was advised that Liberty Aero Oil had been used instead of his pet brand. It was not long until Liberty Aero Oil was successfully introduced to and universally praised by the government aeronautical service.[29]

Pilots were made of sterner stuff in those days! A pilot today would never think of questioning the "spec" of the oil specified for his aircraft.

In summary, it can be said that the Liberty did have some faults, but that the tremendous step forward in engine design and concept more than offset its faults. This fact was more apparent to our Allies than to some of our own people, as evidenced by the following telegram from the British Air Minister to Lord Reading:

> Our technical authorities inform me that Liberty engines have now been subjected to sufficient air experiment in England to warrant confidence in this engine. Excellent results have so far been obtained which place the engine at once in the First Line of High Powered Air Engines. Naturally service experiment in the field is still to be obtained but the Liberty Engine will be a most valuable contribution to Allied Aviation Programmes and the United States should develop production with every confidence.[30]

The construction and testing of experimental engines had been completed, and the tests had convinced most reliable observers that the Liberty engine was ready for production. The following two chapters examine the organization that was established to oversee production, as well as the trials and tribulations that beset the companies which contracted to produce it.

---

[28] RATHBUN, op. cit., p. 248.

[29] History of BAP, loc. cit., p. 1555.

[30] McCook files, telegram, Air Minister, Great Britain, to Lord Reading, 7 June 1918.

Organization for Production

The sum total of organizations for war production during World War I was prodigious; there were organizations for all facets of production for the war effort. This paper refers only to production for the aviation program and, more specifically, to the creation and production of the Liberty engine. One cannot entirely separate the engine from the aircraft, since the engine is the heart of the machine that carries it into the air. The organizations that were developed, one after another, to achieve production were no less complicated than the aircraft and engines they sought to produce. In any event, the United States Government exercised ultimate control over the production of aircraft and aircraft engines. Within the aviation program this paper will be confined mainly to the organization within and for the Army.

When World War I began in Europe, the Aviation Section of the Signal Corps was composed of 28 officers and 166 enlisted and civilian personnel. By the latter part of 1915 aviation was established as coequal with the other divisions of the Signal Corps.[1] When war was declared, the Aviation Division consisted of 65 officers and 1330 enlisted and civilian personnel. Lieutenant Colonel John B. Bennett was made chief of the division on 9 April 1917, and Sidney D. Waldon, vice president and general manager of the Packard Motor Car Company, was asked to take charge of the whole subject of production of aircraft.[2]

On 12 April 1917 the Aircraft Production Board was established by resolution of the Council of National Defense.[3] The council stipulated organization of the board along the following lines:

    1. Airplane and engine engineering;

    2. Specifications and standards;

    3. Production:

        a. Coordination of designs with Allied missions;

---

[1] History of BAP, vol. 1, p. 18. (See Chart I, p. 84.)

[2] Ibid., p. 21. (See Chart II, p. 85.)

[3] Ibid., vol. 3, p. 568.

257-441 O - 78 - 5

b. Arrangements with factories for production;

c. Approved advance of government funds and cost-plus arrangements;

d. Full use of facilities;

4. Inspection;

5. Aviation schools—establishment of sites, building, etc.;

6. Supply depots—establishment of sites, building, etc.;

7. Priority of deliveries.

The first meeting of the board was held in General George O. Squire's office, 17 May 1917. Members were: Howard E. Coffin, chairman; Sidney D. Waldon, vice-chairman; Edward A. Deeds; Robert L. Montgomery; A. G. Cable, secretary; Major Raynal C. Bolling (11 June 1917); Major B. D. Foulois; and Captain N. E. Irwin, U.S. Navy (14 September 1917).

The Aircraft Board succeeded the Aircraft Production Board on 1 October 1917 by an act of Congress. The board now came under the Secretaries of Army and Navy. The net result was the creation of a forum for discussion and routine approval of plans for the production of aircraft and the development of the Air Service. The responsibility for the initiation and success of such plans was left to the military and naval authorities.[4]

Within the Signal Corps in 1917 the Construction Division was formed on 21 May and the Aircraft Engineering Division on 24 May. This was a period of rapid expansion; military personnel were transferred from other branches of the service, and civilian experts were brought in to handle the mountainous production problems that arose.[5] By 1 June the production functions originally contemplated as the responsibility of the Aircraft Production Board were placed under the Chief Signal Officer and the Aircraft Production Board assumed a strong advisory role.[6]

In August 1917, management personnel from the Aircraft Production Board were brought into the Signal Corps and placed in charge of production work. The Equipment Division, resulting from this organization,[7] was organized principally for Air Service work, and it handled all aircraft production. On 8 September 1917, the chief of the Equipment Division, Colonel E. A. Deeds, reorganized it into four departments.[8] Basically, though changes were made, the structure shown in Chart VII (p. 90),

---

[4] Ibid., vol. 3, pp. 616–626.

[5] Ibid., vol. 1, p. 18. (See Chart III, p. 86.)

[6] Ibid., p. 23. (See Chart IV, p. 87.)

[7] Ibid. (See Chart V, p. 88.)

[8] Ibid., p. 26. (See Chart VI, p. 89.)

NASM specimen is of this type.

Figure 10.—Dayton-Wright DH–4, 1918.   (Smithsonian photo A32766A)

continued until the Air Service was separated from the Signal Corps on 20 May 1918.[9]

On 27 April 1918, the Air Service Division succeeded the Aviation Division, and Brigadier General William L. Kenly was placed in command. On 4 May 1918, John D. Ryan became Director of Aircraft Production, and, on 20 May 1918, he was appointed by executive order Director of Military Aeronautics, coequal with the Chief Signal Officer.[10] Under the same executive order establishing the Directorate of Military Aeronautics, the Bureau of Aircraft Production (BAP) was established. This agency was to ". . . exercise full, complete and exclusive jurisdiction and control over the production of airplanes, airplane engines, and aircraft equipment for the use of the Army. . . ."[11]

Ryan and Kenly entered into an agreement that required coordination between their agencies when a ". . . certain type of airplane comes from General Pershing or other source . . . as . . . the director of military Aeronautics alone knows what performance is needed . . . and the

[9] Ibid., p. 34. (See Chart VII, p. 90.)
[10] Ibid.
[11] Ibid., p. 35.

Figure 11.—Handley Page O–400, 1918, bomber.   (Smithsonian photo A554)

Director of Aircraft Production alone knows the production possibilities." [12]

Early in September 1918 the Division of Military Aeronautics and the Bureau of Aircraft Production were brought together as the Air Service. War Department General Order 81, 1918, announced the appointment of John D. Ryan as second assistant Secretary of War and Director of the Air Service.

The Liberty engine was introduced into this maze of organization and reorganization under the Engine Design Section of the Equipment Division (Chart V, p. 88). As the engine moved toward the production phase, that facet of its growth came under the Engine Production Section, Equipment Division (Chart VI, p. 89), and the follow-on design and experimentation came under the successor of the Engine Design Section, i.e., the Engineering Department (Chart VII, p. 90). The Engineering Department moved from the Bureau of Standards to Dayton, Ohio, as the Bureau could no longer contain its expanding facilities. The Engineering Department was to become the primary tenant at a new Army Air Field (North Field, Dayton, later to become McCook Field); however, while the necessary buildings were being constructed at the Field, the Department occupied

---

[12] Ibid., p. 36.

two floors of the Lindsey Building in Dayton.[13] Beginning in early 1918 the operational development of the Liberty engine centered at McCook Field.

The Engine Production Section was organized in the latter part of August 1917 and decentralized into districts to conform to the geographical area in which individual types of engines were being produced. Thus, the Curtiss OX5 was in the Buffalo district; Hall-Scott A–7–A, San Francisco; and the Liberty under the Detroit district, since the largest producers of the engine were located there. Each district had a manager who had complete charge of local problems of production-engineering, production, and inspection. This alleviated the necessity for a large central office in Washington, which was already overcrowded.

The Washington office had a chief, an assistant, and three sections—machinery, spare parts, and distribution. This office exercised complete supervision and control over the entire field of engine production, except in those local matters delegated to the districts. Procurement of tools, material, machinery, and transportation (including priorities), relations with other governmental agencies (including labor and draft deferments), and the settling of district questions are examples of the tasks performed by the central office.

Navy Lieutenant Harold H. Emmons was named Chief, Engine Production Section. Emmons had started his career as a lawyer in Detroit. Through his professional connection with large concerns in legal or financial difficulties, he had mastered the details of their management and organization, and was widely recognized as an outstanding industrial executive. He had been a member of the Michigan Naval Reserve and aspired to

[13] Vincent MSS, "History of the Development of the USA Standaridzed Aircraft Engines."

Figure 12.—Curtiss R4L, 1918.   (Smithsonian photo A47365)

line duty in the destroyer service, but was detailed to the Equipment Division for the engine production job.

Emmons is not well known in connection with the Liberty engine, but his effect on its production was equal to that of any other single individual. He was awarded the Distinguished Service Medal by the War Department, through the Secretary of Navy, and was officially commended by Major General Charles T. Menoher, Chief, Air Service, on 28 May 1919 for his contribution. Emmons built up an organization of 23 engine-construction plants, 79 parts factories, and was instrumental in getting one of the 6 A-1 priorities issued during the war to cover machinery, equipment, and all other facilities for aircraft-engine production.

Figure 13.—Converted H-16, U.S. Navy World War I Flying Boat. Fourteen seat transport Aeromarine 75, 1919. (Smithsonian photo A48123B)

The Producers

Before discussing the problems and accomplishments of individual producers of the Liberty engine (Appendix 2) some common factors should be mentioned.

The Aircraft Production Board was the prime mover in the investigation of manufacturing concerns and in recommending to the Army which companies should receive contracts for Liberty-engine production and the number of engines they should produce. Although this was an advisory board, the indications are that all its recommendations were immediately approved. The Army was the responsible contracting agent, furnishing the Navy and other agencies (as well as the Allies) with engines from the total number produced.

The contract form used to procure engines was cost plus a fixed profit. The cost to build an engine was set by a group of manufacturers who were not involved in the program. Rollin White, of Cleveland, and Henry May, of the Pierce-Arrow Company, were two of the group appointed by the Secretary of War.[1] The cost was set at $6087 plus $913.05 profit; however, the contract was also to include a bonus for economy in production. This bonus was a split of 25 percent to the manufacturer and 75 percent to the government of any reduction in the $6087 established cost per engine. This arrangement was recommended to the Chief Signal Officer by resolu-

---

[1] History of BAP, vol. 4, p. 877. MARCOSSON, op. cit., p. 246, calls this a "bogey" contract, not cost-plus.

Figure 14.—Navy-Curtiss NC–4, 1919.   First airplane to cross Atlantic Ocean.
NASM specimen

tion of the Aircraft Production Board on 31 August 1917.[2] The cost was $17.50 per horsepower to the government for each Liberty engine ($7000 total cost divided by 400 horsepower); the only comparable Allied engine, the Rolls-Royce, cost $23 per horsepower.[3] In December 1917 the cost of building an engine, based on quantity production, was computed at $5000, including a fixed profit of $625. All contracts were subsequently supplemented to include the new figures.[4]

Many problems plagued the manufacturers in their efforts to produce Liberty engines in quantity. The requirement to produce engines with interchangeable parts necessitated a strict program of inspection to ensure a quality product. This caused the tolerances and other specifications set for the Liberty engine to be very rigidly controlled by the government's inspectors in order to make sure that the engine would embody the safety factors designed into it. This was important because the margin of safety had been reduced to a minimum to decrease weight. As the engine was modified to produce more horsepower, adherence to specifications became even more necessary. Unfortunately, the inspectors were not all competent and experienced men; they were apt to insist that the specifications be complied with regardless of the circumstances. The basis for the Liberty series was standardization to achieve economy and ease of maintenance. Laxity in enforcement of the specifications that provided this goal would

[2] Ibid., p. 878.
[3] Ibid., vol. 7, p. 1993.
[4] Ibid., vol. 4, pp. 884–885.

Figure 15.—Dayton-Wright DH–4B, 1923.   (Smithsonian photo A41141A)

NASM specimen

Figure 16.—Fokker T2 (F IV). First nonstop coast to coast flight, 1923. (Smithsonian photo A45288A)

Figure 17.—Loening Model 23 "Air Yacht", 1921. (Smithsonian photo A48355B)

Figure 18.—Douglas World Cruiser (DWC), 1924. (Smithsonian photo A48828)

Figure 19.—Douglas M–1 mailplane, 1925. (Smithsonian photo A46899F)

negate the benefits to be gained from the basic design. On the other hand, some deviations that could have been authorized on the spot would not have adversely affected either safety or standardization. The lack of experienced, competent, and practical government inspectors precluded this flexibility. As production and testing experience was gained, nonvital specifications were relaxed, but much production time was lost in the interim.

Manufacturers were plagued by shortages of natural resources, owing to the demands of a wartime economy. The coal shortage in the winter of 1917–18 was a national problem affecting the entire war effort. It led to transportation, electric-power, and gas shortages, and in some cases caused plants to be shut down completely. Lumber shortages delayed necessary construction, and almost all metals were in short supply. Shortages of tools, jigs, gauges, components, and similar items accounted for an estimated 50 percent delay during the early months of production. Among the most critical shortages were thread gauges, cylinder grinders, water jackets, spark plugs, and insulators.

There was also a lack of workers. The draft initially took all personnel in applicable age groups, which led to the loss of skilled workmen; this impact was felt particularly in highly industrialized areas such as Detroit. Women and others who had not been a part of the prewar labor market entered the war industries, thus creating a formidable training problem. Industrial expansion was so rapid that recruitment and training constantly lagged behind.

Figure 20.—Loening OA-1A Amphibian, 1926. U.S. Army Air Corps Pan-American good-will flight, Dec. 21, 1926–May 2, 1927. (Smithsonian photo A34588)

NASM specimen

One of the most frustrating and costly production problems was the constant stream of design modifications that flowed into the manufacturer's plant. Tests were conducted during the early production period to increase the horsepower of the L–12. The modifications to engine parts resulting from these tests were rushed to the manufacturers so that they could bring their production engines up to date. Changes to blueprints were required to correct clerical errors, to provide for more flexibility in specifications, and to facilitate production. The latter modifications were requested by the manufacturers based on actual production experience. It was generally agreed that most of the changes were improvements; they resulted, however, in delays and the creation of excess scrap. The changes averaged 100 per week and affected 25 percent of all engine parts. The impact on production was so great that manufacturers wrote letter after letter to the chief of Aircraft Production attempting to obtain relief so that production could be expedited.[5]

Notwithstanding the obstacles enumerated, contracts were let for a total of 56,000 L–12 and 8000 L–8 engines, but most of these were cancelled because of the Armistice.[6] The actual production of Liberty engines totaled 20,478 L–12, 15 L–8, 52 L–6, and 2 L–4 engines. Prior to the Armistice, 13,574 L–12 engines were produced, and by 31 December 1918, 17,935 had come off the assembly lines.[7] The United States had agreed to supply the British with 11 percent of the total production of Liberty engines;[8] on the basis of 20,478 total production the British share was 2252. The French received 3575.[9] Before the Armistice 980 had been delivered to England and

[5] HAROLD E. PORTER, WILLIAM R. BENET, and WARNER W. KENT, "History of the Liberty Engine" (MS, The United States Air Force Museum, Wright-Patterson Air Force Base, Ohio, 6 June 1918), pp. 71–82. Cited hereafter as PORTER ET AL. In addition, the listing of production problems was compiled from SWEETSER, op. cit., pp. 178 and 183, and from the McCook files.

[6] National Archives files, letter, Senator G. W. Norris from Brigadier General H. H. Arnold, 1 June 1937. MARCOSSON, op. cit., p. 242, stated that 56,000 was the total. He did not mention the 8000 L–8s, but, taken in context, it can be assumed he meant only L–12s.

[7] Ibid. MARCOSSON, op. cit., p. 248, stated that 24,475 L–12 engines were produced up to the Armistice. Gorrell shows 13,574 by the Armistice, but this figure does not include those not packed or loaded on 11 November 1918. In that Gorrell wrote an official history of World War I, it is possible that General Arnold (footnote 6) got his figure from Gorrell. Marcosson's figure is not compatible with any combination of possibilities, and therefore must be considered inaccurate.

[8] Ibid., United States Army Liquidation Mission, England, from Director, Air Service, 3 March 1920.

[9] Ibid., Norris from Arnold, 1 June 1937.

405 to France; the remainder were delivered after the Armistice. The final settlement with Britain was for $16,589,718 for engines and spares; France paid $21,272,250 for engines and 3310 sets of spares.[10] Assuming Britain received spares to equal her quota of engines, the cost per engine and one set of spares was over $7300. France paid less than $6000 each for her engines, including spares.

The 20,478 engines were built by the following companies: Packard, 6500; Lincoln, 6500; Ford, 3950; General Motors (Cadillac and Buick divisions), 2528; and Nordyke and Marmon, 1000.[11] This production was against an initial procurement of 6000 from Packard, 6000 from Lincoln, 5000 from Ford, 3000 from Nordyke and Marmon, 2000 from General Motors, and 500 from Trego Motors Corporation.[12] The number of engines produced by Trego is a mystery. The only clue indicating that they produced any is found in the minutes of the Aircraft Production Board for 5 June 1918. On this date Lieutenant Emmons stated that the Trego Liberty was not up to standard and recommended that their efforts be diverted into the production of tanks. The board concurred and recommended that all Trego Liberty engines go to the Ordnance Department.[13]

After a slow start the monthly production of Liberty engines increased rapidly. From Table 1, p. 91, it is apparent that, despite formidable barriers, the producers of Liberty engines had reached their stride in October 1918. Had the war lasted longer there is no doubt that American and Allied requirements for the engine would have been met easily. To gain a more personal view of production problems and achievements, short summaries of the production history of the Liberty engine of the three largest producers are presented in Appendix 2, pp. 91–99.

---

[10] GORRELL, op. cit., p. 71. MARCOSSON, loc. cit. (footnote 7), stated that the United States had furnished the Allies with 1089 engines by the Armistice; History of BAP, vol. 7, p. 1903, gives the figure 1022.

[11] GORRELL, op. cit., p. 70. History of BAP, loc. cit., p. 1890, transposed the General Motors and the Nordyke and Marmon production figures. It is believed this was a typing error; however, the initial Nordyke and Marmon contract was for 3000, and the General Motors contract for only 1000. This would indicate General Motors was the producer of 1000. On 3 January 1918, however, the Aircraft Production Board recommended transfer of a 1000-engine Deusenberg contract to General Motors (History of BAP, loc. cit., p. 1888). Gorrell is supported by a letter in the McCook files to the Material Division, McCook Field, from the Marmon Motor Car Company, 28 January 1927, which stated: "We produced 1000 Liberty motors that were numbered 4402 to 5401 inclusive."

[12] BENEDICT CROWELL, *America's Munitions*, *1917–1918* (Washington: Government Printing Office, 1919), p. 274.

[13] History of BAP, loc. cit., pp. 1910–1911.

The Liberty Goes to War

The combat career of the L–12 is inextricably bound to the American-built deHaviland–4. An engine cannot go to war without wings to carry it aloft, and in this case the wings chosen were those of the DH–4.

Strangely enough, the decision to build an all-American engine was not translated to the building of aircraft, although the reasons would appear to be equally applicable. Many American aircraft designers of the time were unable to rationalize the Aircraft Production Board's insistence that the American air-frame effort be limited to copying European designs. Grover C. Loening, one of the bright lights of early American design, expressed the consensus of his contemporaries:

> . . . The fatal error of the Aircraft Production Board of 1917 was in this policy founded on their belief that while they in the automobile business knew motors so well that they could get away with a Federally managed Liberty motor design and production, the American background for building aircraft consisted only of a few young draftsmen and aviators, notably, Chance Vought, Glenn Martin, Thomas-Morse and myself, lacking in the war plane design experience needed.
>
> What they did not know was that the aircraft designers in Europe were also young men of about the same age and training by the names of Fokker, Nieuport, Tommy Sopworth, A. V. Roe, etc.
>
> As a result of this policy (which was fatal to the Aircraft Production Board's program) their labors principally boiled down to the great error of trying to fit an engine to a plane that was not designed for it. . . . But in 1918, due to the great policy of Mr. Ryan and Mr. Potter, who succeeded the automobile group, we had four outstanding American planes about to go into production to win the war—the Martin Bomber (with the Liberty engine), the Thomas-Morse Pursuit Plane, the Loening two-seat Fighter and the Vought VE–7.[1]

Since this is the story of an engine, discussion of the aircraft will be held to that which is relevant to the engine.

When the United States entered the war the only available aircraft were assigned to training use on the Mexican border. These machines were built by Curtiss, Glenn Martin, Standard, and Lowe, Willard and Fowler (LWF),

---

[1] Letter, S. Paul Johnston from Grover C. Loening, 19 April 1965.

and were powered by Curtiss 90 and 160–200-hp, Thomas 140-hp, Hall-Scott 130-hp, and Sturtevant 140-hp engines.[2] Our initial wartime effort was to build up a fleet of training planes for the tremendous pilot-instruction program ahead. The Bolling Commission, meanwhile, was gathering the necessary facts in Europe to recommend a proper course for the United States.

The British mission to the United States recognized our general lack of knowledge in technical matters concerning aircraft, as the following statement indicates:

> The enormous potentiality in technical matters was obvious wherever one went and the immediate necessity for giving the best technical advice was made very evident. The Americans in the Aircraft Administration, although possessing little knowledge of technical subjects, are quick to perceive such in others; this demonstrates clearly the absolute necessity of sending the very best talent available.[3]

At the western front, one of the members of the Bolling Commission, Lieutenant Colonel V. E. Clark, found that the three functions of the airplane in modern warfare were: to help the Army successfully perform its operations on the ground; to prevent enemy aircraft from doing damage in any way; and to inflict direct damage on the enemy. These three functions were performed, respectively, by observation, combat or pursuit, and bomber planes. Observation aircraft in use at this time included the Bristol Fighter (British), the SIA–7B (Italian), the Breguet (French), and the LVG (German), all requiring engines of from 235–365 hp. Combat aircraft, such as the British Sopwith or the French Spad and Nieuport, required 345–375-hp engines; Germany was abandoning this type of plane. Operational pursuit aircraft included the Martinsyde (British), the SVA (Italian), the Spad (French), and the Halberstadt and the Albatross (German). A single-seat pursuit plane required an engine of 325–350 hp; with two seats a 425–445-hp engine was needed. Bombers utilized were the British DH–4 and –9, the Italian SIA–7B and –9B, the French Breguet 14–B2, and the German Gothatwin. A day bomber required an engine with from 495–520 hp, and a night bomber, two or more engines of 400–450 hp each.[4]

---

[2] History of BAP, vol. 6, p. 1654.

[3] SPECIAL BRITISH AVIATION MISSION TO THE UNITED STATES OF AMERICA, June 11–July 29, 1918, *Supplement to the General Technical Report* (British Air Ministry), p. 3. Cited hereafter as "British Technical Report."

[4] History of BAP, loc. cit., p. 1598. This information came from a report "September 17th Status of Military Airplanes Along the Western Battle Front" written by Lt. Col. V. E.

The Bolling Commission's evaluation of the aircraft situation at the front determined that the French and British combat and pursuit types were adequate and offered good production potential. The role of the United States was then to produce the larger observation and bombing aircraft. There were two reasons for this decision. First, the Liberty engine was more suited to these types of aircraft. Secondly, and this was the more important reason, "The primary purpose of war flying is observation. The duels in the air that occurred in large numbers, especially during the earlier stages of the war, were primarily to protect the observation machines or to prevent observation by enemy machines." [5]

The aircraft that fit both of the above criteria was the DH–4. The first sample DH–4 was received in New York on 18 July 1917 and was sent to Dayton for redesigning to take American machine guns, instruments, other accessories, and the Liberty engine. The first American-built DH–4 was ready to fly 29 October 1917.[6] But there was much to do before this airplane which was designed for a certain engine, armament and other accessories, could be considered a finished, operational craft with a different engine, guns, and similar equipment. The trials of the American-built DH–4 were many and difficult. Prior to going into combat it had already been called a "flaming coffin," but actually it was a good machine and gave excellent service.[7] The general impression today is that few, if any, of the warplanes built in the United States ever reached the front during World War I. The facts prove differently:

> The grand total of all DH–4s produced was 4,846. Of these, 3,431 had been completed and shipped from the air plane factories up to the Armistice, November 11th. Of the 4,846 freighted from factories, a total of 2,297 was floated from ports of embarkation. Of this number a total of 1,885 with engines and 204 without engines had been floated up to Armistice date. On November 11th 1918 in addition to those actually floated there were 964 on the docks or en route from factories to ports to be shipped.[8]

Clark. It is difficult to understand his notations of the power required for the different categories of aircraft. At that point in time there were no aircraft engines in existence in the 450–550-hp class, with one exception. The exception was a Fiat V–12 developed late in the summer of 1917, which was rated at slightly below 600 hp. This engine was mounted in the SIA–9B, but so much trouble developed when the aircraft was put in service that it was recalled. In 1918 the aircraft was returned to the front with the same engine, which, in the meantime, had been increased to almost 700 hp (History of BAP, loc. cit., p. 1653).

[5] CROWELL, op. cit., p. 254.

[6] Ibid.

[7] GORRELL, op. cit., p. 43.

[8] History of BAP, loc. cit., p. 1707. In general, Gorrell's figures agreed with the History of BAP.

Tables 8 and 9, pp. 100–101, present statistics showing the actual use of the DH–4 by the American Expeditionary Forces (AEF) in France. Each DH–4 was powered by one L–12 and backed up by another, plus spares.

Fifteen percent of the total casualties of the Air Service occurred in American-built DH–4s. There were 38 killed in action, 8 wounded, 10 missing, and 20 taken prisoner. Total casualties were 76. Thirty-three DH–4s were lost to enemy action. This was 14 percent of the total lost by American Squadrons.[9] The Liberty-powered DH–4s did not go down without a fight. Table 10, p. 102, shows the number of American victories in the DH–4 by squadron.

No greater percentage of DH–4s was lost in flames than that of any other type at the front, although the first self-sealing gas tanks were not installed in this aircraft until 12 October 1918.[10]

Some of the credit for the ultimate success of the American-built DH–4 must go to the British mission headed by Major General W. S. Brancker, which visited the United States from 11 June through 29 July 1918. This group of aviation experts, whose knowledge was based on almost four years of warfare, tested our aircraft and gave valuable advice.[11]

The L–12 was installed in, or considered for installation in, many aircraft; the DH–4, however, was the only one that saw service in France. Worthy of note is the effort that went into the American version of the Handley-Page bomber. Until the summer of 1918 the United States could choose from only two types of bombers: the Handley-Page and the Caproni. The Handley-Page was adapted for production purely because drawings were available. The first set of drawings was received in August 1918, but during the ensuing winter two new sets were sent from England and almost every part was altered.

Owing to the size of the Handley-Page (wing spread of more than 100 feet), it was decided to manufacture the parts in the United States and have them assembled in England. Each machine consisted of 100,000 separate parts and two L–12 engines. The packing for overseas shipment was a major undertaking in itself.[12]

One hundred sets of parts for the Handley-Page were manufactured, packed, and sent overseas between July and October 1918.[13] The Armistice intervened, however, and

---

[9] GORRELL, op. cit., p. 64.

[10] Ibid., p. 68.

[11] "British Technical Report," loc. cit.

[12] CROWELL, op. cit., p. 261.

[13] History of BAP, loc. cit., p. 1797.

the American-built Handley-Page machines never reached the front; but with the two low compression Liberty engines with which they were equipped, the United States, had the war continued, would have been in a good position to do considerable damage by night bombing along the German lines.[14]

Table 11, p. 103, shows the multiplicity of aircraft that our ambitious Air Service was considering for use or had actually produced and tested with the Liberty engine during the short period that the United States was engaged in World War I. Considering the paucity of our knowledge of aircraft and aircraft engines and the difficulties involved in their production, this is truly an impressive list.

---

[14] Ibid., p. 1800.

Post Bellum

After the war was over an overriding emphasis was placed on the return home of the victorious United States Army. The result was an undermanned situation overseas, which led to poor maintenance of munitions left in the field. Fabric covered, lightly built aircraft suffered greatly from exposure to the elements and from lack of care. The DH–4s that were airworthy or could be put in shape to fly received favored treatment, and 612 were shipped to the United States by 20 August 1919, at an average cost of $1125 each. Only 202 had to be salvaged.[1]

Once home, the aircraft from abroad were distributed among the many flying fields that had been built during the war. In joining the aircraft which had not made the Atlantic crossing, however, they caused a surplus of planes for which the only legitimate use was training. Production of Liberty engines, which had reached a peak in October 1918, had been geared to wartime attrition; cessation of hostilities left an enormous surplus of L–12s. In October 1919 the Army had a total of 11,871 Liberty engines, of which 2773 were in service and the balance in storage. At that time the Army's requirement was estimated at 10,000 Liberties, not including engines to be installed in new aircraft.[2] The Post Office Department also had use for Liberty engines in the postwar period in the new and growing Air Mail Service.

Some authorities were concerned with the surplus of Liberty engines. In August 1919 the Air Service announced a policy under which serviceable Liberty engines would be sold to United States citizens for commercial and civil aeronautics or to educational institutions; none were to be sold to foreign governments, however, without approval of the Department of Air Service. This policy was made known to the Air Service agencies but was not released to the public.[3] The Assistant Secretary of War, Benedict

---

[1] GORRELL, op. cit., p. 77.

[2] National Archives files, letter, Major General Burr from Colonel Gilmore, 21 October 1919.

[3] Ibid., memo to Chief of the Supply Group, McCook Field, 8 September 1919.

Crowell, made inquiries about disposing of the surplus but was told that until new engines were available the Air Service could not dispose of "practically the only engine we have of service type."[4] Some, however, were sold. As of 18 October 1919, 58 serviceable Liberty engines had been disposed of—50 to the Post Office Department. Eight serviceable engines had been sold to schools.[5]

Table 12, p. 105, though incomplete, gives an indication of the number of sales and reconditionings of Liberty engines, compared with the number on hand. As this table shows, the Liberty engine died hard. This was a mixed blessing. The L–12 was so far ahead of its time that it took a few years for manufacturers in the United States to overtake and surpass it. During this period it was the bulwark of the Air Service, the Air Mail Service, and commercial aviation. It was available in quantities sufficient for all users even though initially the Air Service tended to be a little sparing with its wealth. Not until 1929 was it necessary to update and recondition used engines, because of the great number of unused engines available.[6]

On the other hand, the very existence of this plethora of engines tended to restrict development of new service aircraft.[7] By 1924 a number of engines were on the market or in the development stage that were superior in performance to the Liberty. At the operating level considerable concern was evident that this situation would stagnate the Air Service at the 1918 period of technology while world aviation continued. It had been only seven years since the United States had awakened to its abysmal ignorance of the progress of aviation and had, at gun's point, so to speak, done something about it. Now, because of plenty rather than famine, the cycle appeared to be repeating itself. The surplus of 11,810 engines in 1924 was calculated to last the Air Service for 26 years. Little Rock Air Intermediate Depot operated exclusively for the storage of L–12s; the disposition of 5000 engines to non-service-connected organizations would have allowed the inactivation of the depot and a concomitant saving in operating costs. The situation was plainly stated by Delos C. Emmons, Chief of Production Engineering at McCook Field, in January 1924:

There is no doubt but what the large stock of Liberty engines is hindering engine development. The plans of the Chief, Air Service on this question are,

---

[4] Ibid., Colonel Pearson from Major General Menoher, 30 October 1919.

[5] Ibid., Chief, Information Group, from Chief, Material Disposal and Salvage Division, Directorate of Air Service, 18 October 1919.

[6] McCook files, memo, Power Plant Branch from Procurement Section, 8 January 1929.

[7] Ibid., letter, Fairfield Air Intermediate Depot from Chief, Production Engineering, McCook Field, 15 January 1924.

however, unknown to this office. It is a fact that at present our only valuable asset in aeronautical supplies is this large number of Liberty engines. With our present limited number of airplanes and the various conditions of decrepitude, the large stock of Liberty engines which we know are successful always looms up as a saving asset in the eventuality of emergency. On the other hand it is more than apparent that if a large number of Liberties are sold it would give a great impetus to commercial aviation. At the present time commercial aviation is built around the old Curtiss training planes to a great extent. The marketing of a number of high powered engines would undoubtedly force the production of a more satisfactory airplane to fly it in commercial life.[8]

This information was amplified and passed to the Chief of Air Service in February 1924 with a recommendation to sell or otherwise dispose of 5000 engines in the next four years.[9]

Not until three years later was there any indication of action on the part of the government to cope with the surplus engine problem. On 2 February 1927, the Assistant Secretary of War directed that a study be made of the "desirability of excluding from future designs of aircraft the use of the Liberty engine."[10] The Air Service pointed out that, with the exception of the LB–1, a stopgap bombardment type, no aircraft had been designed around the Liberty since the Observation Competition in the summer of 1924. It was further stated that with the exception of observation aircraft, there was no requirement for the Liberty. The Curtiss D–12 was the standard engine for pursuit planes and development of aircraft engines was pointed toward air-cooled and more powerful water-cooled types. It is interesting to note, however, that even at this time (February 1927) the Air Service saw "no purpose . . . in obtaining a new design for observation as present types appear to offer all the advantages that could be obtained from new designs."[11]

The question of continuing the use of the Liberty in observation aircraft was more difficult to resolve. The facts were that: the observation aircraft in service were adequate; they were already fitted with Liberty engines; and an abundant supply of engines was available. This made it difficult to rationalize the switch to a different—even though more modern—engine. The study that had been directed by the Assistant Secretary of War attempted to make this rationalization.

It was found impossible to compute an exact cost because "none of the modern motors has been purchased by the Air Corps in sufficient quantity

---

[8] Ibid.

[9] Ibid., Chief, Air Service, from Chief, Engineering Division, 14 February 1924.

[10] Ibid., Chief, Air Service, from the Assistant Secretary of War, 2 February 1927.

[11] Ibid., Chief, Air Service, from Chief, Engineering Division, 16 February 1927.

to indicate what the costs would be on a production scale." [12] Table 13, p. 105, shows the cost of some of the better commercial engines of the period.

The Air Corps had some experience, however, with one modern engine—the Curtiss D–12. The costs of overhauling the D–12 and the Liberty are compared in Table 14, p. 106. The difference in cost was only $58.32 per engine, a total of $29,160 per year based on a consumption of 500 engines. The Liberty engine cost $19.55 per running hour against $20.29 for the D–12. Table 15, p. 107, shows that the higher initial cost of the D–12 was almost completely absorbed by its longer life and cheaper operation. The study points out that, purchased and overhauled in large quantities, its cost should have been less than that of the Liberty. The number of maintenance hours expended on the D–12 was about half those expended on the Liberty, principally because of its accessibility. The D–12 was also considered more reliable than the Liberty since a smaller percentage of crashes was chargeable to engine failure. [13]

On the basis of the study, Major General Patrick, Chief of the Air Corps, wrote to Assistant Secretary of War Davidson, on 25 February 1927, recommending that the government sell as many Liberty engines as possible and continue to build observation planes around the Liberty for the next two or three years. By the end of this period designs were to be made for observation planes with better and more modern engines. Final decision on the use of Liberties would be withheld until the end of the two- to three-year period.

Patrick based his recommendations on the facts that over 9000 usable L–12s were on hand, that no new observation-type designs were necessary for the next several years, and that the Liberty would be acceptable for that period of time. He also pointed out that consumption would not exceed 500 a year, so that the supply would last 18 to 20 years. In a fraction of that time much better engines would be available, and if the Air Service were to continue to use Liberties until the supply was exhausted, its developments elsewhere would be held back. He noted that there would be an increase in cost to keep the fleet modern. [14] On 1 July 1929, the Air Corps finally prohibited the use of Liberty engines in any new aircraft. [15]

---

[12] Ibid., report, "Cost of Excluding Liberty Motors from Future Design," n.d. (probably 1927). This cost study was directed by the Assistant Secretary of War.

[13] Ibid. The initial cost of the L–12 was based on a "bogey". The method of computation was not shown. Actual initial cost was more than $4000, and overhaul cost was from $500 to $1000. The cost study did not cover the cost of redesign and reconstruction of existing Liberty-powered aircraft to accept a different engine.

[14] Ibid., memo, Assistant Secretary of War from Chief, Air Corps, 25 February 1927.

[15] Ibid., Chief, Air Corps, from Commander, McCook Field, 24 January 1929.

In February 1928, W. P. McCracken, Jr., Assistant Secretary of Commerce for Aeronautics, suggested to Assistant Secretary of War Davidson that "it would be of advantage to the government, as well as industry, if you could trade Liberty motors on the basis of $700.00 each in the purchase of modern motors." [16] This suggestion was passed on to the Chief of Air Corps by Captain Ira C. Eaker, executive to the Assistant Secretary of War.[17] The Chief of the Air Corps referred the paper to the Material Division, McCook Field.[18]

The people at operating level had a different view of the proposal to trade L–12s for more modern engines. McCracken had referred to the Curtiss D–12 as the most promising replacement for the Liberty engine, based on an estimated 1200-hour life with four overhauls. The engineers at McCook did not feel that the D–12 would last 1200 hours when subjected to military use. They stated further that "the Liberty has better high speed in the Curtiss observations . . . [and] . . . is slightly more reliable than the D–12." [19] This was quite a tribute to engines that were 10 years old compared with new engines that had the advantage of 10 years of technological research.

The Air Corps engineers did feel, however, that the Liberty could be replaced by high-powered, water-cooled or air-cooled engines. The air-cooled engine appeared to be coming into prominence at this time. Air Corps statistics now showed the overhaul cost of the D–12 to be $737.45, including $572.80 for spares, $125.82 for labor, and $38.83 for overhead. This was more than $200 over the cost indicated by the 1927 study.

In summing up, it was pointed out that cost was not the primary consideration in replacing the L–12. Increased performance of modern engines (other than the D–12) and damage to aircraft caused by Liberty-engine vibration were more pertinent arguments. Information indicated that airlines such as Boeing and Ford rejected L–12s unconditionally because the increased payload lifted by modern air-cooled engines more than paid for increased initial cost. In addition, the airlines believed they were more reliable than the Liberty and much more accessible for maintenance.[20]

Nevertheless, letters were sent to Curtiss, Pratt & Whitney, Wright, Allison, and to Steel Products Engineering Company suggesting a trade-in arrangement. In effect, the letters said that if the L–12s were disposed of

[16] Ibid., Assistant Secretary of War from Assistant Secretary of Commerce, 16 February 1928.

[17] Ibid., Chief, Air Corps, from Assistant Secretary of War, 25 February 1928.

[18] Ibid., General Gilmore from the Material Division, Wright Field, 2 March 1928.

[19] Ibid.

[20] Ibid., Chief, Air Corps, from General Gilmore, 9 March 1928.

there would be increased sales of more modern engines to the government; the cost of overhaul of Liberty engines out of storage was $730; and, although the Liberty was too inefficient for airlines, other uses could be found for it. The answers were not encouraging. The manufacturers could see no advantage in considering the use of obsolete engines in a growing technology either for industry, commerce, or the Air Corps. Commercial operators would not buy water-cooled engines because of their relative inefficiency when compared to the air-cooled type. As F. B. Rentschler, president of Pratt & Whitney, put it:

> Take the Douglas Mail Ship, when a wasp is installed in place of the Liberty engine between 700 and 800 pounds are saved. Take also the Boeing Mail Ships . . . with the Liberty engine the payload was 600 to 700 pounds; with the wasp they are carrying 1500 to 1800 pounds with about the same speed, etc.[21]

Some interest was expressed in a contract whereby the government would permit purchasers free export to foreign countries, stipulating, however, that it would not sell subsequently at a lower price to the same countries.[22]

The manufacturers did, however, recognize the contribution of the Liberty. Rentschler summed it up:

> Let me point out that I am among the ones who have always been great believers in the Liberty engine. At the time it was designed I think it was the finest power plant that was available anywhere, and continued to be the best of its size for a number of years. I believe the Liberty engine constitutes the finest contribution of the War Department during the World War, regardless of the fact that those who had to do with aircraft production during the war were chiefly criticized because they designed and put into manufacture this particular type of engine. If water cooled engines were not more or less obsolete for commercial work the Liberty today would be entirely desirable for either military or commercial operation.[23]

And so it went. The Liberty hung on in a world where its usefulness as an aircraft engine had become dependent solely on its low cost resulting from large surpluses.

Although the L–12 was outdated for use in aircraft, it was used exten-

---

[21] Ibid., letter, Major MacDill, Material Division, Wright Field, from F. B. Rentschler, president of the Pratt & Whitney Company, 19 March 1928.

[22] Ibid., Material Division, Wright Field, from the Curtiss Company, 2 April 1928; Material Division, Wright Field, from the Allison Company, 6 April 1928.

[23] Ibid., Major MacDill, Material Division, Wright Field, from F. B. Rentschler, president of the Pratt & Whitney Company, 19 March 1928.

sively in speedboats. During prohibition rum runners outran the Coast Guard with boats powered by Liberty engines which had been purchased from junk dealers. In consequence, the Coast Guard later equipped some of its own craft with L–12s.[24]

In 1923 the Ordnance Department asked the Commander of McCook Field for any L–8s that were available for installation in 15-ton tanks and learned that all but two (donated to museums) had been sold.[25] In 1929 the Army was testing the Liberty in armored cars which had been modified from World War I Christy tanks.[26] The Christy was the vehicle that took the Liberty to war on the eastern front in 1941. The *New York World Telegram* stated:

> Liberty Motors built in 1918 are now driving Russian tanks against the Germans. The Allison, outstanding liquid cooled motor of the present era, . . . is a direct descendant of the Liberty. In 1929 in order to acquire the crankshaft bearing and other patents as well as the skilled personnel Allison had gathered about him, General Motors bought the Allison Plant after the founder's death. By 1935 the plant began to expand in the Indianapolis location developing a liquid cooled motor whose foundation was in an experimental model built for the Navy's dirigible program in 1930. There were traces of the old Liberty in it yet.[27]

Russia was not the only country that had used the Liberty in World War II. In the United Kingdom the designing of special engines for tanks had been discontinued in 1930 in an attempt to use "lorry" engines.

> The result was that when a belated effort was made to produce tanks quickly just before the war, the only engine design available was the American Liberty aero-engine, which had first seen the light of day in 1916! [sic] This fine old engine, efficient as it was in its time, developed only 320 to 330 h.p.— not nearly enough for the heavier tanks then envisaged—and had such draw backs as exposed valve gear and an extension of the crankshaft for the propeller.[28]

Nevertheless, a great number of Liberties were produced and were used in

---

[24] National Archives files, letter, Commandant, United States Coast Guard, from Chief, Air Corps, 15 January 1937. This mentions a 70-foot patrol boat with four Vimalert marine conversions of the Liberty engine (L–12) in tandem.

[25] McCook files, memo, Commander, McCook Field, from Ordnance Department, U.S. Army, 9 January 1923, and first indorsement thereto, 17 January 1923.

[26] *New York Times*, 24 February 1929, p. 3.

[27] *New York World Telegram*, 25 October 1941, p. 12.

[28] HAROLD NOCKOLDS, *The Magic of a Name* (London: G. T. Foulis and Company, Ltd.), p. 217. Of course, the Liberty "saw the light of day" in 191⁓, not 1916.

British tanks in World War II. General N. W. Duncan, curator of the Royal Armoured Corps Tank Museum, provided the following information:

> The Liberty engine was built under U.S. license by Messrs. Nuffield Mechanisation in 1938. As produced it was rated at 340 BHP and installed in Cruiser tank Mk. III (A.13) which came into service in 1939. This engine was also fitted in Crusader tank Mk II and III (1941 and 1942 respectively).
>
> A.13 was used in France in 1940 with 1st Armoured Division while the Crusader was extensively used in the Western desert.
>
> The Nuffield Liberty engine in its last form was used in the Centaur and Cavalier tanks which were produced in 1943. Neither of these tanks were ever used in action—their weight had risen to 30 tons and eventually the Rolls Royce 600 HP Meteor was installed in the same chassis to become the Cromwell tank.
>
> The Liberty engine in A.13 was exactly the engine I remember in 1920 when it was used in de Haviland aircraft DH 9A (single engine) and DH 10 (twin engine). It was then a very simple engine and in that form, was manufactured by Nuffield Mechanisation. Its later variants were considerably more sophisticated. Up to its rated H.P. it was a good power unit.
>
> The Liberty was used before W.W.II for training. A.13 was received by 1st Tank Brigade early in 1939. As to numbers produced I have no really reliable figures here, but I do know that 560 A.13 were issued to the service and that 6,000 Crusaders were also issued. This means that 600 of the simple Liberty engine were built and that more than 6,000 of the later type must also have been used and this last figure takes no account of the engines used for Centaur and Cavalier tanks.[29]

It is not the province of this paper to relate the records established by Liberty-powered aircraft; this has been adequately covered elsewhere. The first aerial crossing of the Atlantic, however, was made by Navy Commander Read in May 1919 in the NC4 flying boat powered by four Liberty engines. Five years later the first aerial circumnavigation of the earth was accomplished in the "Magellans of the Air," the Douglas World Cruisers, powered by L–12s. This was a flight of 26,345 miles covered in 363 hours of flying time.[30]

This concludes the story of the Liberty engine. Its birth, production, and accomplishments total a remarkable achievement in the technology of the United States that is worth reviewing and that should not be forgotten. In retrospect the history of the Liberty engine is a typically American story. The desire to maintain continental isolation and thereby keep free of the

---

[29] Letter, author from Duncan, 3 December 1964.

[30] MARCOSSON, op. cit., pp. 253–254. Records established by Liberty-powered aircraft may be found in *Aircraft Year Book*, particularly for the years 1919 through 1925.

affairs of the world outside has helped to lead a poorly prepared United States into every major foreign war in its short history. This disease is endemic today. In every case victory—or at least stalemate—has been achieved through the awesome ability of American technology to respond to the needs of the moment and to the abundant natural resources with which the nation has been blessed. Without these two factors the Liberty engine could never have been conceived and produced.

The engine is noteworthy in the boldness of its conception and the dedication of its proponents in the face of adverse criticism. Vincent's unwavering determination that the engine design should not be compromised and Deeds' firm and intelligent leadership were primary factors in its success. The Liberty marked the first attempt to standardize an aircraft-engine series for mass production in the United States. Credit for successful production must go to the automotive industry which utilized production experience gained with auto engines to mass produce the Liberty. The most striking part of the story, however, is that with the Liberty engine the United States moved from a position of gross inferiority in aircraft-engine technology to superiority in less than one year. It has been well said that the Liberty was among America's greatest contributions to World War I victory.[31]

Finally, was the Liberty engine actually designed in six days? This has been one of the legends surrounding the engine; but could it have been done? Not completely. Without the research of a Vincent, or the production experience of a Hall, or the inventive genius of both there would have been no Liberty engine. The six-day session in the Willard Hotel was actually the culmination of the years of experience of the two men, the aggregation of their knowledge into an engine design. But, on the other side of the coin, the Liberty design was a complete departure from the heavy, durable aircraft engines of the day; it was an aristocrat. The ingredient of lightness with power was designed into the engine in six days, and the vision and skill that put it there must ever be respected.

---

[31] Ibid., p. 252. McCook files, telegram, Air Minister, Great Britain, to Lord Reading, 7 June 1918.

Appendix

1. Organization for Production

Chart I ORGANIZATION OF THE SIGNAL CORPS 4 November 1915

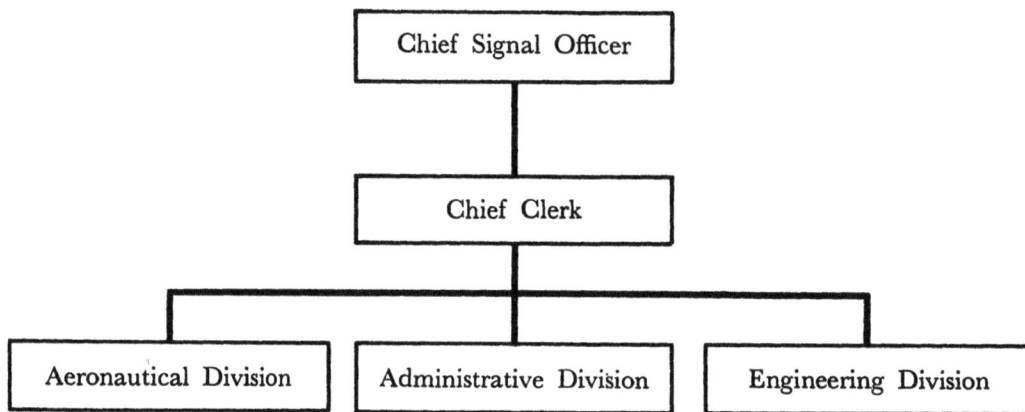

```
              ┌─────────────────────┐
              │ Chief Signal Officer │
              └─────────────────────┘
                         │
              ┌─────────────────────┐
              │     Chief Clerk      │
              └─────────────────────┘
                         │
        ┌────────────────┼────────────────┐
┌───────────────┐ ┌──────────────┐ ┌──────────────┐
│ Aeronautical  │ │Administrative│ │  Engineering │
│   Division    │ │   Division   │ │   Division   │
└───────────────┘ └──────────────┘ └──────────────┘
```

Chart II ORGANIZATION OF THE SIGNAL CORPS April 1917

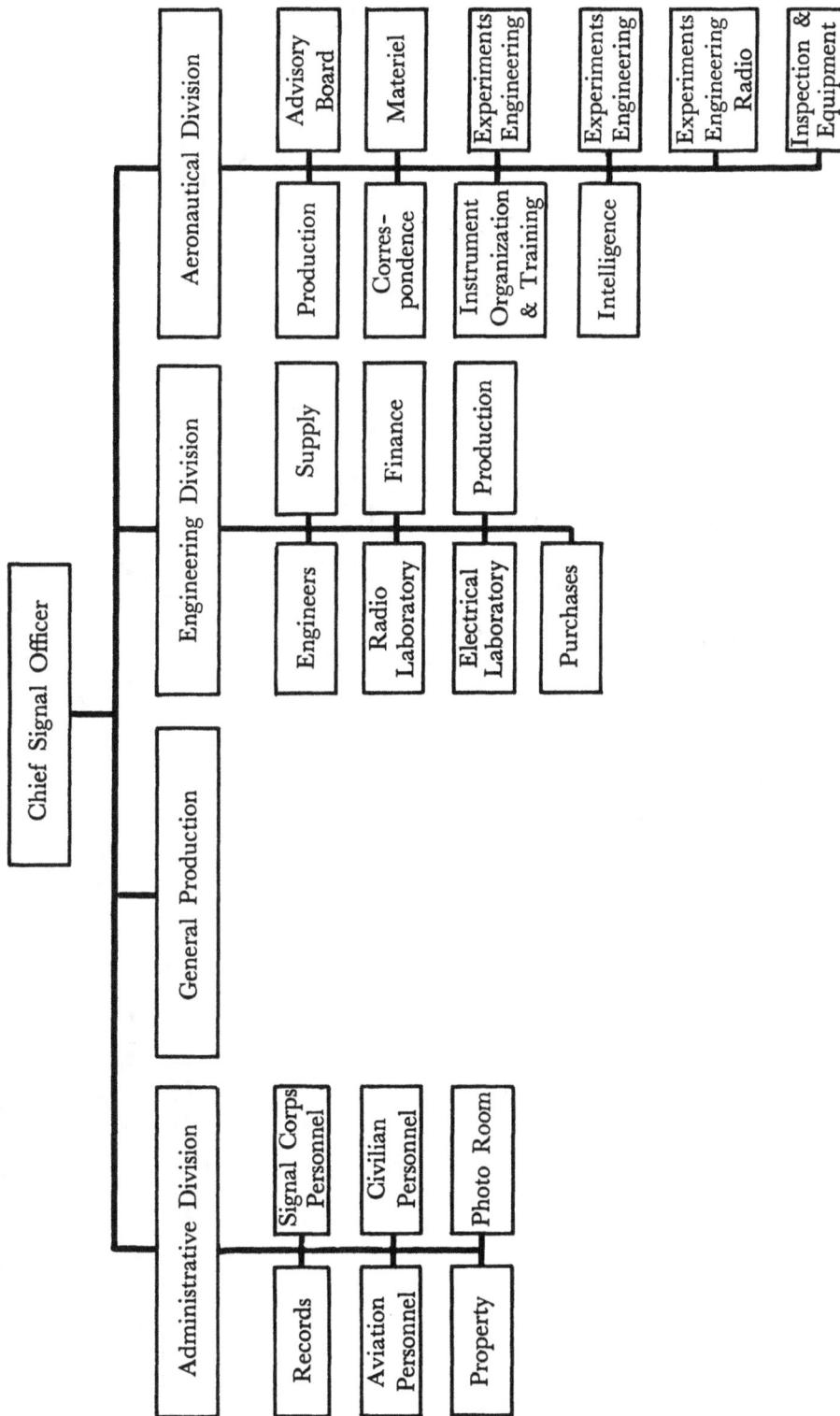

```
                              ┌─────────────────────┐
                              │ Chief Signal Officer │
                              └──────────┬──────────┘
         ┌───────────────┬───────────────┼───────────────┐
┌────────┴─────────┐ ┌────┴───────┐ ┌────┴────────┐ ┌─────┴──────────┐
│ Administrative   │ │  General   │ │ Engineering │ │  Aeronautical  │
│    Division      │ │ Production │ │   Division  │ │   Division     │
└──────────────────┘ └────────────┘ └─────────────┘ └────────────────┘
```

Administrative Division
- Records
- Signal Corps Personnel
- Aviation Personnel
- Civilian Personnel
- Property
- Photo Room

Engineering Division
- Engineers
- Supply
- Radio Laboratory
- Finance
- Electrical Laboratory
- Production
- Purchases

Aeronautical Division
- Production
- Advisory Board
- Corres-pondence
- Materiel
- Instrument Organization & Training
- Experiments Engineering
- Intelligence
- Experiments Engineering
- Experiments Engineering Radio
- Inspection & Equipment

85

Chart III   NATIONAL ORGANIZATION FOR AIRCRAFT PRODUCTION AND USE 1 May 1917

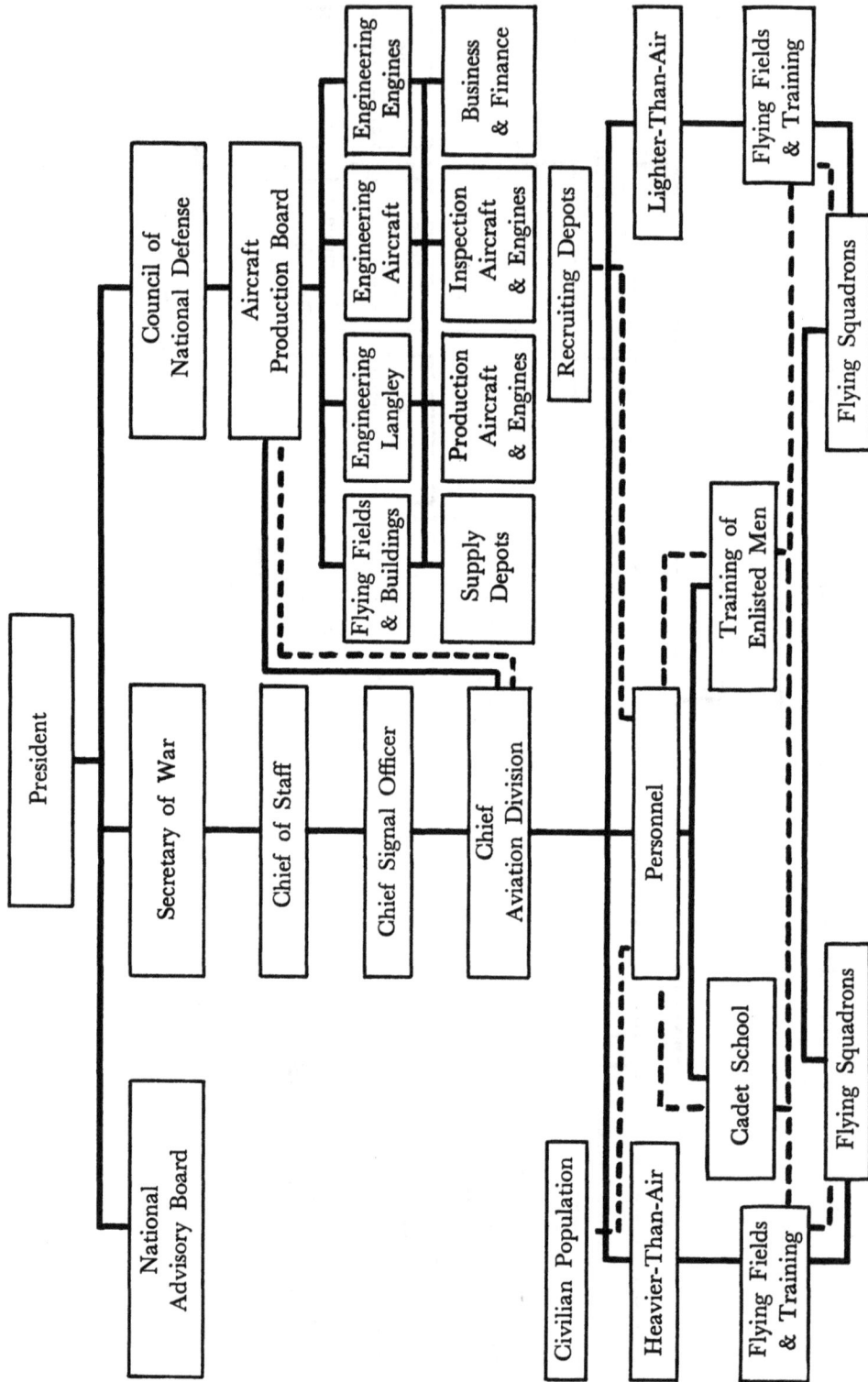

President

National Advisory Board

Council of National Defense

Secretary of War

Aircraft Production Board

Chief of Staff

Chief Signal Officer

Chief Aviation Division

Engineering Engines

Business & Finance

Engineering Aircraft

Inspection Aircraft & Engines

Engineering Langley

Production Aircraft & Engines

Flying Fields & Buildings

Supply Depots

Recruiting Depots

Lighter-Than-Air

Flying Fields & Training

Flying Squadrons

Personnel

Training of Enlisted Men

Cadet School

Civilian Population

Heavier-Than-Air

Flying Fields & Training

Flying Squadrons

86

Chart IV   NATIONAL ORGANIZATION FOR AIRCRAFT PRODUCTION AND USE 2 June 1917

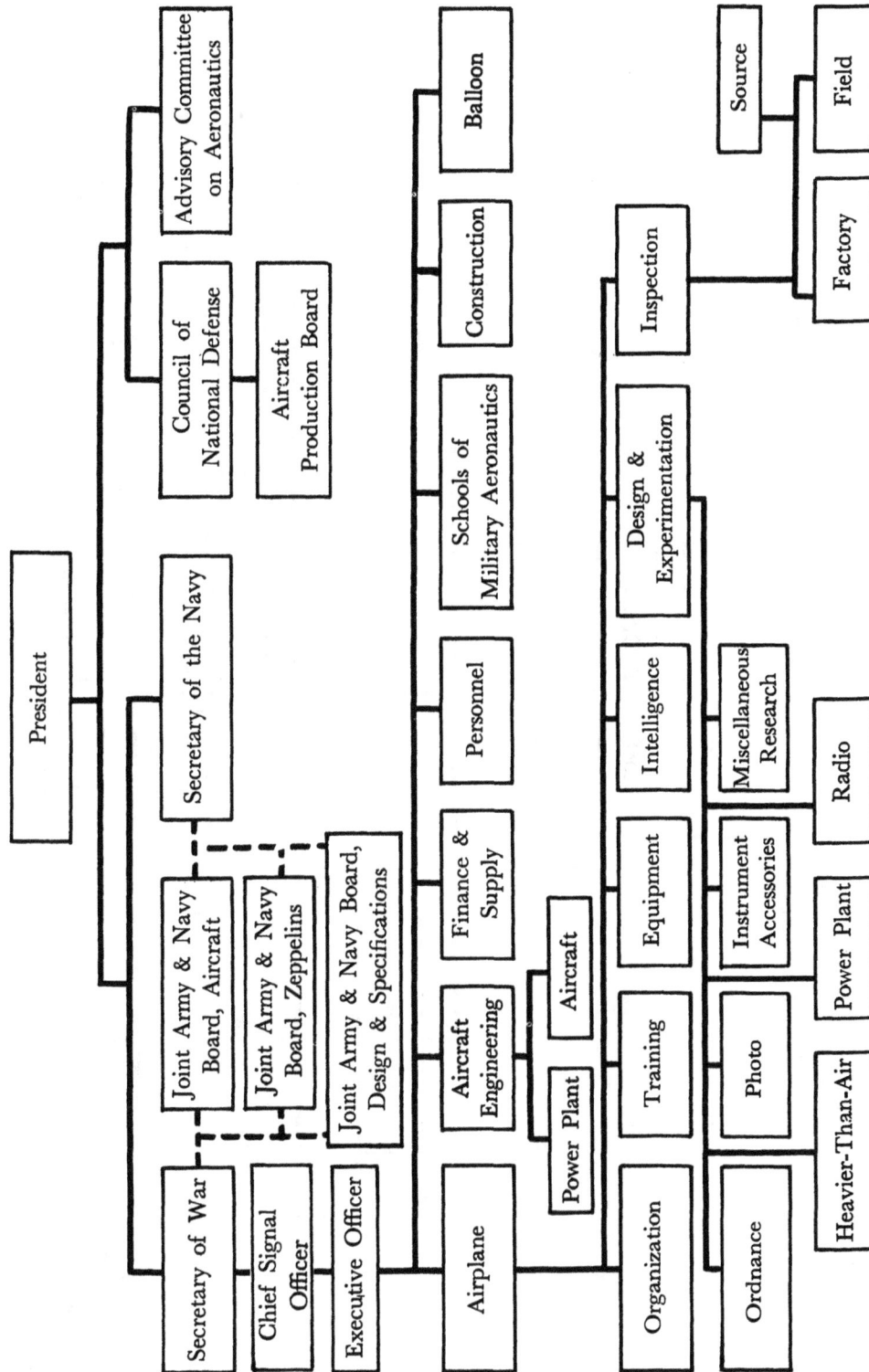

President

Advisory Committee on Aeronautics

Council of National Defense

Aircraft Production Board

Secretary of the Navy

Secretary of War

Chief Signal Officer

Executive Officer

Joint Army & Navy Board, Aircraft

Joint Army & Navy Board, Zeppelins

Joint Army & Navy Board, Design & Specifications

Airplane

Power Plant

Aircraft Engineering

Aircraft

Finance & Supply

Personnel

Schools of Military Aeronautics

Construction

Balloon

Organization

Training

Equipment

Intelligence

Design & Experimentation

Inspection

Source

Factory

Field

Ordnance

Photo

Instrument Accessories

Miscellaneous Research

Heavier-Than-Air

Power Plant

Radio

87

257-441 O - 78 - 7

Chart V   EQUIPMENT DIVISION, AIR SERVICE 15 August 1917

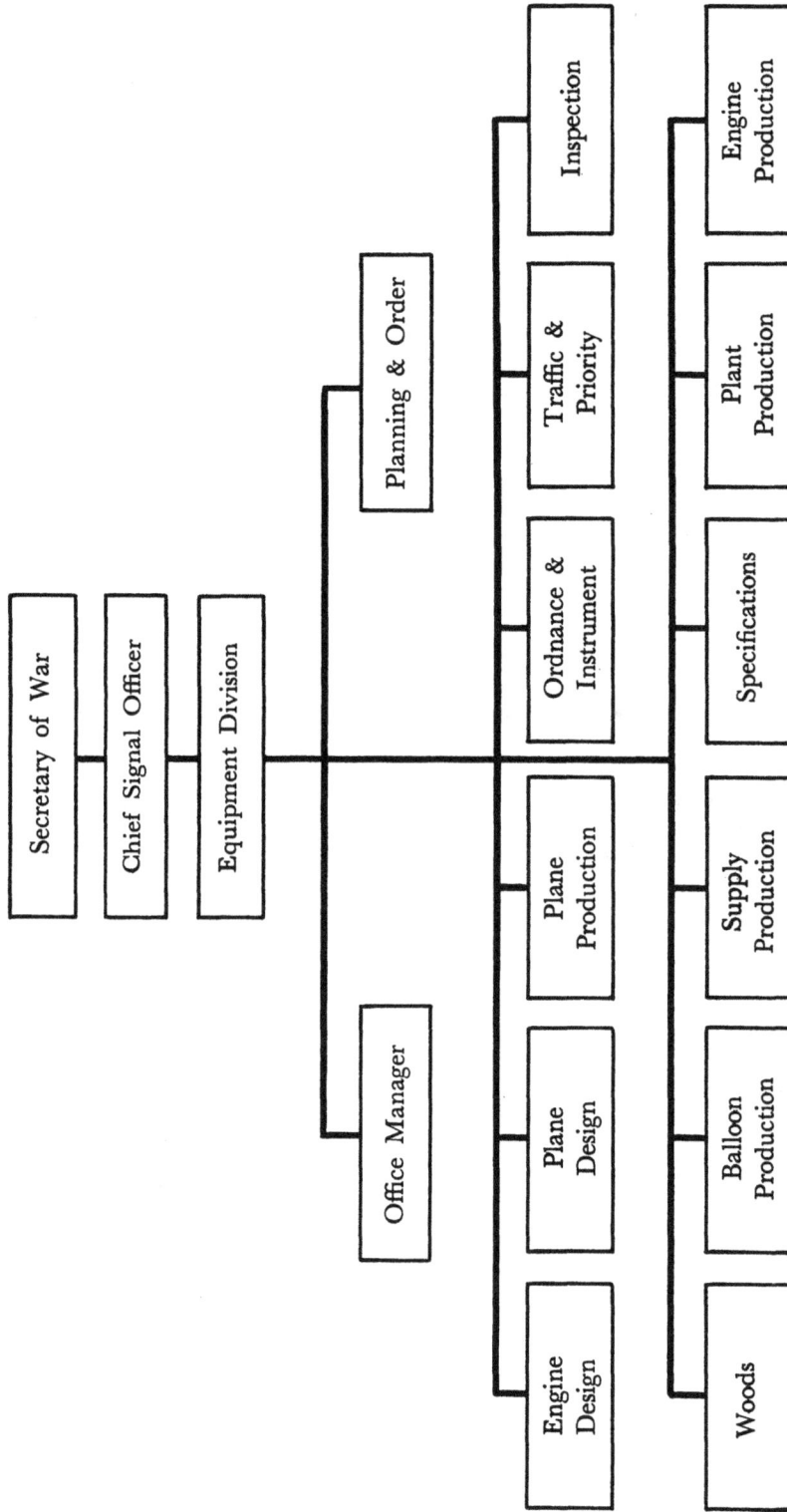

```
                    ┌─────────────────┐
                    │ Secretary of War │
                    └────────┬─────────┘
                    ┌────────┴─────────┐
                    │ Chief Signal     │
                    │ Officer          │
                    └────────┬─────────┘
                    ┌────────┴─────────┐
                    │ Equipment        │
                    │ Division         │
                    └────────┬─────────┘
         ┌───────────────────┼───────────────────┐
 ┌───────┴──────┐                         ┌───────┴──────┐
 │ Office       │                         │ Planning &   │
 │ Manager      │                         │ Order        │
 └──────────────┘                         └──────────────┘

  ┌──────────┬──────────┬──────────┬──────────┬──────────┐
┌─┴──┐   ┌──┴──┐   ┌───┴──┐   ┌───┴───┐   ┌──┴────┐   ┌─┴──┐
│Engine│  │Plane│  │Plane │   │Ordnance│  │Traffic│   │Insp│
│Design│  │Design│ │Produc│   │& Instr │  │& Prior│   │ection│
└──────┘  └─────┘  └──────┘   └────────┘  └───────┘   └────┘

┌──────┐ ┌──────┐ ┌──────┐ ┌────────┐ ┌──────┐ ┌──────┐
│Woods │ │Balloon│ │Supply│ │Specifi │ │Plant │ │Engine│
│      │ │Produc │ │Produc│ │cations │ │Produc│ │Produc│
└──────┘ └───────┘ └──────┘ └────────┘ └──────┘ └──────┘
```

88

Chart VI   Equipment Division, Air Service 29 September 1917

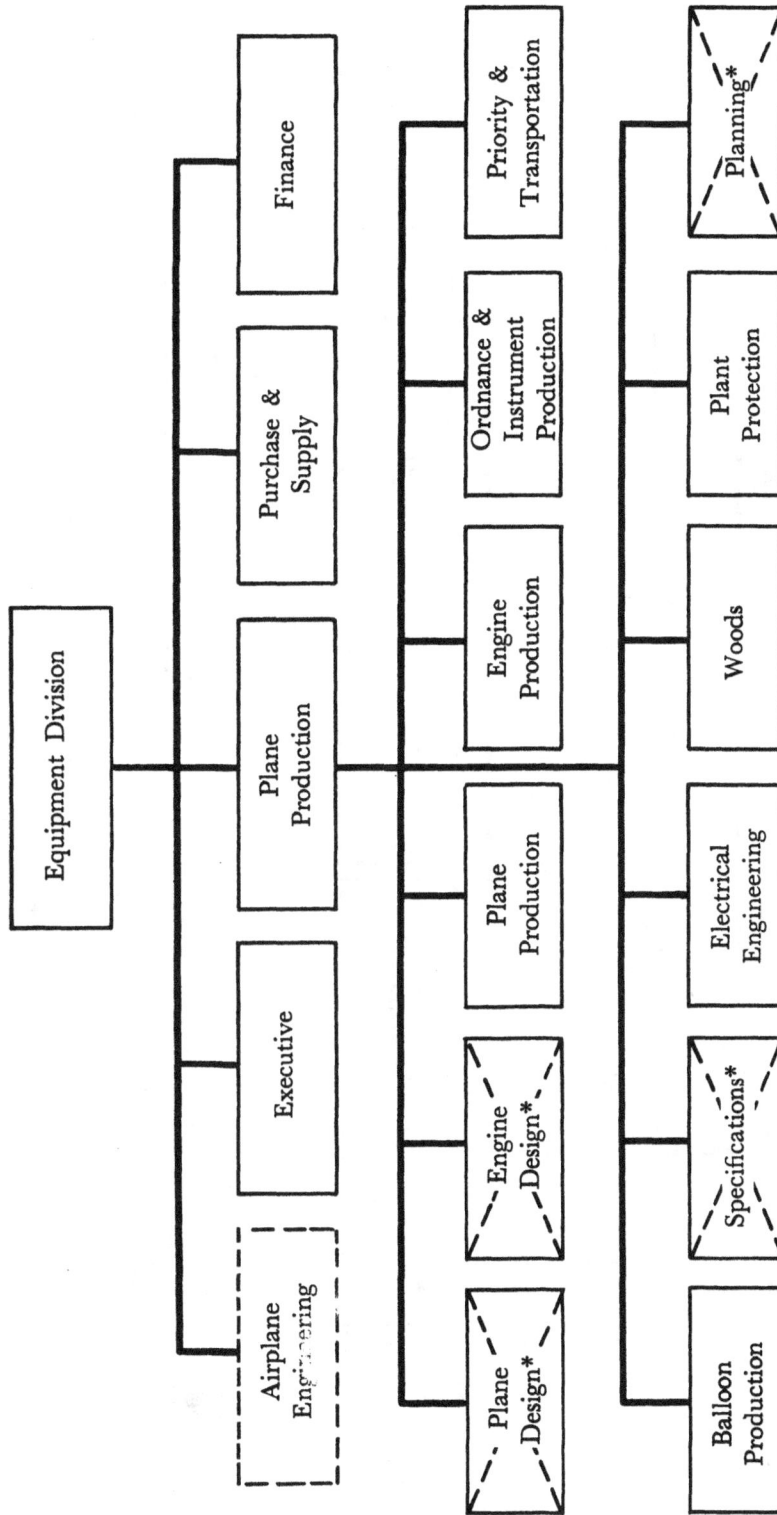

```
                                        Equipment Division
                                                │
        ┌─────────────────┬─────────────────────┼──────────────────┬──────────────┐
        │                 │                     │                  │              │
   Airplane           Executive           Plane Production    Purchase &       Finance
  Engineering                                                   Supply
 (dashed box)
                                                │
   ┌──────────┬─────────────┬──────────────┬────┴─────────┬──────────────────────┐
   │          │             │              │              │                      │
 Plane      Engine        Plane         Engine        Ordnance &            Priority &
 Design*    Design*      Production    Production      Instrument          Transportation
                                                       Production

   ┌──────────┬─────────────┬──────────────┬──────────────┬──────────────┐
   │          │             │              │              │              │
 Balloon   Specifications* Electrical      Woods        Plant          Planning*
 Production              Engineering                    Protection
```

*———————— Changes made 30 October 1917.

89

Chart VII Equipment Division, Air Service 30 October 1917

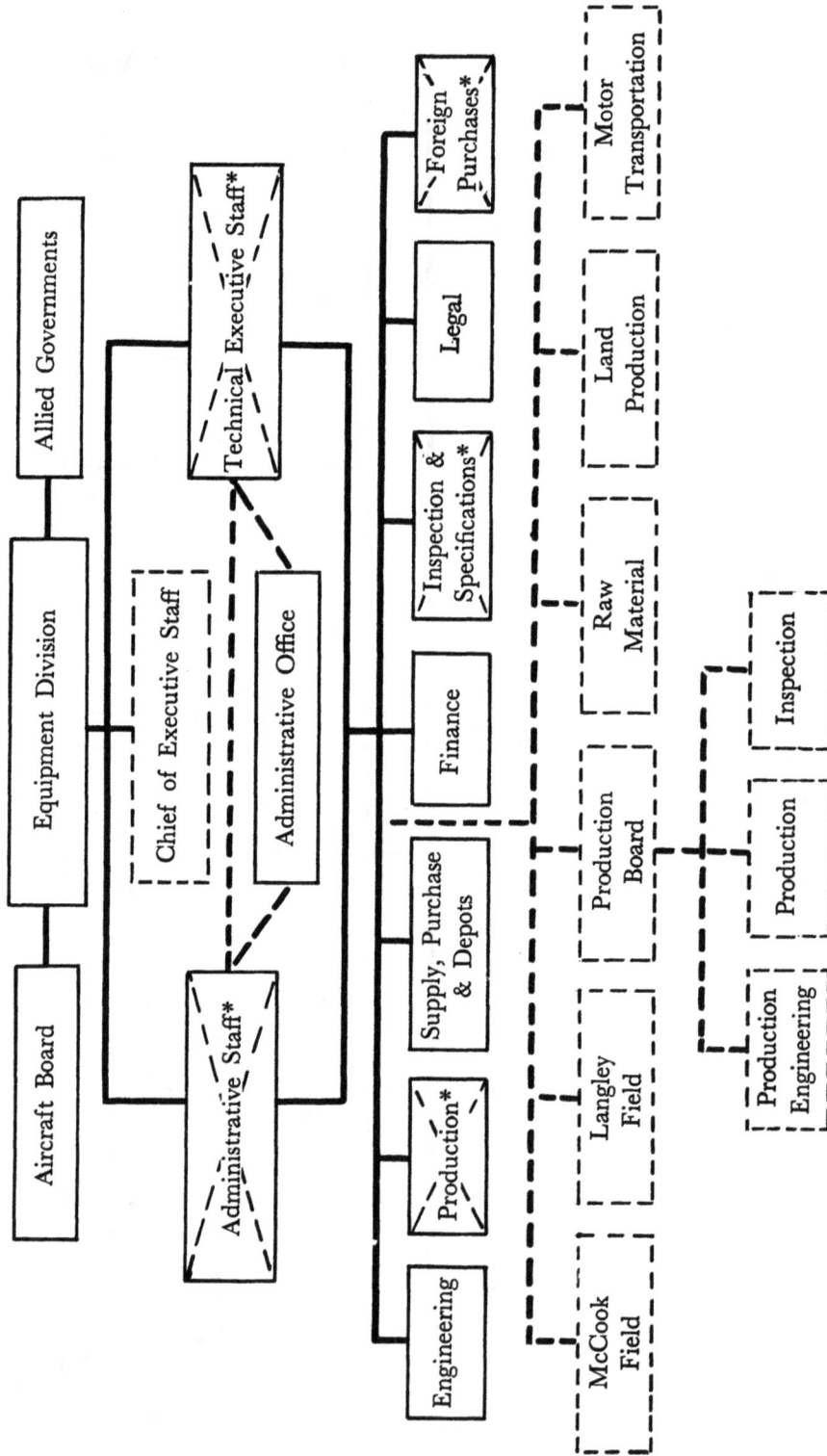

Aircraft Board

Equipment Division

Allied Governments

Chief of Executive Staff

Technical Executive Staff*

Administrative Staff*

Administrative Office

Engineering

Production*

Supply, Purchase & Depots

Finance

Inspection & Specifications*

Legal

Foreign Purchases*

McCook Field

Langley Field

Production Board

Raw Material

Land Production

Motor Transportation

Production Engineering

Production

Inspection

* — — — Changes to 2 February 1918.

2. Production Summary

TABLE 1.—LIBERTY ENGINE PRODUCTION (December 1917–February 1919)

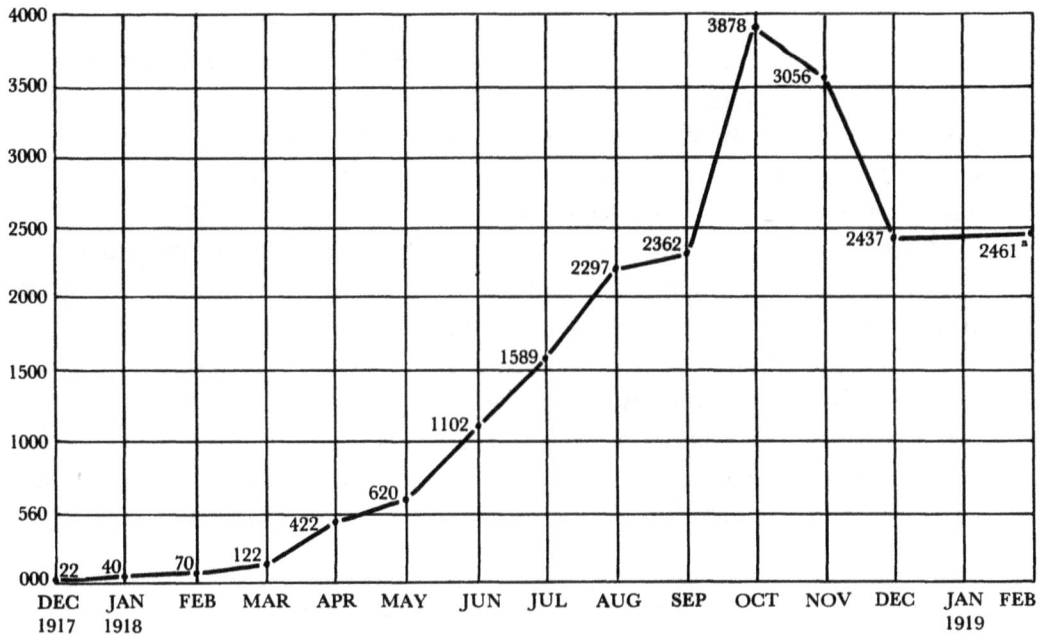

*Crowell did not show production for Jan & Feb of 1919; 2,461 engines have been added to show complete production of 20,478 engines.

Ford

Ford's initial contract was for 5000 engines, but, because of a late start and other work in the plant the company produced only 3950.

Ford's contract, dated 22 November 1917, was number 2129; it was later amended to reduce the estimated cost to $5000, and the fixed profit to $625.[1] At the time the contract was let, Ford cars were being produced at the rate of 3500 per day. The aircraft engine was a different production problem, and only 987 machine tools out of the 14,000 used on auto construction could be used for the Liberty. The original estimate of floor space to produce 50 L–12s per day was 350,000 sq. ft.; the actual space required was 550,000. It was necessary to rearrange over 50 percent of the plant equipment and machinery, including the dismantling and tearing out of several thousand machines, so that one entire building could be used for Liberty construction.

The production of the engine caused Ford to buy over 1500 new machine tools at a time when the machine-tool industry was flooded with orders. In many cases selection had to be based on availability rather than on merit. Ford's best mechanics were diverted to the Liberty program, and all supervisors were given an opportunity to fly so that they would recognize the danger involved for aircraft pilots and, in consequence, would realize the necessity for quality in the product. Ford also picked subcontractors on known ability to produce quality work.

Ford's personnel problems were minimized as curtailment in production of the autos paralleled the increase in production of Liberty engines and as personnel were transferred from one to the other. Personnel growth in L–12 production was:

TABLE 2.—PERSONNEL GROWTH

Month	Number	Month	Number
February (1918)	675	August	7976
March	779	September	9390
April	1550	October	10,654
May	2450	November	11,288
June	3412	December	826
July	5141	January (1919)	543

[1] PORTER ET AL., op. cit., p. 87.

Work was started in October 1917, prior to signing the contract. The initial schedule of deliveries was planned to be:

TABLE 3.—ESTIMATED DELIVERY SCHEDULE (April–September 1918)

Month	Number	Month	Number
April	200	July	1000
May	800	August	1000
June	1000	September	1000

It was impossible to meet this schedule for the following reasons: there was a lack of detailed specifications during early production, and there were constant changes in material specifications. In 14 months 1013 changes were received; as late as December 1918, 8 changes came in. These changes cover only those made to vandykes and blueprints and do not include the volume of detail, such as changing dies, jigs, fixtures, and tools necessary to comply with the changes imposed by the government. For each part changed on a blueprint or vandyke, three to five additional changes were required because an altered engine part required several changes to jigs, dies, or other machine tools.

The coal shortage had an adverse effect on subcontractors (the American Steel and Wire Company had to shut down for five weeks). Railroad embargoes delayed shipment of machines and raw materials, and priorities for purchase of materials were difficult to obtain. The government was to furnish 424 thread gauges, but by March 1918 had only delivered 34 acceptable machines. Training of personnel from auto- to aircraft-engine construction caused production delays, as did the rigid specifications initially imposed. These original working limits were not practical as some very important dimensions were too limited in tolerance for production. As the engine was tested, limits were changed in accordance with the best results attained from the tests. The manufacturers and personnel of the Bureau of Aircraft Production spent many hours going over the engine, piece by piece, to establish practical limits. This effort continued up to the date of the Armistice. A related problem was the shortage of experienced inspectors with professional judgment for the specification problem. Despite these problems, production was maintained (see Table 4).

On Armistice Day 75 engines were assembled, the highest daily production to that date. Plans called for 100 engines per day by 1 December 1918.

TABLE 4.—MONTHLY PRODUCTION

Month	Assembled	Shipped	Month	Assembled	Shipped
May (1918)	8	0	September	705	811
June	65	53	October	1242	1059
July	400	182	November	969	1201
August	550	519	December	10	125
			TOTAL	3950	3950

The overall production of the Liberty engines benefited by several distinctly Ford developments. Cylinder forgings made from steel tubing introduced an innovation which did more to attain quantity production than any other manufacturing development. The result was an enormous saving in the initial cost and in the cost of machining.[2]

A special process of making bronze-backed, babbit-lined bearings in the crankcase and connecting rods reduced bearing failures which had been one of the biggest problems with the Liberty engine. Ford spent several thousand dollars in research to solve the bearing problem. The new process used a Ford-designed machine which formed the bearing by centrifugal molding, which produced a more dense and heavy metal per unit of volume. Molding time was only one minute.

Electric butt welding of the inlet and exhaust elbows to the top of the cylinder forging modified the former method, which had heated the whole dome of the cylinder. The dissipation of this heat collapsed the dome, which then required straightening so that the inlet and exhaust valves could be aligned. The new method localized the heat and solved the problem.[3]

[2] History of BAP, vol. 7, p. 1913. LOENING, op. cit., p. 81, while giving Ford credit for this production advance, says that the cylinders ". . . poured out at the rate of 2,000 . . . a day, and entirely out of proportion to what could be done on plane production or, for that matter, on the training of aviators in sufficient numbers to fly sufficient planes using enough engines to use a production of 2,000 cylinders a day. . . ."

[3] Ibid., pp. 1906–1914. This information is contained in a letter to the BAP from Ford, 2 April 1919, quoted in full.

Packard

Packard's initial contract was for 6000 engines and spares. Contract number 1646 was signed on 4 September 1917; it was later supplemented for the $5000 cost plus $625 fixed-profit arrangement. A later contract was number 1646–4.[4]

Packard had started experimenting with aircraft engines in 1914. This experimentation, carried on primarily by Vincent, had resulted in the development of a 12-cylinder aircraft engine of 905 cubic inches, which was tested in December 1916. The engine was too heavy and not powerful enough for wartime use.

After Vincent and Hall had completed the design of the Liberty (at that time called the USA Standardized engine), Deeds asked Alvan McCauley, president of Packard, to produce five L–8 and five L–12 engines, to loan Vincent to the government for 90 days, and to give up Packard rights until the end of the war. McCauley agreed and subsequently completed testing the L–8 on 28 July 1917 and flew it on 21 August 1917. The L–12 completed its 50-hour acceptance test on 25 August 1917, after one of the fastest acceptance tests on record.

During late 1917, continued development on the engine resulted in the increase of its horsepower from 315 to 400. Because of this increase, Hall and O. E. Hunt of the Packard Company ran a series of tests at the Packard plant from November 1917 through February 1918. These tests resulted in changes to the connecting rods, crankshaft, connecting-rod bearings, piston-pin retainer, and the oil system from scupper to forced feed.

The changes put Packard in the position of doing experimental manufacture and design-development work at the same time.

> In early February, this effort to produce engines under conditions of constant change, and in response to the insistent demand for them on the part of the government, had resulted in a chaos in the Packard shops that was almost unbearable. Changes were so frequent that it was almost impossible to get tools finished and hand-made parts made necessary by lack of tools were below the desired standard, and the personnel of the organization were consequently being educated to the wrong standard.[5]

Packard asked the government for permission to stop production so it could regroup, but this was denied. Consequently, many of the early engines did not compare in quality with those of other manufacturers.

---

[4] PORTER ET AL., op. cit., p. 119.

[5] History of BAP, loc. cit., p. 1938.

In March, April, and May 1918 Packard was occupied with the final revision of tools, the building of stock reserves, and the gradual increase of production volume. The work of the previous six months started to bear fruit, and by early June the Liberty engine was acknowledged a success and large volume production was assured. Packard led all other manufacturers until late July 1918, and at the Armistice had shipped 4727 accepted engines. This was 25 percent more than the next largest producer.

The company had the vision to see the need for a fighting engine and placed the talent, facilities, and almost a half million dollars into the effort to develop it prior to the start of the war. It had obscured its own identity to further the national cause, struggled through the developmental stage alone, and smoothed the way for others.[6]

The results of Packard's patriotism in submerging its role as the developer of the Liberty were unfavorable to the company. The developmental engines they had built caused the Packard image of quality to become tarnished, as they were not of the quality of later production; they were used, nevertheless, due to the vital need for engines. Others were not as circumspect in their adherence to the play down of individual achievement to promote the effort as a whole, and publicity and credit were sometimes given to people who had nothing to do with the engine. Vincent felt strongly that Packard was being victimized.

> When I took hold of this job you made it quite clear to me that in order to obtain proper co-operation, the Packard Company as well as myself should be content to work under cover so to speak. I believe you will agree this has been done. The Packard Company has followed my earnest request in this connection, with the result that they are about the only people who are seldom heard of in connection with the Liberty engine.
>
> You are, of course, familiar with the fact that it was the money which they spent—more than any other thing—that made the Liberty engine possible. [Packard had financed the initial development work on the engine until the government appropriation was available.] The last time I saw Mr. McCauley he was, I believe justly, very much put out at the way this entire situation has been handled and I must admit that I could not justify the situation in any sense of the word.[7]

---

[6] Ibid., pp. 1934–1939. This information is contained in a letter to the BAP from O. E. Hunt, of the Packard Company, 5 March 1919, quoted in full.

[7] McCook files, letter, Deeds from Vincent, 30 October 1917. This is only one of a series of letters on this same subject. There does not seem to be any doubt that Packard was poorly treated, based on the all-out effort the company made. Even though struggling with make-

Lincoln

Due to their experience in developing the Cadillac motor car and high-speed, multi-cylinder engines of high quality, Henry M. and Wilfred C. Leland decided, when they resigned from General Motors on 1 May 1917, that they would build Liberty engines for the government. To this end they organized the Lincoln Motor Company on 29 August 1917 with a total of 142 employees.

Lincoln signed its first contract, number 1647, on 31 August 1917, the first Liberty contract to be signed.[8] The Lelands financed their undertaking with private and government money, and bought one plant and built another. The new plant was started on 21 September 1917 and was finished on 12 February 1918. It was 1275 feet long, 68 feet wide, 4 stories high, and contained 615,959 square feet of floor space. The Lincoln Company's total investment was $8,500,000.

Within its first year of operation Lincoln increased its personnel strength to 6000 and produced 2000 Liberty engines—50 per day. Equipping for this production called for a total of 91,087 special tools, among which were

TABLE 5.—LABOR INCREASES

Month	Number employed	Month	Number employed
August (1917)	52	March	1667
September	142	April	2331
October	180	May	3391
November	248	June	3944
December	349	July	4920
January (1918)	755	August	5600
February	977		

shift tools and handcrafted engines, Packard was forced to accept the $5000-cost/$625-profit arrangement along with companies who benefited from Packard's developmental efforts. McCauley said in a letter to the Chief, Purchase, Storage, and Traffic Division, BAP, 22 August 1918, that ". . . we seriously doubt whether we can produce the first 6,000 motors within two or three hundred dollars each, of the cost at which they can and will be manufactured by the other contractors."

[8] PORTER ET AL., op. cit., p. 115.

97

6522 separate and distinct designs. Design changes caused many delays. The number of changes received from 8 September 1917 to 25 June 1918 amounted to 1398. Labor problems, both in the increased employment necessary and in the turnover of personnel, also caused delay.

TABLE 6.—LABOR TURNOVER, JANUARY–JULY 1918

Month	Resignations	On Payroll	% Turnover
January	186	755	.246
February	171	977	.175
March	237	1667	.142
April	714	2331	.306
May	838	3391	.247
June	728	3944	.185
July	694	5600	.122

The number of temporarily unemployed persons in Detroit during the most intensive period of the war program—occasioned by men moving from one job to another—was more than 7000 above the average number of unemployed in normal times. The "work or fight" order which was promulgated about the middle of 1918 caused men who had moved to nonproductive fields to seek employment in the essential industries. This immediately increased the skilled labor market.

Lincoln found sabotage to be a problem: emery dust was found in machines; screws were loosened and machines thrown out of adjustment;

TABLE 7.—LINCOLN PRODUCTION

Month	Assembled	Shipped	Month	Assembled	Shipped
February (1918)	7	0	August	851	761
March	24	9	September	556	687
April	134	100	October	1111	1050
May	106	127	November	940	818
June	351	344	December	301	1109
July	533	533	January (1919)	586	1011
			TOTAL	6500	6500

oil-feed lines were plugged and loose nuts found in crankcases; cans of gun powder were found in the coal supply; and fire extinguishers were plugged with cotton.

Lincoln made the following production records:

1. Largest daily average for a month—December 1918..... 52;
2. Largest single month—December 1918............... 1301;
3. Largest six consecutive work days—24–31 December..... 378;
4. Largest single day—30 December 1918............... 86;
5. Largest number built in 1918....................... 5850.[9]

---

[9] History of BAP, loc. cit., pp. 1981–2023. It should be noted that the Lincoln records were made, with one exception, in December 1918. It appears that the reason for this is that the other large concerns involved in Liberty manufacture were anxious to return to building autos as soon as the Armistice was declared, whereas Lincoln, which had been formed exclusively for the production of Liberty engines, could gain only by continued production.

3. Statistical Charts

TABLE 8.—DH–4s AVAILABLE TO AEF ON 11 NOVEMBER 1918

At the front		196
In the zone of advance:		
Advance depots	24	
Fifth depot	41	
First depot	64	
Total in zone-of-advance depots		129
TOTAL		325
In service-of-supply depots:		
Orly depot	25	
Remorantin depot	178	
Total in service-of-supply depots		203
TOTAL		528
In use for advance training		270
TOTAL		798

TABLE 9.—STATUS OF DH-4s ON 11 NOVEMBER 1918

In use:		
Observation squadrons (2)	33	
Day-bombing squadrons (5)	93	
Corps observation squadrons (5)	86	
TOTAL		212
Attached to pursuit squadrons	1	
TOTAL		213
Out of commission:		
Lost over enemy lines	37	
Crashed at front (prior to 11 Nov. 1918)	249	
TOTAL		286
Delivered to squadrons at front	499	
In zone-of-advance depots	129	
TOTAL		628

101

TABLE 10.—LIBERTY-POWERED DH-4 VICTORIES

Squadron	Combat Victories
8	4
11	13
20	11
50	1
85	0
96	14
100	0
135	8
163	0
166	6
168	2
278	0
354	0
TOTAL	59

Aircraft	No. produced

L–8

Combat:

USB–2	1
USP–2	Designed
USXB–2 (observation type)	1 (under construction)
Victor D–8	Considered
VL–8	6

Other:

Ordnance model D	Considered

L–12

Bombing:

Caproni (3 engine)	5
Corps d'Armee (2 engine)	3
Curtiss	Designed
H–P (2 engine)	107 (393 partial)
J V Martin (2 engine)	1
LePere triplane (2 engine)	2
Martin Bomber (2 engine)	10
Sperry	Designed
Standard E–5B (5 engine)	Designed
Standard E–8	Designed
USD–9B	1
Victory	1
VL–12	6

Combat:

Berckman's	Considered
Bristol Fighter	27 (failure)
Hittle	Designed
J V Martin	Designed
Lavison Battler	Designed
LePere	Considered
Liberty Fighter	Considered

(continued on p. 104)

257-441 O - 78 - 8

TABLE 11.—LIBERTY-POWERED AIRCRAFT PROPOSED OR PRODUCED BY 11 NOVEMBER 1918 (*continued*)

Aircraft	No. produced
L–12 (*continued*)	
Combat: (*continued*)	
Loening	1
MB–1	1
MB–2	2
McCook Field	Preliminary data
USAC–1	1
USAC–2	Designed
Observation:	
DH–4	3431
DH–4B	1
LePere 11	25
USD–9A (successor to DH–4)	8
Other:	
Curtiss R–4–L	6 (mail service)

TABLE 12.—LIBERTY ENGINES ON HAND IN 1942

Year	On Hand	Reconditioned	Sold
1921	. . . .	275	. . . .
1922	. . . .	1000	. . . .
1924	11, 810	600	. . . .
1925	. . . .	500	. . . .
1928	. . . .	1942	813
1929	8756	2000	. . . .
1930	7133	301	2022
1931	6289	. . . .	. . . .

TABLE 13.—AIRCRAFT ENGINE COSTS

Manufacturer	Model	Description	Price
Curtiss	D–12	435 hp, water-cooled	$8, 000
Curtiss	V–1550	600 hp, water-cooled	15, 000
Packard	1500	500 hp, water-cooled	10, 155
Pratt & Whitney	Wasp	400 hp, air-cooled	7, 500
Curtiss	1454	400 hp, air-cooled	13, 500

TABLE 14.—COMPARATIVE COST OF OVERHAUL (JULY 1925–DECEMBER 1926)

Number overhauled	Average cost per engine	Total cost
	LIBERTY	
109	$475. 81	$51, 863. 29
159	651. 77	103, 631. 43
47	630. 87	29, 650. 89
315	TOTAL $587. 76	TOTAL $185, 145. 61
	D–12	
16	$474. 32	$7, 589. 12
11	609. 62	6, 705. 82
27	TOTAL $529. 44	TOTAL $14, 294. 94

TABLE 15.—COMPARATIVE COST PER RUNNING HOUR

Liberty:	
Initial cost	$2, 500. 00
Three overhauls @ $587.76	1, 763. 28
TOTAL	$4, 263. 28
Cost per hour (estimated life: 320 hr.)	$15. 16
Gas (24.52 gal/hr @ 15¾ cents/gal)	3. 85
Oil (7 qt/hr @ 31 cents/gal)	. 54
TOTAL COST PER RUNNING HOUR	$19. 55
D–12:	
Initial cost	$8, 000. 00
Four overhauls @ $529.44	2, 117. 76
TOTAL	$10, 117. 76
Cost per hour (estimated life: 600 hr.)	$16. 86
Gas (20.2 gal/hr @ 15¾ cents/gal)	3. 18
Oil (3.25 qt/hr @ 31 cents/gal)	. 25
TOTAL COST PER RUNNING HOUR	$20. 29

Bibliography

Aircraft Files. National Air and Space Museum, Smithsonian Institution.

Aircraft Yearbook. Vols. 1–7 (1919–1925). New York: Manufacturers Aircraft Association (1919–1921); Aeronautical Chamber of Commerce (1922–1925).

BARNES, JOHN K. The Vindication of Squier and Deeds. *World's Work* (July 1921), vol. 42, pp. 300–306.

BASSETT, B. V. *Instructions for the Installation, Inspection and Maintenance of the U.S.A. Standardized Engine.* U.S. Signal Corps, Equipment Division, n.d.

Central Decimal Files, Record Group 18 (Army Air Forces), 452.8. Washington, D.C.: National Archives of the United States.

CROWELL, BENEDICT. *America's Munitions 1917-1918.* Washington, D.C.: U.S. Government Printing Office, 1919.

DAVID, JOHN EVAN. *Aircraft.* New York: Charles Scribner's Sons, 1919.

Dayton Journal, 1 November 1918.

DECKER, WILBUR F. *The Story of the Engine.* New York: Charles Scribner's Sons, 1919.

Detroit Free Press, 5 November 1918.

Detroit News, 2 November 1918.

Elbert John Hall. New York: James T. White & Co., 1924.

GORRELL, EDGAR S. *The Measure of America's World War Aeronautical Effort.* Norwich University, Northfield, Vermont (James Jackson Cabot Professorship Lectures, no. 6), n.d.

History of the Bureau of Aircraft Production. Vols. 1–8. MS, The Air Force Museum, Wright-Patterson Air Force Base, Ohio, 1951.

Jesse G. Vincent files. MSS, The Air Force Museum, Wright-Patterson Air Force Base, Ohio.

LOENING, GROVER CLEVELAND. *Our Wings Grow Faster.* Garden City, N.Y.: Doubleday, Doran and Co., Inc., 1935.

MARCOSSON, ISAAC F. *Colonel Deeds; Industrial Builder.* New York: Dodd, Mead, and Company, 1948.

McCook Field Decimal Files, 452.8 (1917–1936). U.S. Air Force Depository, St. Louis, Missouri.

New York Times, 24 February 1929.

New York World Telegram, 25 October 1941.

NOCKOLDS, HAROLD. *The Magic of a Name.* London: G. T. Foulis and Company, n.d.

Pertinent Facts About the Liberty Motor. San Francisco: Hall-Scott Motor Car Company, n.d.

PORTER, HAROLD E., BENET, WILLIAM R., and KENT, WARNER W. History of the Liberty Engine. MS, U.S. Air Force Museum, Wright-Patterson Air Force Base, Ohio, 1918.

RATHBUN, JOHN B. *Airplane Engines in Theory and in Practice.* Chicago: Stanton and Van Fliet Company, 1921.

SPECIAL BRITISH AVIATION MISSION TO THE UNITED STATES OF AMERICA, June 11–July 29, 1918. *Supplement to the General Technical Report.* British Air Ministry, n.d.

SWEETSER, ARTHUR. *The American Air Service.* New York: Daniel Appleton and Company, 1919.

U. S. GOVERNMENT PRINTING OFFICE : 1978 O - 257-441

www.ingramcontent.com/pod-product-compliance
Lightning Source LLC
Chambersburg PA
CBHW080518110426
42742CB00017B/3157